RACE TO POWER:
The Struggle for Southern Africa

ABOUT THE AUTHORS

The Africa Research Group was an independent research and educational collective whose primary focus was to promote a more informed concern with and protest against the role the United States plays in the economic domination of Africa. Established in 1968, the Africa Research Group was an outgrowth of the anti-war movement in the United States. Opposition to American involvement in Southeast Asia led to an understanding of the extent and impact of American penetration around the world. The Africa Research Group worked to expand this understanding to include Africa by examining United States corporate expansion, United States Government intervention on the African continent, and the international dimensions of racism.

As part of its educational work the Africa Research Group spoke widely in high schools and colleges, published pamphlets, wrote articles and news analyses for journals and newspapers in the United States and Africa, and actively encouraged popular concern with American foreign policy. *Race to Power* is a continuation of this effort to bring the issues of domination and liberation in Africa to the attention of the American public.

RACE TO POWER:
The Struggle for Southern Africa

THE AFRICA RESEARCH GROUP

ANCHOR BOOKS
ANCHOR PRESS/DOUBLEDAY
GARDEN CITY, NEW YORK, 1974

A portion of RACE TO POWER was previously
published by the Africa Research Group in 1971.

Anchor Books Edition: 1974

ISBN: 0-385-04368-6
Library of Congress Catalog Card Number 73–16969

The authors make grateful acknowledgment for use of material from the
following sources:

Don Barnett and Roy Harvey, *The Revolution in Angola: MPLA, Life Histories and Documents,* copyright © 1972 by Don Barnett and Roy Harvey.
Reprinted by permission of The Bobbs-Merrill Co., Inc.

James Boggs, *Racism and the Class Struggle,* copyright © 1970 by James
Boggs. Reprinted by permission of Monthly Review Press, Inc.

Selected texts by Amilcar Cabral, *Revolution in Guinea,* copyright © 1969
by Stage 1. Reprinted by permission of Monthly Review Press, Inc.

Gérard Chaliand, *Armed Struggle in Africa: With the Guerrillas in "Portuguese" Guinea,* copyright © 1969 by Monthly Review Press. Reprinted by
permission of Monthly Review Press, Inc.

Basil Davidson, *The Liberation of Guiné* (Penguin African Library), copyright © 1969 by Basil Davidson. Reprinted by permission of Penguin Books
Ltd.

Eduardo Mondlane, *The Struggle for Mozambique* (Penguin African Library), copyright © 1969 by Eduardo Mondlane. Reprinted by permission
of Penguin Books Ltd.

FRELIMO, *Mozambique Revolution,* official publication of FRELIMO.

MPLA, *Angola in Arms,* official publication of MPLA.

PAIGC, *Actualités,* official publication of the PAIGC.

In January 1973, Amilcar Cabral, leader of Guinea-Bissau's national liberation movement (PAIGC), was assassinated in Conakry, Republic of Guinea. As with the assassination of Eduardo Mondlane, leader of Mozambique's liberation movement (FRELIMO) in 1969, Cabral's loss is a serious blow to the PAIGC. But, as the material presented in this book makes plain, nothing can undo the effective independence which the people of Guinea have won for themselves from Portuguese colonial rule.

Race to Power was prepared before 1973; no changes have been made in the text of the book to indicate Cabral's murder or subsequent developments. Cabral's spirit lives stronger than ever in the ongoing struggle of the Guinean people. This book is dedicated to him, and to the people who continue the fight to govern themselves in freedom.

CONTENTS

PREFACE   xiii

PART ONE
   WHITE DOMINATION: APARTHEID,
   COLONIALISM, AND INTERNATIONAL
   CAPITALISM

CHAPTER ONE. SOUTH AFRICA: LIFE UNDER
               APARTHEID   3

   I. What Is Apartheid?   5
   II. White South Africans: The Minority Rulers   14
   III. How Apartheid Prospers   22
   IV. Resistance, Repression, and the Police State 29

CHAPTER TWO. LIFE UNDER PORTUGUESE
               COLONIALISM   41

   I. The Overseas Provinces: The Last of the
      Colonies   41
   II. Portugal and the Colonies   43
   III. Resistance to Colonialism   53

CHAPTER THREE. PORTUGAL AND THE WEST   61

I. *Portugal's Dilemma*   61
II. *Western Involvement Takes Many Forms*   69
III. *South African Involvement in the Colonies*   75
IV. *Cabora Bassa: Power House of Southern Africa*   77
V. *The Wars in the Colonies*   79

CHAPTER FOUR. APARTHEID TAKES THE OFFENSIVE:
THE REGIONALIZATION OF SOUTHERN
AFRICA   85

I. *Military Regionalization*   85
II. *Economic Regionalization*   89
III. *South Africa Looks Across the Buffer Zone*   93
IV. *South Africa: Savior of the Free World*   99

CHAPTER FIVE. SOUTH AFRICA AND THE WEST   101

Part 1. *Corporate Interests and South Africa*   103

I. *A Survey of Corporate Involvement*   103
II. *Corporations and Apartheid*   110
III. *South African Views on Foreign Corporations*   117
IV. *Corporations and Foreign Policy*   120

Part 2. *National Interests and South Africa*   122

I. *World Opinion*   122
II. *Military Ties*   123
III. *Strategic Considerations*   126
IV. *Economic National Interests*   127

PART TWO
BUILDING FREEDOM: LIBERATION
IN THE PORTUGUESE COLONIES

INTRODUCTION 135

CHAPTER SIX. MOZAMBIQUE 139

    I. *Prelude to Armed Struggle* 140
    II. *The War* 145
    III. *The New Mozambique* 157
    IV. *Mozambique Today* 165

CHAPTER SEVEN. ANGOLA 183

    I. *Prelude to Armed Struggle* 185
    II. *The War* 199
    III. *The New Angola* 209

CHAPTER EIGHT. GUINEA-BISSAU 235

    I. *Armed Struggle* 236
    II. *Life in Liberated Guinea-Bissau* 247
    III. *The Development of Revolutionary
        Strategy in Guinea-Bissau* 258

CONCLUSION. THE WORLD LOOKS AT SOUTHERN
        AFRICA 289

REFERENCES AND SUGGESTIONS FOR FURTHER
    READING 297

INDEX 321

PREFACE

Race to Power was written with the memory that popular ignorance about the Vietnam situation once allowed massive government commitments to go unchallenged until it was too late. We have written this in the hope that Americans will never have to say, "It was a mistake to get involved in Southern Africa in the first place, but now that we are there . . ."

The war in Indochina has been the world's major conflict in the last decade. The growing confrontation in Southern Africa threatens to be as grave a crisis in the next decade: the forces of White domination in that region rigidly confront the African people who are moving to regain control over their lives and lands.

This book is about that confrontation. Its two parts juxtapose an examination of White rule with African liberation struggles that have grown out of opposition to that rule. *Race to Power* is about the power relationships in Southern Africa. It focuses on the major bastion of White minority strength in the region, South Africa, and on the Portuguese colonies, where, through armed struggle, African people have won more and more control of their countries. Guinea-

Bissau, although not geographically in Southern Africa, is included in *Race to Power*, since it shares a colonial history with the other Portuguese colonies and plays an important part in the political dynamics of the region. As the book seeks to indicate, it is *politically* part of Southern Africa. For reasons of space and clarity we have limited discussion primarily to these areas, although the role of other countries in the region is briefly examined in relation to the dynamics of the entire southern portion of the continent.

The first part of the book looks at the White governments who have power—how they got it, how they use it, and how they hope to preserve it. This section is a survey of the power structure and, as such, does not aim to present a systematic cultural and political history of African peoples or their traditional states in Southern Africa. Chapters One and Two are overviews of the conditions of life under apartheid and colonialism. In each, the arguments used by the White regimes to justify their rule are presented; each examines the most obvious social, political, and economic effects of these two systems and includes a brief history of the roots of African resistance.

It is not possible fully to understand Southern Africa by looking only at each country or territory separately. While the Republic of South Africa is the most widely known stronghold of White power in Africa, it does not operate in isolation, nor does the power struggle end at its borders. Chapter Four examines the regionalization of the conflict throughout Southern Africa and the particular role of South Africa in this process. It emphasizes the commonality of interest of all the minority regimes in the region. Chapters Three and Five specifically examine foreign interests in the Portuguese colonies and South Africa, with special emphasis on American involvement there. These chapters look at the types of Western economic, political, and military aid that operate in Southern Africa. They analyze not only the importance of this involvement to the minority regimes but also the importance of Southern Africa to Western capitalist interests. Chapter Five outlines many of the issues which confront policy makers and raises questions about how policy is made. It asks: What is the basis of African nationalist assertions that White minority domination is perpetuated by support from the United States, Britain, Japan, and other powerful countries?

Part Two presents the other side of the situation in Southern Africa: the new societies, free of White domination, which African people are building. Each of the chapters discusses a liberation movement in the Portuguese colonies —in Mozambique, Angola, and Guinea-Bissau—relating the development of their wars against colonialism and their struggle to create a new life. Detailed accounts of the process of revolutionary change are presented, often in the words of people engaged in this process. This part begins, in Chapter Six, with an overview of the struggle for liberation in Mozambique. Chapter Seven contains an in-depth look at the role of racism in Portuguese colonialism and discusses how education has been transformed in liberated Angola. Chapter Eight considers the interaction of theory and practice in the development of Guinea-Bissau's revolution.

The concluding chapter sketches recent developments in the world-wide reaction to this conflict in hopes of mobilizing American people's concern for the future of Southern Africa. It situates the struggle in Africa in the context of the global conflict of the last decade.

Race to Power examines the key issues that confront the governments and peoples of Southern Africa. It also looks at the international dimensions of the conflict there and tries to raise the question, What do the dynamics of domination and liberation in Southern Africa mean, not only for that region, but for the rest of the world as well?

A NOTE ON TERMINOLOGY

Terminology is an often unnoticed form of bias. This problem arises when we seek a suitable designation for the United States and its allies. American politicians often use the term "Free World." This usage generally refers not only to the industrial countries of Western Europe and America but to all countries outside the Communist bloc. Thus the "Free World" includes such totalitarian states as Portugal, Brazil, Nationalist China, and Greece. Such countries may be "free" from Communist rule, but they hardly qualify as states whose citizens enjoy any political freedoms.

Another common label is simply "The West." Since the world is round, this term is arbitrary. It developed among European peoples, from whose perspective Turkey and China appeared to the east. In common usage, the "West" connotes not so much a geographical concept as a social system based on private enterprise. Its corollary, the "East," refers to a system in which the state controls the means of production. Japan is a leading capitalist country, but it is obviously located in the "East." Cuba is a Communist country in the "West."

The only neutral terms seem to be those which refer to the social systems directly. Therefore, this book uses "capitalist powers" to indicate what are often called simply "the leaders of the Free World." The terms "West" and "Western powers" are used for purposes of variation, but they should be understood as social rather than geographical designations.

RACE TO POWER:
The Struggle for Southern Africa

PART ONE

WHITE DOMINATION: APARTHEID, COLONIALISM, AND INTERNATIONAL CAPITALISM

CHAPTER ONE

SOUTH AFRICA:
LIFE UNDER APARTHEID

At one time or another, most Americans have heard or read about South Africa and its policy of apartheid, or complete separation of the races. The word "apartheid" (pronounced *apart-hate*) comes from the Afrikaans language spoken by the descendants of the Dutch settlers in South Africa. It literally means separation. The system of apartheid determines the conditions of life in South Africa. It has to be the starting point for any discussion of that country.

Today this system has become too complex to describe in full detail; this chapter is only an introduction to the conditions of life in South Africa. It traces the gradual development of White control of the country and its Black majority.

The first Europeans arrived to settle in South Africa in the 1600s. From the beginning they sought to enslave the indigenous African population and make them subservient to White rule. As the White settlers moved from the coastal regions further inland, as they sought to own and control African lands, they encountered powerful opposition from the African people. In subjugating the African people they instituted from the beginning a series of laws that excluded Africans from any social, political, or economic control over the country.

Over the centuries as the economy grew in prosperity and the population grew in size, the "separation" of Africans from the political and social power of the Whites was extended, while forcing the Africans to provide the cheap labor necessary for the economic growth of the country. For example, Whites were able to mine the country's minerals profitably only by forcing large numbers of Africans to work for low wages. The system of requiring Africans to live in areas where they could support themselves only by working for Whites became even more highly refined with the development of industry in South Africa and the subsequent need for a large unskilled or semiskilled labor force.

Largely because of superior weapons, Europeans won the continual wars against Africans which died down only in the twentieth century. White domination was a centuries-old fact, with many laws ensuring that power remained in the hands of the Whites. In 1948 the present Nationalist party was elected to office. As in previous elections the maintenance of White supremacy was the key issue and the party was explicitly elected on a platform of "apartheid"—a new word for an old system. Since 1948 the Nationalist government has systematically revised and extended the laws making Blacks subservient to Whites. Each year in Parliament the government has passed more discriminatory legislation. In addition, stringent legal measures enforced by police terrorism have forced the continuing political opposition underground. Today White control is the most complete it has ever been.

The system of apartheid now defined by South African law was created and passed only by Whites. Africans have no representation in the South African Parliament and have never been consulted about making separation of the races into the legal policy described in this chapter.

1. What Is Apartheid?

Apartheid starts from the premise that all power must remain in the control of the Whites. To maintain this, all other peoples must be separated from the Whites, except when they are needed for their labor. In South Africa every person is classified by race—that is, by the color (or alleged color) of his or her skin. The different racial groups are segregated from each other as much as possible. These two facts are the cornerstones of apartheid as a legal system.

A. Race Classification

Skin color governs every single aspect of life in South Africa: where people live, what employment they may seek, where they can travel, what political rights they have, who can attend school, who can own property, whom they can marry, where they may be buried. Whites have the most rights and privileges. Africans have the least.

The South African government recognizes four main racial groups:

Africans—persons of African descent	15 million
Whites—persons of European descent	4 million
Coloreds—persons of racially mixed descent	2 million
Asians—persons of Asian (almost entirely Indian) descent	⅔ million

Final authority to decide a person's race rests with the government-appointed Race Classification Board which is made up only of Whites. The classification is sometimes quite arbitrary, relying mostly on "looks" and heritage. A brother may be classified as a Colored, for example, while his sister is classified as an African. Under apartheid laws they would not be allowed to associate with each other or live in the same house. Enforcement of racial separation is rigid even to the point of breaking up families.

B. Geographical Segregation:
The Group Areas Policy

The physical separation of people of different races is the most observable fact of life in South Africa. It applies to the country's land as well as its people.

Since the nineteenth century White governments have tried to divide the land into "White areas" and areas for Blacks. Today the entire country is so divided. The areas for Africans are called "reserves" or "Bantustans." This term gets its title from the word "Bantu" which is actually the name of the family of languages spoken by Africans in Southern and Eastern Africa. The South African government refers to all Blacks in South Africa as "Bantu" or "Natives"; it calls the areas reserved for them "Bantustans." Most Africans, however, despise being called "Bantu" and would rather be known as "Blacks" or "Africans," terms that acknowledge their race, their history, and their claim to land.

Although Africans are roughly 70 per cent of the population, only 13 per cent of the land of South Africa has been "reserved" for them. Individual Africans cannot own land even in these reserves. The reserves contain few industries and no important sources of employment. The land, from which most of the reserve inhabitants derive their income, is very poor—eroded in most parts, desert in others. The areas of the country reserved for Whites include all the large cities, the seaports and airfields, the gold, diamond, and other mineral mines. There is no land set aside for Asians and Coloreds.

	White (Europeans)	Black (Africans)
Per capita income (1968)	$3,144	$117
Average wage in mining (1968)	$4,740	$285
Ages subject to tax	21–60	18–65
Income exempt from tax	$840	none
Education expenditure per pupil	$159	$18
Infant mortality per 1,000 births	27	200
Percentage of population	19	70
Percentage of land reserved	87	13

The Bantustans are similar to Indian reservations in the United States in many ways. In both cases the land set aside for the indigenous people of the region is only a small proportion of the area taken by the European invaders. In both cases the inhabitants are supposed to be able to develop their societies independently of the dominant White civilization, despite the limitation of space and the poverty of available natural resources. In reality, the reservations act as potential reserves of labor for the dominant economy rather than reserves of land for the people who live there. Because the reserves have the poorest land and there are no jobs on them, Africans are forced to come to White areas to seek work. They have no rights in these areas.

All Africans living outside the reserves must have official permits to stay in any White region of the country. Even if they have lived in such an area all their lives, they can be "endorsed out" (ordered to leave) at any time. Here is the case of one such eviction order.

The Trial of Mr. Nana Sita

For forty-four years Mr. Nana Sita, an Indian, and his family lived in Pretoria, the administrative capital of South Africa. His house was in an area which had been inhabited primarily by Indians for many years.

Most of the Indians in South Africa were brought there as indentured servants and laborers and after fulfilling their contracts worked to establish small businesses. Mr. Sita was one such merchant.

On June 6, 1958, the government issued a proclamation declaring the whole of Pretoria a White area. No Indians were to be allowed to continue living there. Residences and businesses had to move. Mr. Sita refused. For over ten years he fought lengthy court battles, spending months in prison. In the meantime his home and business were destroyed, his community dispersed. Found guilty of breaking a law that had destroyed his life, he made the following statement at his trial:

"Those of us on whom the axe has fallen are undergoing untold hardships through having been uprooted from business and residences, causing misery, suffering, and unhappiness resulting in financial loss and insecurity for the future . . . Implementation of this policy [apartheid] brands us as inferior people in perpetuity, degrades our self-respect as human beings, condemns us as uncivilized barbarians. It degrades and humiliates my race to which I am proud to belong, a race which has produced eminent men in all walks of life . . . It has branded the fourteen million non-Europeans of South Africa, Africans, Indians, and Coloreds as inferior lest their proximity and shadow contaminate and pollute the members of the ruling race . . ."

The rural areas are also affected by the government's land reservation policy. Groups of Africans living on land reserved for Whites are called "black spots" by the government. Although they may have lived there for generations, these Africans are gradually being evicted. The evicted families are moved to "resettlement villages" such as Morsgat. Morsgat, which means "mess-hole," is about ninety miles northwest of Pretoria in one of the most desolate areas of the country.

More than a million Africans have been uprooted and sent to resettlement villages since 1959. Morsgat is only one of many resettlement camps.

At Morsgat—more than 300 families are living there in tents and shacks after having been moved off "White" land.

—the first people were taken there in December 1968. Nine months later, and only after a public outcry, did the government start building some crude houses.

—some people were moved from slate quarries where they worked, others came from locations in White towns.

At Morsgat—there is no employment and the men have to leave the camp to find work. Most breadwinners earn no more than $5.00 a week.

—round-trip bus fares to work vary from $1.54 to $2.52 a week. Most men cannot afford to pay these fares often for weekend visits—this forces the men to stay away from their families for long periods of time.

—before coming to Morsgat, the men lived with their families near their work. Now they can no longer live with their families.

At Morsgat—there is one water tank for the whole community—over 1,200 people. The water is bad.

—there are no latrines and subsequently there is much disease.

At Morsgat—there is evidence of malnutrition.

—there are no medical facilities available there.

There are many Morsgats in South Africa. They exist because under the design of apartheid everyone has to be moved off the land belonging to another race. But unlike Africans, Asians, and Coloreds, Whites have never been forcibly evicted. Those few who have moved have been well compensated by the government.

C. Migratory Labor and the Pass Laws

Two thirds of the Africans and all of the Coloreds and Asians in South Africa still live in White areas where they can be evicted, resettled, or ordered to move at any time. Most of these people who live in White areas have to go either to the mines or to the cities and towns to find work.

In the large cities, Africans have to live in ghettolike areas called "townships" which are physically separated from the rest of the city. Men who come to the cities seeking employment are not allowed to bring their wives and families with them. As a result, they move constantly between the cities and the rural areas. Sometimes they work for a year or more before returning home for a short time.

Africans are also required to have special permits to enter a city to find work. They lose their permit if they leave the city to return to their family and have to re-apply for a new permit the next time they need to find work there. The government uses this system of permits to regulate the labor force in different cities. If there are few jobs available in a city, few Africans will be allowed to enter it. This often puts Africans in the position of having to choose between keeping their jobs or seeing their families.

By depriving them of the right to settle in one place and the right to own property, the government makes Africans (and to a lesser extent Asians and Coloreds) into a vast pool of "migratory labor" that can be easily channeled to satisfy the needs of the South African economy. Prime Minister John B. Vorster recently expressed the government's view of this situation:

> The fact of the matter is that we need them [Africans] because they work for us, but after all we pay them for their work . . . But the fact that they work for us can never entitle them to claim political rights. Not now,

not in the future, under no circumstances can we grant
them those political rights in our own territory, neither
now nor ever.

This system of migratory labor destroys family life for
the majority of Africans. It forces them to live as isolated
individuals in a permanent state of uncertainty. And it deprives them of their cultural heritage. Traditional ways of
associating with friends and relatives, wives and children,
traditional ways of cooking, of dressing, of worshiping,
traditional arts are made impossible in the modern industrial environment of the cities where Africans are often
isolated strangers who stay but a short time before having
to move somewhere else.

But while the system of migratory labor destroys the
traditional African culture, and with it their ties to their
past, Blacks are not allowed to participate in the dominant
White culture. They are prevented from having access to
the benefits that living in a city normally brings.

The physical separation of the races that is the basis of
migratory labor is effectively enforced by a system of "pass
laws." All Africans, men and women, have to carry a pass
(something like a passport) on their person at all times. The
pass books contain personal biographies, details of employment, and records of permits to travel or reside in a certain
place. They have to be always kept up to date: in practice,
this means hours of standing in line every few weeks to be
photographed or to get the signature of employers and of
the petty government officials who are in charge of keeping
track of the movement of individuals.

Africans may be stopped by any policeman at any time,
even in their proper residences; and if they are found to be
without a pass, they are automatically arrested. If the pass
book does not contain the necessary permits to reside or
work in the place, they are stopped; if any of the required

information in the pass is out of date or if some required signature is missing, they are also arrested. Over 3,000 Africans are arrested *each day* for pass offenses.

This large number of arrests is the government's most obvious method of regulating the movements of the population. Even without the arrests, the pass laws are a continuous harassment that prevents the African population of South Africa from ever feeling secure. The fear of being arrested, the long waits to obtain required certification, and just the necessity of carrying a pass book at all times are only more subtle measures that make the Nationalist government's extensive control of people possible.

Africans who are arrested without being able to show that they have permits to work in a particular city are sent back to the reserves. The following case is typical of millions of others:

Mrs. Bukane left Lady Frere, the small village where she was born, in 1946 and had never been there since. She joined her husband in Paarl (a large town) where he worked and lived with him there for twelve years—until 1958. Then his firm transferred him to Cape Town and she was allowed to accompany him and lived with him in temporary housing in Guguletu, an African "location." [A "location" is a settlement of Africans usually on the edge of a town; also called a "township."] on the outskirts of the city. They lived there until 1966 when she was suddenly endorsed out after twenty-one years of marriage. By then she had five children, all of whom had been born either in Cape Town or Paarl and who had gone to school in Guguletu. The youngest had polio and was being regularly treated at the Guguletu clinic. She and her children were told to return to Lady Frere. By leaving Paarl and moving to Cape Town she had lost all her "rights" to live in an urban area. The law demanded that she leave her husband and return to her "home." When she refused to go, she was arrested, found guilty, and sentenced to prison. Her attorney said at her trial: "Nothing the court can do can punish her as severely as the prospect she faces of having to leave her husband." If she remained in Cape Town, she would be arrested again. Her husband could not follow her as there was no possibility of his finding work in Lady Frere. Their marriage of twenty-one years was destroyed.

Because most Africans, Asians, and Coloreds are not allowed to settle in one area and individual Africans are not allowed to own property, they are prevented from developing their own businesses or industries or other ways of supporting themselves. This forces them to take whatever jobs are available, regardless of the location or the wages. The system of separation of the races thus in practice ensures that there is a constant supply of cheap African, Asian, and Colored labor. The need to have a pool of cheap labor available, first for large-scale agricultural production, then for mining operations, and now for industrial manufacture, has been one of the primary reasons for the development of apartheid.

There are other important reasons. The Whites who were the architects of apartheid believed that only complete separation of the races would allow them to survive—politically, economically, and culturally—in a country where they were a small racial minority. Furthermore, they viewed apartheid as a just and morally responsible policy—as part of the responsibility that Whites had, to lead Africans to self government.

II. White South Africans:
The Minority Rulers

The complex social relations that have emerged in South Africa derive in part from the earliest contacts between Europeans and Africans. The first White settlers arrived in the Cape in 1652 and within fifty years several hundred Europeans had decided to settle permanently in this new land. Whites have lived in South Africa from that time— longer than most Americans have lived in the United States. Their "home" is no longer England, Holland, or France, which were the countries of their forefathers. They no longer think of themselves as "settlers" but as White Africans.

Before the Whites arrived at Cape Town and began to move northward, South Africa was inhabited by migratory or stationary African nations. The area around Cape Town itself was occupied by the Khoi people, who were conquered by the European settlers and enslaved. There was miscegenation between these two groups from the beginning. The descendants of this racial intermixture comprise the Colored population of South Africa who still live primarily around the Cape area.

In those early days most Whites were farmers of Dutch descent, living isolated and difficult lives. These Boers, as they were called (boer means farmer in Dutch), were similar in many ways to the American frontiersmen. They were rugged individualists who had to rely mainly on their own resources for survival. When the Cape was annexed by the British after the Napoleonic Wars, most of the Dutch farmers began to move inland to escape British rule.

In 1836 the Boers began their "Great Trek" northward, which again brought Whites into violent conflict with the

African nations whose land they sought to occupy. Leaving the settled areas of the Cape, these trekkers saw the Africans as the greatest danger to their own survival, just as the American pioneers moving westward feared the attacks of Indians. The African nations of the region, however, saw the White invaders as a threat to *their* existence.

Colonist attempts to take over the land and cattle of the indigenous Africans led to a series of almost continuous wars. Although they only had arrows and spears to use against the Boers' rifles, Africans frequently routed the invaders. The powerful Zulu empire, for example, led by King Tshaka, one of the most outstanding military leaders of the nineteenth century, cut off the eastward expansion of the Whites and forced them to migrate north instead. Tshaka's successor, Dingane, also led such fierce resistance that the day he was finally defeated—Dingaan's Day, December 16, 1838—is still a national day of thanksgiving for the descendants of the Dutch. The Boer trekkers, who called themselves "Afrikaners" as if to justify their claim to the land, were able to defeat Africans in the end only with the help of British military efficiency and equipment.

The two republics—the Transvaal and Orange Free State —that the Afrikaners finally established were heavily influenced by their hatred and fear of Africans as a formidable enemy. Survival depended on "keeping the Black man in his place." The constitutions of the two republics spelled out not only the separation of the races but the subservience of Africans to Europeans.

A. Marching to Pretoria

By the mid-nineteenth century, with the aid of British military power, Europeans had established four independent states in what is now the Republic of South Africa. Cape Colony and Natal in the south and east were under the control of Britain; Orange Free State and the Transvaal, central and to the north, were controlled by the Afrikaner trekkers. The British states had outlawed slavery and allowed a few Africans and Coloreds the right to vote (those who had property or educational qualifications). The Afrikaner states insisted on segregation, with only Whites having the right to vote.

The discovery of diamonds in 1867 and then gold in 1887 in the Afrikaner states led to British intrusion in the north. Relations deteriorated until, at the end of the century, the Afrikaner states declared war on Britain, which was attempting to take over the Boer territories. The Boer War (1899–1902), one of the most bitter wars of its time, is still remembered today through the familiar song "Marching to Pretoria" which came from this war. British soldiers sang the song on their way to Pretoria, the capital of the Afrikaner state of Transvaal (and the present administrative capital of the Republic of South Africa). Superior British military strength finally prevailed and the Afrikaners signed a peace treaty, but their antagonism toward the British remained strong.

In 1910 Britain united the four states into the Union of South Africa and granted it independence as a dominion of the British Empire. The government of the new country gradually worked to bridge the conflicts between the Afrikaners and the English-speaking South Africans. Both groups had to make significant concessions before the new nation's constitution was accepted. When it was finally adopted in 1910, the terms of racial discrimination spelled out by the constitution provoked little opposition among Whites because the system of low paid African labor had proven so lucrative to them. It would be difficult to maintain a steady supply of cheap Black labor if Africans, Asians, and Coloreds were to be granted citizenship rights.

B. The White View of Apartheid

Successive English-Afrikaner coalition governments passed more and more legislation restricting the rights of Africans, Asians, and Coloreds. In 1948 the Nationalist government was elected to office (by Whites only) and, in addition to the racial legislation it enacted, introduced a series of laws that established South Africa as a *de facto* totalitarian state in which all opposition to White supremacy was outlawed.

The program of apartheid legislation enacted by the Nationalist party formalized and refined a system of practices that had been in operation in South Africa since the coming of Europeans.

From their first meeting, Europeans looked on Africans as savages devoid of culture and religion. Whites in South Africa have always used the derogatory term "Kaffir" (unbeliever) to refer to Blacks, while calling themselves true "Afrikaners." Moreover, Europeans believed Africans to be inferior beings because their skin was black.

With the missionary sentiments of a people convinced of their superiority, White South Africans believed it was their duty to govern or "care for" Africans. This idea that they had to "take up the White man's burden," as Rudyard Kipling put it, helped White South Africans rationalize the way they subjugated the peoples of other races. White South Africans, English and Afrikaner alike, were convinced that their control of Africans was a just, responsible, and even divinely directed program.

From the seventeenth century to the present, the Dutch Reformed Church, to which nearly all Afrikaners belong, has played an important role in supporting and justifying apartheid. The Dutch Reformed clergy maintain that all Negroes are descendants of Ham (Genesis 9:22–25) and like him have been condemned to be "a slave of slaves . . . to his brothers"—eternal servants of all other men. This interpretation of the Bible has long been at the root of Afrikaners' belief that they are right to control Africans.

English-speaking White South Africans, who do not accept this theological justification of White superiority, nevertheless believe that apartheid—at least in theory—is a morally responsible policy. Today, most White South Africans explain the design of apartheid this way: Whites and Africans are two different races which cannot live together in one political state without one group destroying the other. The language and culture of both races would be destroyed by intermingling. The pride of both races in their language and culture makes this undesirable. Therefore, the different races must develop separately and to do this must be physically separated.

This policy of "separate development" demands that Africans have their own states. To meet this need the South African government has designated 13 per cent of the total area of South Africa as "African homelands" or Bantustans. According to the official plan, the entire African population is someday to be relocated in these "reserves." There, the argument continues, Africans will have full human rights and will be able to govern their society as they see fit. They will be granted no rights, however, if they leave the Bantustans to travel in White areas.

The Nationalist government has stipulated that it will have to act as trustee over the Bantustans until Africans reach a level of civilization sufficient for self-government. Whites must also assume the responsibility of helping the Bantustans industrialize. Only eventually will the reserves become completely independent states within greater South Africa.

C. Is the Bantustan Policy Meant to Work?

The Nationalist government claims that the Bantustans are the traditional homelands of Africans. The majority of Africans, however, do not live in Bantustans and never have. Many Africans have lived for generations in the cities.

The Bantustan policy means that Africans will someday have political and economic rights—but only in 13 per cent of their country. And even then the White President of South Africa will continue to have the final constitutional control over the affairs of the reserves.

AFRICAN RESERVES

Black South Africans, who make up 70 per cent of the population, are forced to live on 13 per cent of the land.

The promised independence to be granted to the Bantustans leaves the Whites in a commanding position in another

way as well. According to the government's African homeland policy, land will be set aside for eight separate African
states; and each state will be divided into several territorial
areas for each of the many ethnic groups of African people
in South Africa. This divides the economic and political
power of the African population into isolated units and thus
puts Africans in a weaker bargaining position with the uni-
fied White South African nation.

More importantly, the Bantustans do not and never will
possess the economic resources to support the entire African population of South Africa. They occupy some of the
most desolate parts of the country and have a very limited
potential for either agricultural or industrial development.

The Bantustan policy is designed to maintain a plentiful
supply of cheap Black labor for South Africa's growing
economy. As that economy expands, more and more Africans are drawn into the "White" urban areas. The South
African economy is totally dependent on African labor. It
is thus impossible to separate Africans and Whites without
destroying the economy. It is impossible to force all Africans to live in the Bantustans—but in the meantime Africans
have no rights at all in the urban industrial and mining
areas and are therefore extremely vulnerable to exploitation.

D. Signs of Strain in the Policy of Apartheid

Apartheid legislation reserves jobs classified as "skilled labor" for Whites only. But if South Africa's modern industrial
economy is to expand, it needs more skilled labor than
South Africa has White workers. Big industrialists constantly pressure the government for permission to employ
Africans in positions that have up to now been reserved
only for Whites. This is one area of tension in the present
application of apartheid.

Another concerns the enforcement of the migratory labor system. Because African workers have to move in and out of towns frequently, it is difficult for employers to find people to work at one job for any length of time. Productivity suffers because migrant laborers generally do not stay at one job long enough to develop expertise and because indus-trialists are constantly having to train new people. Consequently, many big employers feel that Africans should be allowed to settle in one place. But this is against the apartheid policy.

Finally, because Africans are paid so little, they have hardly any buying power. South African businesses, on the other hand, have more products to sell today and need more consumers than just the country's wealthy White popula-tion can provide. Many businessmen would like to pay Africans, Indians, and Coloreds higher wages so that they could then buy more and keep the South African economy expanding.

These contradictions in the South African economy—for example, the fact that the working of the country's social system denies businesses the skilled labor they need to ex-pand—are a significant challenge to the stability of the policy of apartheid. If the country is to continue to develop along its present industrial line, growth of these contradic-tions could someday force the government to relax some of its present discriminatory laws.

The conflict between the needs of the economy and the ideology of apartheid also creates conflicts between groups of White South Africans. The industrialists, whose interests lie in the expansion of the economy, continuously pressure the government to relax the application of apartheid laws to allow more flexibility in how the African population can be regulated. They clearly favor a less rigidly defined system of laws which would allow Africans more freedom but guarantee continued White economic and political control.

Most of the big businessmen and other Whites who favor this proposal are English-speaking.

There are many Afrikaners in rural areas removed from the needs of a modern industrial, predominantly urban, economy who fear any changes in apartheid. Most successful Afrikaner businessmen, however, realize that rigid application of apartheid policy could interfere with the economic growth of South Africa. The last twenty years of industrialization has narrowed the gap between the Afrikaners and the English-speaking South Africans. For both, economic gain is of primary importance: modification of apartheid will only be tolerated if it maintains or strengthens White economic domination in South Africa.

III. How Apartheid Prospers

Unlike other African countries, South Africa is highly industrialized. It has several large cities similar in size to San Francisco, Boston, and Milwaukee. Up to the late nineteenth century, both European settlers and Africans were engaged primarily in agricultural production. Africans grew mainly what they needed for survival and relied on barter; Europeans, using African labor, produced cash crops for sale on a market based on money exchange. The growth of this money-based agricultural trade led to the development of cities and towns.

The South African economy mushroomed with the discovery of diamonds, gold, copper, and an extensive wealth of other minerals at the end of the nineteenth century. The mining industry, which has been largely under British control since the Boer War, created some fabulous fortunes and generated the financial power South Africa needed to further industrialize.

A. Labor

The South African mines could be worked only by using vast amounts of labor. But they could be operated profitably only when labor costs were low. This meant paying African laborers low wages. To persuade Africans to work for low wages, the South African government, in co-operation with the English-speaking mine owners, did two things. It imposed taxes on Africans that had to be paid in cash, thus forcing Africans to work for cash wages instead of continuing to produce only what they needed for survival. And it classified any African outside a reserve not working for a European as a vagrant liable to prosecution, thereby forcing many African men to accept whatever work Whites provided.

This system still furnishes the South African mines with their labor force today. South Africa also imports Africans from other Southern African countries to work in the mines. These laborers are forced to immigrate temporarily to South Africa. They do not go to South Africa because working conditions there are good—any more than southern Blacks in the United States go to live in ghettos in the Northern cities because conditions there are good—they go only because it is the only way they have of earning wages.

Most Africans work in the mines on nine-month contracts. Because it is more efficient, the mining companies provide some minimal housing and food. But no African miners are allowed to bring their wives or families to live in these mine compounds which are usually just bunkrooms crowding sixteen men into a twenty-by-thirty-foot space. This forced separation of African miners from their families keeps Africans moving constantly from the mines back to the countryside. Under apartheid legislation, the pass laws regulate this population flow to provide for the labor needs of the South African mines and industries.

An abundance of cheap labor and the profits from selling its mineral wealth helped South Africa develop from a mineral-exporting outpost into a modern manufacturing economy. Africans who had worked primarily in the mines were now drawn into the factories as South Africa began to industrialize rapidly. Throughout the history of modern economic growth in South Africa, measures had been enacted to protect White workers from the threat of African competition. In the 1950s, under pressure from White workers, more laws were enacted to safeguard the position of Whites. The government was further induced to apply apartheid laws to labor policies by big mining and industrial employers who argued that both Black and White workers would be easier to govern if they could be dealt with separately in racial groups instead of collectively as workers, regardless of race.

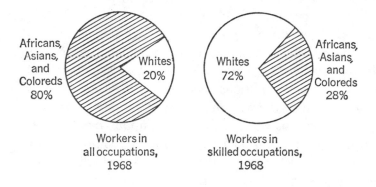

Workers in
all occupations,
1968

Workers in
skilled occupations,
1968

The recent laws that have applied apartheid to labor policies have some important historical precedents. The Cape Masters and Servants Law of 1865, for example, defined the relation of master to servant and servant to master in quasi-legal terms and set the tone for successive legislation. The Mines and Works Act of 1911 was passed to satisfy white miners' demands that skilled positions be reserved only for them. The most important modern apartheid labor legislation includes:

TRADE UNIONS. Multiracial trade unions were prohibited in 1956; successive laws now prevent African trade unions from exercising any rights. This means Africans have absolutely no bargaining power with their employers. All details of employment such as working conditions and wages are controlled by the employers or by government committees. The low wages Africans are paid result partly from this lack of representation.

THE RIGHT TO STRIKE. White and Colored workers have some rights to strike, but African workers are denied the right altogether. Africans who strike or participate in any work stoppage or slowdown face a three-year jail sentence and a fine of $1,500. Despite the penalties, Africans have continued to strike. The police have opened fire on striking Africans several times.

JOB RESERVATION. Labor laws specifically reserve certain occupations for Whites only. The intention of the Job Reservation Act is to keep skilled positions in general open for Whites. This had led to a shortage of skilled labor; but rather than allowing Africans to move into some of the reserved positions, the government is attempting to solve the shortage by bringing in immigrants from Europe.

EMPLOYMENT SUPERIORITY. Under apartheid, no African may occupy a position senior to any White in a company. Africans may never give orders to Whites. The few African doctors, for example, are not allowed to work with White nurses because they would have to give them instructions.

Average Monthly Salaries and Wages in South Africa, 1967–68

Industry	White	Colored	Asian	African
Mining (1967)	$396	$ 83	$ 98	$24
Construction (1968)	357	142	172	61
Manufacturing (1968)	340	87	93	64
Public service (1967)	208	74	93	33

(Source: *Survey of Race Relations in South Africa,* 1968)

B. Wages

There are many more such laws. One rough measure of how this apartheid labor legislation affects the people of South Africa is wages. In the mining industry, wages for Whites are sixteen times greater than wages for Africans. In manufacturing, the average monthly salary for Whites is over five times that of Africans.

The discrepancy between wages paid to Whites and those paid to Africans has increased over the last fifty years. The benefits of South Africa's increased economic prosperity in that time have gone mainly to Whites. South African Whites have one of the highest standards of living in the world. Although there is some poverty among them, the amount of material wealth—cars, houses, and swimming pools, for example—owned per person is more than that of any other country.

But Africans in South Africa have to struggle just to subsist. Surveys conducted by the South African Institute of Race Relations in 1970 found that an average African urban family of five, even with two wage earners per household, had a monthly income that was 10 to 15 per cent short of what they needed just to buy basic necessities. Many Africans are malnourished—those in the reserves as much as those in urban areas. Housing is uniformly bad. No African may own a house, and the government's housing projects offer only shoddy, usually very small units in desolate townships. Streets are neither lit nor paved. Electricity is uncommon, and the water supply for African living areas is minimal. These are the conditions that exist on the outskirts of some of the most prosperous and modern cities in the world.

The government has made no effort to force employers to pay a living wage even though it is well aware of the chronic underpayment in the country. The Minister of Labour summed up the government's attitude this way:

> To plead that you must pay the Natives who are employees a civilised wage means only one thing in this country—White wages. To want to pay Natives White wages fails in the first place to take account of their productivity; in the second place it does not take their living standard into account.

C. The Educational System

Education plays a major role in preparing Whites to lead the economy and in simultaneously preventing Blacks from having influential positions in the labor force. Apartheid applied to education means that schooling for Whites is free and compulsory until the age of sixteen. White schools have excellent facilities, and a large percentage of the White population complete diplomas in higher education at the government's expense.

At the other end of the scale, apartheid means that educational opportunities for Africans are very limited. In 1953 the Nationalist government brought all education of Africans under state control. The government itself spends nine times more per pupil for the education of White children than it does for the education of Africans. And unlike Whites, Africans must pay even to go to public school. Although there are three "Bantu" universities (with very small enrollments), most Africans never get to school at all. Most who do start in Grade One do not have more than three years of schooling. And in the last several years, government expenditure per capita for "Bantu" education has decreased. When the state took complete control of Black education, the Minister of Education put the government's case this way:

> Education will be suitable for those who will become the industrial workers of the country. . . . What is the use of teaching a Bantu child mathematics when it cannot be used in practice? That is quite absurd. Education must train and teach people in accordance with their opportunities in life . . .

The South African government often says in its own defense that more Africans in South Africa attend school than in any other African country. This comparison is misleading, not only because it attracts attention away from actual opportunities for Africans to attend school in South Africa, but because it does not contrast African education to White education in South Africa. This is like defending the quality of education for Black people in the United States by comparing it with education in Zaire (formerly the Republic of the Congo). South Africa, like the United States, is a rich, industrialized country. Other African countries are not. But the real difference between most independent African countries and South Africa is that the former are committed to free, universal education for all citizens. In South Africa this is for Whites only.

Today South Africa is one of the most prosperous modern industrial countries in the world. Its economy has been expanding so rapidly that almost 1,000 corporations in the United States and West Europe have decided to invest there to take advantage of the low labor costs and high profit rates.

But South Africa's economic prosperity depends on discriminatory labor and educational policies and on the general control of the population that apartheid makes possible. The government has had to increase its control in recent years because resistance to its exploitative racial policies still continues strong. The next section examines how making the country an economic success has meant creating a totalitarian state in South Africa.

IV. Resistance, Repression, and the Police State

White South African society has been built up on the expectation of racial warfare. The townships where Africans live have been physically separated from the cities so they can be easily surrounded. Pillboxes and road blocks have been built all over the country. Expenditures for defense and police have increased every year; South Africa now has more military might than all other nations in Africa —excluding Egypt combined. There is even an extensive program of volunteer small-arms training for White women.

The present tension in South Africa has a long history. Ruling South African Whites have had to fight every inch of the way to establish themselves in power and to maintain their position against continuous opposition. This short section only sketches the range of this opposition. It does not mention many of the individuals and organizations that have led the fight, nor can it hope to convey its real weight and intensity.

A. Resistance to White Invasion

The first Europeans found Africans willing to coexist peacefully with them. They responded by enslaving the indigenous peoples and claiming their land. In the next hundred years as the Europeans gradually expanded away from the coast by plundering Africans, taking over their land, and often burning their villages, Blacks mounted a fierce resistance to defend their land. Black South Africans have never submitted willingly to White rule.

The advance of first the Dutch and then the British into the interior of the country precipitated almost continuous fighting. Africans' determination to keep control of both their land and their people presented the colonists with much more than skirmishes; nine full-scale wars were fought between 1779 and 1879. Even without guns, different groups of Blacks often routed the invaders and in some cases made them respect Africans' territorial rights until the twentieth century.

When the Boers began their Great Trek away from the Cape, they were turned back from Natal in the east after being severely defeated by the Zulu nation. They were forced north by successive defeats at the hands of King Mshoeshoe in the area of Lesotho and King Sekhukuni in what is now the Transvaal. The Boers were able to defeat the Africans only with the military help of the British. And the British, even with their phenomenally superior fire power (including the machine gun for the first time), had to rely on playing rival ethnic groups off against each other to finally establish military control over Africans.

B. Protest Against Continued Occupation

By 1910, when the Union of South Africa was formed as a British Commonwealth nation, Whites controlled most of the land of the country and had been successful in making many Africans dependent on jobs offered by Whites. The act of union further united all Whites in South Africa. One of the first acts of the new Union government was to consolidate White ownership of the land by declaring 87 per cent of South Africa "White" land—and the remaining 13 per cent native reserves.

Africans, who were allowed only token representation in the new nation's government, turned to protest. When petitions before both the South African government and the British government met with no success, Blacks formed the African National Congress (ANC). In 1912 Africans from almost every ethnic group and every region of South Africa met together on the question of White domination. Dr. P. I. Seme, one of the founders of the ANC, declared: "The demon of racialism, the aberrations of Xhosa-Fingo feuds, the animosity that exists between Zulus and the Tongas, between the Basuto and every other Native, must be buried and forgotten . . . We are one people."

Since that time, the ANC has been one of the major leaders of African resistance to White domination. In 1913 the ANC organized protest against the Natives Land Act, which set aside 87 per cent of the territory of the country for Whites only. It has conducted continual demonstrations against the government, involving hundreds of thousands of Africans at one time or another, and has been especially active in opposing discriminatory legislation.

In the 1920s, 1930s, and 1940s, Africans organized their own trade unions. One of the biggest and most successful of these was the Industrial and Commercial Workers' Union (ICU) which conducted several major strikes. Trade unions united Africans and made them a significant political force, but the election of the Nationalist government in 1948 slammed the constitutional door on their appeals for a lessening of racial discrimination. African trade unions are not permitted to exercise any trade union rights—it is illegal for Africans to strike, for example, as we have seen.

The continued implementation of apartheid legislation after the 1948 elections was vigorously opposed by Black

South Africans, as it had been since the first White occupation in South Africa. Africans, Asians, and Coloreds made it clear over and over again that they were not prepared to accept the continuation of White supremacy. A small White minority joined this opposition but soon discovered that White skin, which was usually a passport to extensive privilege, no longer made so much difference. The government moved quickly to try to eliminate all serious opponents of apartheid.

In 1950 the government reacted to the anti-apartheid protests with the Suppression of Communism Act. This move to eliminate political opposition was not something new in South Africa, but a modern version of laws that had been used each time the White government felt its political security threatened. The Suppression of Communism Act entitles the Minister of Justice to "ban" any person who is active in opposing apartheid. Thousands of people have been banned, many on the pretense that they were communists. The government is not required to prove that the banned people are actually communist and is seldom able to do so. The effect of the legislation, however, is to define anyone who is seriously against apartheid as a communist.

People who receive a banning order, which is usually in effect for five years but can be extended, are placed under the following restrictions:

1. They may not belong to any organization (including, for example, even sports clubs) or hold any public office. They may not attend any gathering, social or political. Banned people may not attend weddings or funerals or political rallies.

2. They may not communicate in any way with another banned person. This restriction has only been lifted when a husband and wife were both banned. It is illegal to take a message from one banned person to another.

3. They may be forbidden to receive any visitors. Banned

people can only be with one other person at the same time.

4. They must report regularly to the police.

5. They may not teach in a university and are frequently forbidden to attend universities as students.

6. They may not work as attorneys. By banning many lawyers who defend people charged with political crimes, the government has made it almost impossible for such people to be defended.

7. They are restricted to particular towns or parts of towns in large cities. They may not leave the towns at any time.

By banning people, the government forces them to be prisoners in their own homes. This has proved to be an extremely effective way of stopping political opposition. Banning orders are arbitrary; they may not be appealed, and the police do not need a court order to apply them. Bannings are punishments without trial for "crimes" that the government cannot prove.

Despite the increased political repression, opposition to apartheid did not decline. In 1950 the few Coloreds in the Cape who were allowed to vote were removed from the common voter rolls. They were (and are still) allowed to continue to vote but now on separate rolls, which deprives them of any direct representation in the government of the country. (The seven representatives of Africans in Parliament—who were White—were removed in 1959, thus abolishing all African representation in Parliament.)

In response to the 1950 restrictions, organized Africans decided that they would defy those laws that administered unequal treatment to them instead of only protesting them. The "defiance campaign," as it came to be known, started June 26, 1952. Before the end of the year thousands of African men and women were arrested for entering "Europeans Only" post offices, railroad stations, and other facilities. No one resisted arrest: the idea was to fill the jails with passive resisters.

The government responded swiftly by banning African, Indian, and Colored leaders. It also passed new legislation making passive resistance illegal, thereby giving police more effective measures with which to deal with resisters. The grievances of the Africans, Indians, and Coloreds were never considered.

In 1955 the ANC called for 50,000 volunteers to collect "freedom demands" from all sectors of the South African people. The thousands of demands that came from virtually every economic and racial sector of the country were incorporated into a Freedom Charter for South Africa. The government's response to this showing of anti-apartheid sentiment was to arrest over 100 people in 1956 and charge them with high treason for their role in the freedom charter campaign.

The following is an excerpt from the 1955 Freedom Charter issued in Kliptown, near Johannesburg:

> We, the people of South Africa, declare for all our country and the world to know:
> That South Africa belongs to all who live in it, black and white, and that no government can justly claim authority unless it is based on the will of all the people; that our people have been robbed of their birthright to land, liberty and peace by a form of government founded on injustice and inequality;
> That our country will never be prosperous or free until all our people live in brotherhood, enjoying equal rights and opportunities;
> That only a democratic state, based on the will of all the people, can secure to all their birthright without distinction of colour, race, sex or belief.

One of the Africans' major grievances has always been the system of pass laws which are responsible for the daily arrests of thousands of Blacks. In 1960 the Pan Africanist Congress (PAC), another major African political party, organized a nationwide "stay-at-home" to challenge these laws. In the township of Sharpeville, not far from Johannesburg, several thousand Africans gathered in one such peaceful demonstration. Although no order to disperse was given, the police opened fire on the crowd without warning, killing sixty-nine and wounding several hundred. The country was outraged. Protest—including a highly successful general strike—was so intense that many foreign businessmen believed that a major civil insurrection would break out.

The government responded immediately by declaring a state of emergency, banning all meetings, curtailing the press, and arresting several hundred people without bringing charges against them. But the government's most important action by far was to ban the two major African political parties—the ANC and the PAC. From that time on, there has been no way for Africans to voice their political opinions legally.

C. Repression

There have been many massacres of Africans in South Africa and innumerable political murders. But as the world watched Africa in 1960—the year many Black states were granted independence from colonial rule—Sharpeville finally made people see that a massacre in South Africa was not an aberration, an accident. Maintaining apartheid has always meant government by violence.

The South African army is the ultimate enforcer of the government's apartheid policies. A former Minister of Defense (and now State President of South Africa) made this quite clear when he declared: "Do not think we are arming

to fight a foreign enemy, we are not. We are arming to shoot
down the Black masses."

All White males receive compulsory army training for one
year, and in each of the succeeding nine years must complete two weeks further training in camps. They then pass
into the reserve unit of the army. The entire White male
population is thus equipped to be a citizens' militia which
can be quickly mobilized. The army enforces martial law
(such as imposed after Sharpeville, for example) and is increasingly trained in anti-guerrilla actions. There are no
Africans or Asians in the army.

As apartheid has been more and more strictly enforced
in recent years, South African defense expenditures have
skyrocketed. The government spent $61 million on defense
in 1960 and $356 million in 1968. South Africa's arsenal in-
cludes three brand-new French nuclear submarines, French
Alouette helicopters, and Mirage jet fighters with air-to-
surface missiles; thirty-six F-86 Sabrejet interceptors, Sikor-
sky helicopters, and C-47 and C-130B transports from the
United States; and armored cars, machine guns, and over
500 airplanes (including both short- and long-range bombers) from Great Britain. In addition, Prime Minister Vorster
has said recently that "South Africa does not need one
penny's worth of gunpowder to attack any Black state in
Africa . . . we can manufacture enough weapons of our
own to deal with any of these countries."

South Africa's police expenditures have increased, too—
from $50 million in 1960 to $120 million in 1968. The police
and the Security Branch (similar to the FBI) have extremely
wide powers. The government, through the police, controls
all of the following things: the right to hold public meetings
or public and private protests; what individuals may say,
what they may read, where they can travel, who they can
visit; who can attend a university and what can be studied
there. The police may enter and search anyone's home at

any time of day or night without a warrant. They may arrest anyone without bringing charges against them. They may keep people in solitary confinement without allowing anyone, even a lawyer, to visit them. They may send people to live in remote parts of the country and may forbid people to either enter or leave an area. The police may forbid teachers to teach and prevent writers and journalists from writing. They may wiretap telephones, open and scrutinize all letters, and in countless other ways keep any given individual under close surveillance.

The laws which give the police these wide powers are called repressive legislation; they deny all citizens fundamental human rights. The government has outlawed freedom of speech and of assembly, for example, and has provided for punishment without trial. The Security Branch which enforces these laws is actually a political police force. It is extremely efficient in finding and physically suppressing opposition to the government. The system the Security Branch uses to force people to be informants and to maintain a network of spies is very similar to that of the Gestapo under Hitler in the 1930s. And like the Nazis, the Security Branch is ruthless in exercising its powers; its use of torture has been documented in thousands of cases. It is for these reasons that South Africa is called a police state.

Throughout most of the twentieth century all opposition to apartheid, whether strikes, rallies, or petitions, has had to evade the growing power of the police. Finally in 1960, with apartheid more rigidly enforced than ever, the government made all forms of opposition, including peaceful demonstrations, strikes, picketing, and lobbying, illegal. By banning all African political organizations, and especially the two largest voices of African opposition to apartheid (the ANC and the PAC), the government left Africans with two alternatives: either give up all opposition or continue it by illegal, extraparliamentary networks.

For the preceding twenty years, Africans had repeatedly warned the government against forcing them into the position of having either to submit or to fight. Faced with that decision in 1960, Africans did not submit. Following the bannings, the PAC formed Poqo (Pure) and the ANC formed Umkhonto We Sizwe (Spear of the Nation)—the military organizations of the two parties. In the government's campaigns of repression, aimed at eliminating the nationalist groups taking military action, thousands of Africans were brought to trial and sentenced to death or long prison terms. At one such political trial in 1964, Elias Motsoaledi explained his reason for joining the underground movement:

> When I was asked to join Umkhonto We Sizwe, it was at a time when it was clear to me that all our years of peaceful struggle had been of no use. The government would not let us fight peacefully any more, and had blocked all of our legal acts by making them illegal. I could see no other way open to me. What I did brought me no personal gain; what I did I did for my people and because I thought it was the only way left for me to help my people.

Many ANC and PAC members left South Africa secretly to train as guerrilla fighters in Black African countries. The ones who stayed behind initiated planned acts of sabotage against government buildings and electrical installations. At his trial for political offense, Nelson Mandela, one of the main leaders of the outlawed ANC, explained that this policy had been undertaken to pressure the government to change its policies of apartheid: "Umkhonto, by its policy of controlled sabotage, hoped to bring the government and its supporters to their senses before it was too late." The ANC's

creed, Mandela explained, was based on a "concept of freedom and fulfillment for the African people in their own land,
but not of driving Whites into the sea." And he continued:

> During my lifetime I dedicated myself to this struggle
> of the African people. I have fought against White dom-
> ination and I have fought against Black domination. I
> have cherished the ideal of a democratic and free so-
> ciety in which all persons live together in harmony,
> and with equal opportunities.

The pressure of these sabotage incidents did not move
the government one inch from its committed path; it only
introduced even more severe legislation. The Sabotage Act,
passed by Parliament with only one dissenting vote, allows
for the arbitrary arrest of any suspect for an indefinite period of time, makes people accused of sabotage guilty until
they prove themselves innocent, and defines sabotage so
broadly as to include painting slogans on walls.

Throughout South Africa's history, apartheid has been
more and more harshly enforced. The reality of White supremacy has forced African people to resist. The government has responded to popular pressure and protest only
by enacting even more repressive measures. As a result, the
government today has wide control over *all* South Africans,
Black and White.

The number of political trials continues to grow each
year. But this is also an indication of the strength of the
struggle for freedom in South Africa in the face of the police
state. In the first years of the 1970s, resistance of all kinds—
strikes, protests, guerrilla activity—has expanded. The huge
workers' strike in Durban in the winter of 1972–73 is just
one example of this activity; it reveals only the tip of the
resistance struggle that also includes stepped-up guerrilla

fighting on South Africa's borders. Although severe censorship of the press rarely allows news of this continuing opposition to get out of the country, things are not quiet in South Africa. The people sing "Mayibuye i' Afrika"—"Africa must come back to us."

CHAPTER TWO

LIFE UNDER PORTUGUESE COLONIALISM

I. The Overseas Provinces: The Last of the Colonies

Portugal was the first modern European country to invade Africa and it is the last major colonial power there today. Four hundred and fifty years have gone by since the Portuguese first landed in Africa in search of better trade routes to Asia.

Today, the Portuguese are still holding tight to Mozambique and Angola in Southern Africa, Guinea-Bissau in West Africa, and the Cape Verde Islands in the Atlantic. Although Guinea-Bissau and the Cape Verde Islands are geographically set apart from the other two Portuguese colonies, they are administered under the same colonial policy. (Guinea-Bissau—so called to distinguish it from the neighboring Republic of Guinea, a former French colony—is, thus, politically a part of the Southern Africa complex although geographically it is in West Africa.)

The Portuguese do not call their holdings in Africa "colonies." Since 1952 Portugal has referred to them as "overseas provinces," maintaining that they are an integral part of the Portuguese nation. This change in terms was designed to avoid United Nations resolutions which apply to colonized territories. Now Portugal refuses to debate questions relating to colonialism on the grounds that the African territories are Portuguese provinces.

To the Africans under Portuguese rule, however, it makes little difference what the label is. For them the present relationship between Portugal and the provinces is just an alternative form of the old colonial relationship, where an outside government imposes its rule on a local people; the Portuguese have political, administrative, economic, and social control over the lives of Africans.

PORTUGUESE AFRICA

Guinea-Bissau and the Cape Verde Islands are geographically set apart from the other Portuguese colonies in Southern Africa. However, they operate under the same colonial policy: in each area land, labor, educational, and administrative policy have been similar.

II. Portugal and the Colonies

A. Economic and Political Relations

Portugal is the poorest nation in Western Europe. It has been governed by a dictatorship since António de Oliveira Salazar came to power in 1926. Portugal imposes on its colonies a rigid administrative structure which is designed to extract economic benefits for Portugal from its African "possessions."

The colonies themselves are agricultural societies. Traditionally, most Africans engaged in subsistence farming, growing just what was needed for family or community consumption. There was little production for market exchange.

Portuguese colonialism has changed this pattern, however, because Portugal's industry is heavily dependent on raw materials produced in the colonies. The colonial system has been geared toward extracting certain crops from Africa which are needed in Portugal. Africans have been forced to change the kind of farming they do in order to meet these Portuguese demands.

Colonial authorities frequently compel Africans to produce a certain crop. Millions of Africans have been pushed off their land by Europeans who want it for plantations. Often these same farmers have been forced to work the land they once owned, for the minimal wages paid by plantation owners.

Cotton production in Mozambique illustrates how the Portuguese control African production. Portugal's textile industry employs over one third of all Portuguese labor. Cotton is one of Mozambique's chief export crops; 82 per cent of it is bought by these textile mills in Portugal. For Africans, who can neither use it themselves nor make a profit from it, there is little incentive to grow cotton; the

Portuguese have had to force them to cultivate it. A young Mozambican, Gabriel Mauticio Nantombo, describes how this was done in the Cabo Delgado district:

> When the company came to exploit our region, everyone was forced to cultivate one field of cotton. . . . The time of cotton growing was a time of great poverty, because we could only produce cotton; we got a poor price for it, and we did not have time to grow other crops. We were forced to produce cotton. The people didn't want to; they knew cotton is the mother of poverty, but the company was protected by the government. We knew that anyone who refused to grow it would be sent to the plantations on São Tomé where he would work without any pay at all. So as not to make our poverty any greater, then, so as not to leave the family and leave the children to suffer alone, we had to grow cotton. The company and government work together closely to enforce the system.

Quoted in Eduardo Mondlane, *The Struggle for Mozambique,* 1970

African cotton producers are legally bound to sell what they cultivate to concessionary companies. By contrast, Europeans who produce cotton in Mozambique can sell theirs on the open world market at much higher prices. The companies which buy African-produced cotton have a monopoly in each region and can set prices as low as they wish. They then supply the Portuguese textile industry, assuring Portugal of getting the raw material it needs at low prices.

Most other crops are produced on plantations, where Africans are paid for their labor rather than for what they produce. The company and the government work together, assuring products for the government, profits for the company, and low wages for the workers. Labor recruitment is based on force, either direct or indirect.

Africans are made to work for Europeans indirectly in

order to earn money to pay taxes levied by the colonial regime. Subsistence farming involves no cash, so Africans must turn elsewhere to get money. They have the choice of either producing the cotton which the Portuguese want to buy or hiring themselves out to work on plantations. If they are not able to pay taxes, they can be sentenced to forced labor, with no pay at all.

Legalized forced labor in the Portuguese colonies followed a long period of slavery which lasted in some cases into the twentieth century. One of the first things Salazar did when he came to power was to ensure that forced African labor was written into law. This was done by making it illegal to be idle. The Portuguese defined "idleness" as any work which did not benefit them (e.g., subsistence farming).

By the mid-twentieth century, unfavorable world opinion induced the Portuguese to change the forced labor law. Under a new law Africans could be forced to work only if it was in the "public interest" to do so. But the Portuguese determined what was the "public interest" and, in effect, perpetuated the old system after it was illegal. An American businessman who worked for years in Angola wrote anonymously in *Harper's Magazine* in 1961:

> According to law, it is only in cases where the "public interest" is involved that labor may be requisitioned and such requisitioning must be done by the government, operating through the *chefes de posto*.* Under this heading falls the forced labor on roads, which is done without benefit of wages. Most of the local road work in a given district is performed by women, who are taken from native villages nearby. It is a common thing in the interior to pass gangs consisting of twenty or thirty women of all ages, some in pregnancy, raising and

* Local Portuguese administrator.

letting fall their mattocks in unison as they clean ditches or repair the roads. For major government projects, men and boys are customarily recruited, often spending six months or a year many miles from home.

Today labor can be extracted from Africans in many ways, some more subtle than direct coercion but having the same effect:

1. CORRECTIONAL LABOR. One may be forced to work instead of serving a prison sentence for non-payment of taxes.

2. OBLIGATORY LABOR. Until 1961 all "natives" had to work six months of the year for the state, a company, or an individual. Since then, the law allows such labor to be used to "redress economic ills." The workers receive minimal pay.

3. CONTRACT LABOR. The employee is contracted to do a job. If he does not fulfill some part of the obligation, he can be forced to do correctional labor.

4. FORCED CULTIVATION. The farmer is paid for what he produces rather than for his labor. Most of the earnings go towards taxes.

5. EXPORT LABOR. For work in South African mines, South Africa pays Portugal a recruitment fee of six dollars per African worker. Over 200,000 Mozambicans are recruited this way every year. In 1960 nearly one third of all Mozambican males worked in South African mines.

In addition to forcing Africans to work for them, the Portuguese often claim land which has been occupied by Africans for centuries. In Angola the average land occupied by Europeans is six times that owned by Africans. A Mozambican woman, Natacha Deolinda, describes this system.

At Buzi the Portuguese bought all the land. There were some villages on the land, and the people in them were driven out and had to leave their homes, their land, and look for another place to live. They received no compensation for their houses; they were just driven out. In our area we were forced to leave, abandoning our fields, and the Portuguese planted sugar cane everywhere. We were not allowed to use the wells we had dug; all the water was reserved for the cane. If one of us was found with some sugar cane, they arrested us and made us pay fifty escudos for a tiny piece of it. They said we had stolen it, and if we didn't have any money the administration made us work for a week in the plantation, supposedly to pay for the bit of sugar cane.

Quoted in Mondlane, *The Struggle for Mozambique*

Thus, the Portuguese can force Africans to work, force them to do a particular kind of work, regulate the amount they get paid for their work, and take their land away from them. The effect of this system has been to totally disrupt the normal economic and social life of the African. In southern Mozambique, more than half the Mozambican males live away from their families, working on plantations or in mines. The forced production of cash crops has severely limited the amount of crops grown for food, causing frequent famines.

In Guinea the situation was slightly different, mainly because the swampy terrain discouraged settlers, but also because the small land area provided few mineral and natural resources for exploitation. This meant that there was relatively little forced labor, although in general conditions were the same as those in the other colonies.

A Mozambican peasant, Joachim Maquival, tells how Portuguese colonialism affected his life:

. . . the company paid money to the . . . government, and then the government arrested us and gave us to the company. I began working for the company when I was twelve . . . The whole family worked for the company; my brothers, my father—my father is still there. My father earned and still earns 150 escudos a month ($5.30). He had to pay 195 escudos tax yearly. We didn't want to work for the company, but if we refused the government circulated photographs and a hunt was started. When they caught them they beat them and put them into prison, and when they came out of prison they had to go and work but without pay . . . Thus in our own fields only our mothers were left . . . All we had to eat was the little our mothers were able to grow. We had to work on the tea plantations but we didn't know what it tasted like. Tea never came to our homes.

Quoted in Mondlane, The Struggle for Mozambique

B. Social Relations

1. THE POLICY OF ASSIMILATION

The Portuguese say that, unlike in South Africa, there is no racial discrimination in the Portuguese colonies. Instead, they claim, there is equal social and economic opportunity for anyone who is assimilated into Portuguese culture, regardless of color. This policy of assimilation is based on the assumption of the superiority of Portuguese civilization. According to this philosophy, it is the mission of the Portuguese to "civilize" the Africans, which is to be accomplished by the spread of Portuguese culture in the colonies. In the words of the late Prime Minister Salazar:

> We should organize more and more efficiently the protection of the inferior races whose call to our Christian civilization is one of the most daring concepts and sublime tasks of Portuguese civilization.

In this philosophy, it is culture rather than color which determines the rights and status of an individual. Unless an

African gives up his own culture and adopts the Portuguese culture in full, he is not considered worthy of equal rights.

Until 1961 there was a legal distinction between those who had assimilated (*assimilados*) and those who had not (*indigenas*). For most Africans, the effect of this classification system was the same as South Africa's classification by race. Indigenas got lower wages, were restricted in job opportunities, political rights, and property rights. All Europeans in the colonies were automatically classified as citizens in Portugal. But Africans had to prove that they were "civilized" to become citizens. They had to show that they could read, write, and speak Portuguese fluently; that they had sufficient means to support their families; that they were of good character (as defined by the Portuguese); that they had the necessary education and social habits to fit into Portuguese culture. In addition, they had to get approval from the local administrative authority and the district governor to get *assimilado* status. Some governors required that Africans stand in the public square of their villages and denounce their African heritage and ancestry. In essence, becoming assimilated meant rejecting one's people and one's past. An African high school student tells about the pain he felt at having to denounce his African identity and yet not being accepted as a White:

> By the end of secondary school, I was almost the only African left in class. I used to get lower marks than the Portuguese boys for the same work. My White companions could not see anything wrong with this. At the same time they used to talk in front of me about "those ignorant blacks," referring to unassimilated Africans, and they could not see how this might be painful to me as an *assimilado*.
>
> Quoted in Mondlane, *The Struggle for Mozambique*

The assimilation system was a false hope to most Africans. In order to become assimilated, one had to be educated, but in order to gain access to the educational system, one had to speak Portuguese (which presupposed in most cases, coming from an *assimilado* background). By 1960, after five centuries of the influence of Portuguese culture, only 0.08 per cent of the population of Mozambique and 0.7 per cent of the population of Angola were assimilated.

In the early 1960s the legal distinction between *assimilado* and *indigena* was abolished but the philosophy behind it remains. Assimilation into Portuguese culture is still a goal offered to Africans by the Portuguese, and the prize is still higher wages, greater job opportunities, and elevated social status. In the last decade the Portuguese have realized the psychological importance of offering upward mobility to Africans. New schools have been opened, more Africans have been given administrative posts, new jobs are being made available, and more Africans are being integrated into the social structure. These developments are a direct response to growing discontent and organized resistance by Africans. The Portuguese realize that they can only hold on to their colonies if they promise concrete improvements in conditions to Africans. The campaign for reform is directed toward creating a class of Africans who are loyal to Portugal and who will serve the needs of Portuguese interests in Africa. As such, it is an attempt to pacify Africans who might otherwise turn against the Portuguese. The effects of the campaign are, however, largely limited to urban areas. The masses of rural Africans remain uneducated, outside of the administrative structure, and unable to change their economic position. For them the changes are paper reforms.

Thus, the assimilation philosophy is a strategy designed to give Africans the illusion that they can gain equal status to the Portuguese and that conditions for them are improving. It is used to keep Africans quiet by offering them hope.

2. EDUCATION IN THE COLONIES

The education system in the Portuguese colonies has traditionally reinforced the differential status of Europeans and Africans. Until recently, there were few public schools and these were attended primarily by Europeans. The education of Africans was left in the hands of missionaries. The number of Africans who actually got any education at all was very small. In 1950 in Angola, for example, there were a total of 737 African primary school students; the number who went on to secondary school was negligible. The fees for attending secondary school were high and advancement in school depended on knowledge of Portuguese (since all classes were taught in Portuguese). An indication of the impact of the educational system is the fact that in 1960 the rate of illiteracy in Mozambique was over 95 per cent; in Angola it was 99 per cent.

What education Africans did get was designed to make them good workers and loyal servants of Portugal. A Portuguese cardinal described the goals of African education as follows in 1960:

> We try to reach the native population both in breadth and depth to [teach them] reading, writing, and arithmetic, not to make "doctors" of them . . . To educate and instruct them so as to make them prisoners of the soil and to protect them from the lure of the towns. . . . Schools are necessary, yes, but schools where we teach the native the path of human dignity and the grandeur of the nation which protects him.

It must be remembered that the school system was the primary tool for becoming assimilated. Thus the limited educational opportunity meant a limitation in the possibilities of assimilation. African children whose parents were not assimilated were cut off because their parents could often not afford school fees (since their wages were low) and because they did not speak Portuguese. The school system did not provide a way to break into the closed circle of assimilation.

With the change in assimilation policy came a change in educational policy. New schools were opened and expenditure on African education increased. However, the content of the education remained unchanged. Today all classes are still taught in Portuguese; the curriculum focuses on Portuguese history, geography, and culture, Christian morals, agriculture and handicrafts. African history and geography are ignored.

Josina Muthemba, a Mozambican girl who was at technical school only a few years ago, talked about her school experience:

> The colonialists wanted to deceive us with their teaching; they taught us only the history of Portugal, the geography of Portugal; they wanted to form in us a passive mentality, to make us resigned to their domination. We couldn't react openly, but we were aware of their lie; we knew that what they said was false; that we were Mozambicans and we could never be Portuguese.
>
> Quoted in Mondlane, *The Struggle for Mozambique*

The new educational reforms do not change the basic fact of African education: that it is designed to create the kind of citizens who will serve the needs of Portugal. The Portuguese realized the need for a broader base of middle-class Africans (for reasons outlined in the preceding section) and expanded the educational system accordingly, but the ultimate goal—maintaining the Portuguese in a position of power—remains the same.

III. Resistance to Colonialism

Africans have resisted Portuguese penetration since the initial contacts between them in the fifteenth century. Portugal was able to establish itself firmly along the coasts of Africa because of its superior naval power. Traditional African states and kingdoms organized the defense of the interior; they were usually able to hold off Portuguese efforts to conquer inland territory. But the lack of unity between African states sometimes enabled the Portuguese to benefit from divide-and-rule tactics. Portuguese forces, sometimes in alliance with Africans, engaged in extensive inland warfare to capture many thousands of slaves for export to the Americas. During four centuries of such sporadic warfare, Portugal was never strong enough effectively to conquer and control all of Angola and Mozambique but had sufficient power to prevent any African states from restoring peace and unity to the area. By the early twentieth century, the old African states were demoralized and weakened beyond recovery, and traditional forms of resistance collapsed.

With the passing of the old order, new organizations developed among the African people who joined together on the basis of common suffering under Portuguese colonialism rather than the old ethnic and regional relationships. People began to understand their common oppression through tax collection, forced labor, and land seizure.

Resistance took several forms in the early decades of the century. In rural areas people tried to counter Portuguese exploitation by setting up co-operatives, but such new economic structures were soon crushed by colonial authorities. In the cities Africans had closer contact with the Portuguese and weaker ethnic ties among themselves. In these urban conditions the seeds of African nationalism germinated. In 1920 urban Africans organized the African League, whose goals included national unity, unity between the peoples of different colonies, and unity of oppressed Black people everywhere. Other nationalist organizations crystallized during the 1920s in Angola and Mozambique. When Salazar came to power, however, these organizations were outlawed and broken up.

After World War II there was a general movement for independence and an end to colonialism throughout Africa. In the Portuguese colonies, three groups of Africans were struggling against Portugal through secret political organizing and actions.

The first of these were intellectuals, usually *assimilados*, who had come to regard the Portuguese notion of "national unity" as hypocritical. Many were students who met at Portuguese universities and through these early associations laid the groundwork for later political organizations. Their political consciousness took the form of cultural expression, since overt political action was illegal. Through poetry and prose they played on three main themes: (1) reaffirmation of Africa as their mother country and cultural heritage, (2) the call to revolt of Black people all over the world, and (3) the sufferings of ordinary Black people throughout Portuguese Africa.

José Craveirinha, a Mozambican nationalist, wrote of the colonial relationship during this period of cultural resistance:

> I am coal!
> You tear me brutally from the ground
> and make of me your mine, boss
>
> I am coal
> and you burn me, boss
> to serve you forever as your driving force
> but not forever, boss

I am coal
and must burn
and consume everything in the heat of my combustion

I am coal
and must burn, exploited
burn alive like tar, my brother
until no more your mine, boss

I am coal
and must burn
and consume everything in the fire of my combustion

Yes, boss
I will be your coal.

José Craveirinha

The second group of resisters were secondary school students, who, for example, in Mozambique, formed an organization called NESAM (Nucleus of African Secondary Students of Mozambique) and worked to build a sense of pride in their African heritage and Mozambican nationhood. NESAM was banned in 1964, but from it came many of the nationalist leaders who are today fighting the Portuguese.

Workers from the towns and plantations formed the third group. In 1947 and 1948 they conducted a series of strikes on Mozambican docks and plantations. Several hundred people were deported in retaliation by the Portuguese. In 1956 the police killed forty-nine striking dock workers. In Angola three nationalist leaders were arrested in that year. Hundreds more were arrested, secretly tried, and sentenced to prison in 1959.

By the late 1950s it became clear that sporadic local resistance would result only in repression and death and that it was necessary to organize into larger political units. Nationalist political parties were formed in all of the Portuguese colonies by 1960. The founders of these parties had come from a common political background, had studied together in Portugal, and later had worked together to establish organizations in their respective homelands.

In June of 1960 an Angolan nationalist party, the Popular Movement for the Liberation of Angola (MPLA), sent a memorandum to Portugal requesting a peaceful solution to the colonial question. The Portuguese responded by arresting fifty-two Africans, including MPLA leader Agostinho Neto. When villagers from Neto's region went to demand his release, they were fired upon. Thirty were killed; many more were wounded.

In early 1961 a group of cotton workers protested low wages and bad working conditions in southern Angola. The Portuguese immediately bombed their villages. When Angolans attacked a police station in Luanda, the Angolan capital, the Portuguese responded by killing 3,000 in that city alone. By mid-March, a nationalist organization called UPA (Popular Union of Angola) was able to lead an area-wide rebellion in northern Angola sparked by a revolt against an employer who had killed African workers. In the aftermath of this widespread protest, 20,000 Africans were reported killed by the Portuguese in a systematic campaign of repression.

In Guinea-Bissau, the workers at the river port of Pijiguiti went on strike on August 3, 1959, for better working conditions and decent salaries. In response, the Portuguese government sent in troops, who killed fifty workers in fifteen minutes.

In Mozambique about 600 Africans were killed on June 16, 1960, in a peaceful gathering outside a government official's office in the town of Mueda. The story of that massacre is told by an eyewitness, Alberto-Joaquim Chipande:

> How did that happen? Well, some of these men had made contact with the authorities and asked for more

liberty and more pay . . . After a while, when people were giving support to these leaders, the Portuguese sent police through the villages inviting people to a meeting at Mueda. Several thousand people came to hear what the Portuguese would say.

Then the governor invited our leaders into the administrator's office. When they came outside, the governor asked the crowd who wanted to speak. Many wanted to speak, and the governor told them all to stand on one side.

Then without another word he ordered the police to bind the hands of those who had stood on one side, and the police began beating them. When the people saw what was happening, they began to demonstrate against the Portuguese, and the Portuguese simply ordered the police trucks to come and collected these arrested persons. So there were more demonstrations against this. At that moment the troops were still hidden, and the people went up close to the police to stop the arrested persons from being taken away. So the governor called the troops, and when they appeared he told them to open fire. They killed about 600 people. Now the Portuguese say they have punished that governor, but of course they have only sent him somewhere else.

Quoted in Mondlane, *The Struggle for Mozambique*

By the early 1960s it had become clear to nationalist leaders that their struggle would have to go beyond appeals to the UN and protest demonstrations which ended in massacre. Political organization by itself was not sufficient. In the words of the leader of the Mozambican independence movement, Eduardo Mondlane:

By 1961 two conclusions were obvious. First, Portugal would not admit the principle of self-determination and independence or allow for any extension of democracy under her own rule, although by then it was clear that

her own "Portuguese" solutions to our oppressed condition, such as assimilation by multiracial *colonatos,* multiracial schools, local elections, etc., had proved a mean-
ingless fraud. Secondly, moderate political action such as
strikes, demonstrations, and petitions would result only
in the destruction of those who took part in them. We
were, therefore, left with these alternatives: to continue
indefinitely living under a repressive imperial rule or to
find a means of using force against Portugal which would
be effective enough to hurt Portugal without resulting
in our own ruin.

Quoted in Mondlane, *The Struggle for Mozambique*

Liberation movements dedicated to ending Portuguese
colonial rule developed in Portuguese Africa by the early
1960s. Military operations began in Angola in 1961, in
Guinea-Bissau in 1963, and in Mozambique in 1964.

Nationalist leaders spent several years making political
preparations for this new stage of struggle. They studied
the specific characteristics of every region of the country.
They talked at great length with the people in each region
to convince them that by working together they could defeat their foreign rulers. They explained that their enemies
were those who opposed the freedom of the colonies rather
than the Portuguese people or all White people in general.
In a message to the Mozambican people, the Mozambican
liberation front (FRELIMO) explained:

The purpose of our struggle is not only to destroy. It
is first and foremost aimed at building a new Mozambique, where there will be no hunger and where all
men will be free and equal. We are fighting with arms
in our hands, because in order to build the Mozambique
that we want we must first destroy the Portuguese colonial system . . . only after this will we be able to use
for ourselves our labor and the wealth of our country . . .

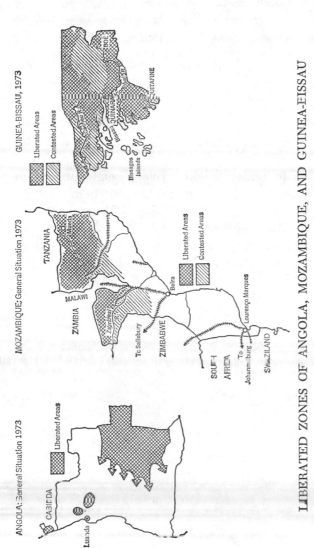

ANGOLA: General Situation 1973

Liberated Areas

CABINDA

Luanda

MOZAMBIQUE: General Situation 1973

TANZANIA

Muéda

MALAWI

ZAMBIA

Zambesi

To Salisbury

ZIMBABWE

Beira

Liberated Areas

Contested Areas

SOUTH
AFRICA

To
Johannesburg

Lourenço Marques

SWAZILAND

GUINEA-BISSAU, 1973

Liberated Areas

Contested Areas

BOE

Cacheu

Bissau

GUINAPA

Bissagos
Islands

QUITAFINE

LIBERATED ZONES OF ANGOLA, MOZAMBIQUE, AND GUINEA-BISSAU

In Angola most of the eastern half of the country is no longer under the control of the Portuguese. In Mozambique the three northern districts are free, and FRELIMO has recently penetrated south of the Zambesi. In Guinea-Bissau the entire country except for the cities is liberated territory, controlled and administered by the people. These victories reflect the determination of the people who have fought under incredible hardships with few supplies or weapons from the outside.

The liberation movements have now been involved in armed struggle for a decade. These wars have been fought by the entire populations of the colonies. Everyone is not armed, but the few people who have weapons are supported by the rest of the people. Unarmed people help by raising food, by giving shelter for those fighting, by transporting supplies, and, most important, by changing their own society.

In the liberated areas of Guinea-Bissau, Angola, and Mozambique, four times as many children are attending school than were able to under colonial rule. Social patterns in general are changing. There is greater participation by everyone in the running of each village. Farming is now co-operative, with the workers sharing the produce between them. Women are moving out of their subservient positions and are taking part in all aspects of building the new society.

CHAPTER THREE

PORTUGAL AND THE WEST

1. Portugal's Dilemma

Today African movements in the Portuguese colonies are fighting for their independence. Over the past thirteen years Portugal has had to face increasingly expensive wars in attempting to defeat these nationalist movements. It spends a higher percentage of its gross national product on defense than any other Western country except the United States. But America is the richest country in the world; Portugal is the poorest country in Europe. Half of the population of Portugal remains illiterate. The average yearly income for a Portuguese citizen is $360. Ten per cent of that meager income must be paid to the government as a defense tax. Portugal has an annual defense budget of $400 million. This represents over 50 per cent of the country's state revenues.

African revolts in the early 1960s caught Portugal unaware. In 1961 it had only 3,000 troops stationed in Angola. During the next six months Portugal sent 50,000 soldiers there and spent 15 per cent of its gold reserves in emergency expenditures. Revolts in Mozambique and Guinea-Bissau brought a dramatic increase of troops to these colonies as well. But Africans responded by strengthening their opposition to the Portuguese—resistance continued to grow each year.

Like Portugal, Britain and France had also faced local demands to give independence to their colonies. However, both countries, unlike Portugal, were in a position to grant political independence without giving up their economic control of the colonies. For one thing, the British and French had trained African administrative elites to oversee the commercial operations established under colonial rule. Decolonization did not present the same threat to them that it does to Portugal.

Portugal, on the other hand, does not have the financial resources of Britain or France. Without the protection of colonial trading relations with the colonies, Portugal would be squeezed out of its business in Africa. For example, the Portuguese textile industry cannot compete with foreign companies buying cotton from Angola or Mozambique at higher prices. Portugal would have no basis for continued economic domination of the colonies if they were to be granted independence.

Furthermore, Africans were never raised to managerial positions in the Portuguese colonial administration. In recent years the Portuguese have conceded some social benefits to the Africans. But in spite of these measures, no client class of Africans has emerged which could carry out the present administrative functions. While the French and British made colonial reforms in times of relative peace, social reforms in Portuguese Africa are now being instituted in a time of war. Africans cannot be sure that the Portuguese have the welfare of the people in mind when for every new school built, ten villages are destroyed by bombs. At this point, decolonization would mean the loss of Portugal's political influence in Africa.

Portugal chose not to follow the wave of decolonization in Africa and is firmly committed to defending its colonies there. It now has about 160,000 well-equipped troops in the colonies. The cost of maintaining these forces has drained Portugal's economy. Unable to cope with the financial burden of a sustained war effort, Portugal has had to turn to other Western countries for assistance.

At the outbreak of the wars, Western countries were hesitant in aiding Portugal. This was a time when anti-colonial movements were growing elsewhere in Africa, and Western powers saw no future in the perpetuation of an old-style colonial regime. So Portugal had to offer attractive reasons for Western support.

A. Portugal Looks for Help

In the early 1960s Portugal passed a series of laws which gave foreign companies generous incentives to invest in her colonies. An account in the West German weekly *Die Zeit* (1961) explains this new policy of actively attracting foreign investment:

> In a kind of last minute panic Portugal has in the past few months opened wide its hitherto almost hermetically closed doors to foreign investments. The reason for this changed course is . . . the knowledge that Portugal will inevitably lose the struggle now beginning for its colonial empire if it is not able in time to win powerful allies for itself in the struggle . . . in this dangerous situation Salazar has radically changed his economic policy without much noise, with a minimum of publicity even, he set out economically to internationalize, to the greatest possible extent, his empire. It is in particular the Americans, the Germans, and the Japanese who are called upon in connection with the industrial development in Portugal's underdeveloped African possessions. Today this policy is securing the intended results . . . lately there has been a growing realization that the involvement of foreign capital in Portuguese Africa has its effects on the attitudes of foreign governments to the nationalist revolts.

The inflow of Western capital into the colonies has provided Portugal's weak economy with foreign exchange necessary to cover its military expenditures. Portugal receives part of the profits of every company that is given permission to operate in the colonies. The Portuguese share of the profits comes from land rental, income taxes, concession rights, and royalties which each corporation must pay to the local administration where it is doing business.

This accumulation of foreign capital allows Portugal the flexibility to import military supplies as they are needed.

In the interest of maintaining their lucrative operations in the colonies, corporations have lent financial backing to the Portuguese war effort. In this way Portugal has implicated Western corporations in its policies and derives political support for continuing the wars.

As Portugal began to solicit Western support by opening the colonies to foreign investment, some Western powers were still reluctant to take an unpopular stand on the side of colonialism and aid the Portuguese. The Angolan revolts in 1961 and the ensuing bloody Portuguese reprisals brought international condemnation to the Portuguese regime. In January 1962 the United Nations passed a resolution confirming Angola's right to independence. This blow to Portugal's image in the world was sharpened by the fact that the United States voted in support of the resolution.

In an effort to pressure the United States to reverse its policy on the Portuguese colonies, Portugal threatened to cut off U.S. military base rights in the Azores. During this period United States strategists viewed the Azores bases as indispensable for American security in Europe. Nearly 80 per cent of U.S. military transport en route to Europe refueled there.

The Portuguese threat elicited the intended response from the United States. In December 1962 the United

States voted against a United Nations General Assembly resolution condemning Portuguese policy and calling for a ban on the sale of arms to Portugal. The following year the American Under Secretary of State for Africa, G. Mennen Williams, stated that: "It is neither in our interest to see the Portuguese leave Africa nor to curtail their influence out there." Ever since then, the United States has voted in the United Nations against resolutions demanding that measures be taken against Portugal.

Owing to the development of longer-range aircraft, the strategic value of the Azores to the United States has been declining steadily since the crisis of the early sixties. But U.S. business interests in the colonies have increased tremendously over the same period. Although strategic considerations have ceased to dictate United States policy towards Portugal, the future stability of American business operations in the colonies has demanded that the United States maintain friendly relations with the Portuguese regime.

Perhaps this second consideration explains why, in spite of the Azores' minimal strategic importance, the United States government gave Portugal a five-year $436 million economic aid package in late 1971 in exchange for continued use of the Azores base. The deal confirmed Portugal's hopes that the United States would not return to its former anti-colonial stance in the United Nations. As the *U.S. News and World Report* said:

> For years the Portuguese complained that the U.S., their ally in Europe, worked against them in Africa. There is less of that kind of talk now and the Portuguese expect the relationship to keep on improving under Nixon.

In 1969 Portuguese Foreign Secretary Nogueira confirmed that this change in attitude towards Portugal was not

unique to the United States but applied to the rest of the
Western world as well:

> For a long time it seemed as though the big powers
> had united against Portugal; meanwhile, however, the
> Western big powers have recognized the value of Por-
> tugal's Africa policy . . . I can confirm that we have
> information from reliable sources that the military lead-
> ers of the Western big powers would become very
> anxious should Portugal's position in the world be im-
> paired.

But along with this pledge of political support from the
West, Portugal has had to accept further external control
over its domestic economy. In order to hold on to its colonial overseas provinces, the Portuguese regime has become dependent on those countries supporting it. Members
of the anti-colonialist movement in Portugal wrote about
this development as early as 1962:

> West Germany is now, even more than the U.S.A. and
> Great Britain, the country from which Salazar is trying
> to get economic support for his barbarous policy in Por-
> tugal and the colonies. This support, as usual, is acquired
> in exchange for important concessions—which are plac-
> ing Portugal more and more in the absurd position of
> having to be a colony in order to keep on being a colo-
> nialist country.

The financial invasion of the colonies is an extension of
the situation in metropolitan Portugal. For years, foreign
capital—primarily British and more recently West German
—has permeated all sectors but the agricultural sector of
the Portuguese economy. The major iron mines belong to
a German steel trust. Another critical industry, tungsten
production, is controlled by British capital. In the service

industries, the production and distribution of electricity is dominated by a United States firm while the urban transport, radio, and telephone systems are run by British companies.

Portugal's Minister for Industry voiced his concern about this situation in 1969:

> The gap between the economically advanced countries and underdeveloped countries is increasing. The good wishes formulated by governments are not followed by the private activities of those who hold economic power. And the main question is still to know if, within the pure logic of a market economy, it is possible to find a solution to that problem . . . Recently some foreign investments have been made in our country, mostly to take advantage of the relatively cheap labor force, which is rare and expensive in industrialized countries. There is therefore no implementation of productive techniques, design, commerce, or management techniques. Business is dominated in all its aspects by foreign investors, and all that remains Portuguese is the range in occupational hierarchy from shop floor to assistant foreman.

Portuguese colonialism survives today because Western powers have offered the economic and political support necessary to sustain the war effort. But by allowing intense Western involvement in its economy, Portugal has sacrificed a large measure of control over both its domestic and colonial economies.

B. New Plans for the Colonial Economics

Since 1960 the Portuguese military presence in the colonies has pumped large amounts of new money into the local economies. This money has been concentrated in the development of roads and other communications networks in order to increase the mobility of the Portuguese army and also to pave the way for foreign investment. In Angola, for instance, the 1961 overseas development expenditure was $40 million. Two years later $164 million was allocated for development, half of which was spent on a crash program for roads, airports, and communications. Of the remaining funds, $10 million was spent on geological and scientific surveys to determine raw material potential.

This allocation of development funds points to a change now taking place in the economies of both Angola and Mozambique from agricultural production to mineral extraction. In 1968 agriculture accounted for 60 per cent of Angola's exports, while diamonds, oil, and iron ore accounted for only 28 per cent. In 1969 however, while 90 per cent of the population was still engaged in agricultural production, the total value of mineral exports exceeded that of agricultural exports.

The mining industry in the colonies is being rapidly developed by the joint effort of Western corporations and the Portuguese government. Portugal has had to prepare the colonies for investment by determining the potential for mineral extraction and by building facilities such as roads leading to valuable mineral reserves. This kind of preparation has absorbed a large portion of development funds. Foreign companies in turn have provided the capital, equipment, and know-how to develop the industry. A portion of the profits are then paid to the Portuguese government, but the largest part remains in the hands of foreign corporations. The colonies have no control over their foreign currency earnings. While the colonial economies have been radically altered by this development, the people of Angola and Mozambique receive none of the natural resources of their land.

II. Western Involvement Takes Many Forms

A. Trade

The United States has played a prominent role in absorbing agricultural produce from the Portuguese colonies. It buys more than 80 per cent of Mozambique's major cash crop, cashews. It also buys almost 50 per cent of Angola's coffee (1970)—which is to say nearly half of the country's agricultural produce. This trade in coffee makes the United States the second largest consumer of Angola's total exports.

The United States became Angola's second largest source of imports in 1968, a position Britain had held for years. The United States and West Germany have replaced Britain because of huge purchases of equipment for their new mining and oil enterprises in Angola.

B. Investments

More and more companies have been attracted to invest in the Portuguese colonies as rich and untapped reserves of oil, minerals, and hydroelectric power have been discovered. Already thirty U.S. companies are operating in Angola.

In 1957 Gulf Oil Company received a concession for exploration off the northwestern tip of Angola, in the district of Cabinda. A rich oil strike was finally made in 1966. Portugal will receive 50 per cent of the profits, providing it with much needed revenue. In 1970 Gulf's payments to the Portuguese government totaled $16 million. Only about $5 million was in the form of royalties on actual 1970 oil production. But because of expanding military expenditures Portugal requested advance cash payments. So Gulf complied by granting the Portuguese $11 million in payment for future royalties and taxes on anticipated oil production. By the end of 1972 Gulf's investment in Angola had reached $209 million. Gulf's payments to the Portuguese for 1972 operations reached $61 million, an amount which represents 13 per cent of the total Angolan provincial budget for that year and 60 per cent of the province's 1972 military expenses.

The Gulf operation also makes Portugal self-sufficient in oil and gives Angola the potential to become the fourth largest oil producer in Africa. In 1970 it began to export oil, primarily to Japan and a few northern European countries. The Cabinda oil discovery is of special importance to South Africa, which has no oil of its own; any cut-off of oil could cripple its economy. But thanks to Gulf, South Africa can continue to get oil from its Portuguese ally to offset the impact of any sanctions that might be applied by other nations.

A ready supply of oil is crucial for the maintenance of Portugal's modern war machinery. Angolan liberation movements have attacked the Gulf installations several times. Because of this, the Portuguese government has forced Africans who were living in the Cabinda area to leave. The Gulf camps are surrounded by barbed wire fences and spotlights and are well patrolled. This enables Gulf to continue expansion of its activities protected from attacks. As the Johannesburg *Star,* a South African newspaper, said:

> It is probably the prevailing peace that has made it possible for the American Cabinda Gulf Oil Company to step up its production from 745,000 tons to 2,457,000 tons in the past year. Nobody says it out loud that possibly Americans have found that a few dollars a day keep the terrorists [African guerrillas] away.

West Germany has taken a prominent position in Angola's trade because of the Cassinga iron ore center, which was built by the Krupp firm at the head of an international consortium. West Germany has had connections with Angola since World War II, when about 1,100 German landowners moved there. They strongly influence German policies in Angola.

A Portuguese company owns the mines but Krupp took over the financing of investments, delivered the equipment for the mining plant, and generally co-ordinates the project. A 130-mile railway line was built, with help from Krupp, along which the ore reaches the coast. Most of the ore is then exported to Krupp steel mills in West Germany.

C. Law and Order and the Corporations

All companies with mining rights in the Portuguese colonies have a contractual obligation to help "maintain law and order" by contributing to the national defense. For example, a huge diamond consortium, DIAMANG, extracts 40 million carats a year in an area in northeastern Angola. All foreign investors have to pay a special defense tax initiated in Angola in 1963, amounting to 28 per cent of their earnings. In addition, DIAMANG has its own private mercenaries led by South African professionals. In 1963 and again in 1964 DIAMANG spent $600,000 on these "security personnel and facilities."

D. Loans and Aid

Revenue derived from foreign companies in the colonies is only one source of Western support for the war effort. Portugal also relies on direct loans for military assistance. A large portion of Western loans are booked as "development aid." In 1969 Portuguese Prime Minister Marcelo

Caetano admitted the close connection between the colonial wars and international financing:

> All the military effort overseas has been and will go on being supported from the ordinary income which before was largely used to cover development expenses. Now we have to face many of these expenses with money obtained by loans.

Of all the development funds allocated to the colonies, half is contributed by the Portuguese government while the other half is derived from foreign loans.

E. The North Atlantic Treaty Organization

The most significant amounts of military aid to Portugal have been delivered in the name of the North Atlantic Treaty Organization (NATO). In 1949, at the instigation of the United States, fifteen European countries signed an agreement stipulating that member countries would grant protection to each other from internal and external attacks against their governments. NATO military integration includes operational planning and joint management of supplies and communications. NATO countries supply each other with weapons for mutual forces. This defense treaty gives Portugal access to the advanced weaponry and sophisticated techniques of its more powerful allies. In return for this, other NATO countries secure rights for strategic military bases in Portugal and the colonies. They also get preferential trading agreements with the colonies.

Portugal has never paid its share in the NATO alliance. It has also consistently broken the terms of the alliance by using NATO arms in the overseas provinces, which are outside the NATO defense area. Here again Portugal has defended its breach of the treaty by playing upon the strategic value of the territories for the West. Portuguese foreign

policy statements continuously stress the importance of
Angola and Mozambique in securing Western control over
the Atlantic and Indian Oceans. To implement this control
Portugal has called for an extension of the NATO defense
area to cover its colonies. In practice, this demand has been
met. NATO assistance continues:

> Portuguese Guinea is the last territory in West Africa
> possessed by a NATO power and should be considered
> in relation to the vital Cape route and to the strategy of
> Western resistance to tricontinental subversion.
>
> *NATO's Fifteen Nations,* 1968

Western powers have attempted to abdicate responsibility for assisting Portugal in its colonial wars in Africa by
denying that arms furnished by NATO are used in Africa
and asserting they are kept in Portugal for internal defense.
But this argument is based on the assumption that the role
of Portugal's military in Europe is separate from its role in
Africa, so that co-operation in one area has nothing to do
with co-operation in the other. It ignores the fact that arms
supplied by NATO can free other Portuguese arms for use
in Africa. The Portuguese themselves make no distinction,
since they claim that the wars in Africa are being waged in
defense of national territory, which includes the overseas
provinces.

After the outbreak of the colonial wars, Portugal began
a major expansion of the navy as a part of a long-term overseas defense program. In addition to its crucial function of
transporting troops between Portugal and Africa, the navy
has an important role in controlling the colonies by patrolling the long coastlines and many navigable rivers and
lakes. One of the first steps in building up the navy was an
agreement with France, under the auspices of NATO, for a
long-term loan of $125 million for the construction of

twenty vessels. In 1967 a new agreement with France
granted the navy $4,740,000 for installations and training
centers. Generally, Portugal builds its own small patrol ships
and is supplied with larger transport ships by NATO allies.

In Angola and Mozambique, where there are few roads
and long distances for troops to cover, the airforce is a crucial part of the war machinery. Portugal is dependent on its
NATO allies for all its aircraft and heavy weapons. It is
able to produce its own light weapons in its NATO-
supported armaments industry. Portugal's airforce is composed of a variety of transport aircraft and jet fighters
supplied primarily by the United States and West Germany.
It receives helicopters from France and South Africa. The
United States also supplies napalm as documented by Professor John Marcum:

> By January 1962 outside observers could watch Portu-
> guese planes bomb and strafe African villages, visit the
> charred remains of towns like Mbanza M'Pangu, and
> M'Pangala [in Angola], and copy the data from 750-
> pound napalm bomb casings from which the Portuguese
> had not removed the labels marked "Property of U. S.
> Air Force."

Portugal uses the income derived from military bases in
Portugal and the Azores, leased to France, Germany, the
United States, and Britain as members of NATO, to defray
its military expenditures. NATO installations alone are
valued at $30 million, with Portugal's contribution less than
$3 million. As the Portuguese Minister of Defense com-
mented:

> Although Portugal did not contribute on a large scale
> to the work of NATO due to our struggle in the overseas
> territories, our allies always show much comprehension
> for our position.

F. Training the Army

The United States plays an important part in the training of the Portuguese army through its Military Assistance Advisory Group stationed in Portugal. One hundred and thirty-three Portuguese received training under this program in 1969 and a similar number in 1970. In addition, Portuguese officers come to the United States for special training in such fields as communications, electronics, maintenance, administration, and missiles. By 1971 Americans had trained nearly 2,700 Portuguese soldiers in the United States and in Portugal.

In the summer of 1965 West Germany, Portugal, and South Africa signed a military agreement providing for West Germany to train officers from Portugal, South Africa, and Rhodesia. In Lisbon the Permanent German Military Mission offers military trainers and advisers and also has an important voice in the utilization of the Portuguese military budget.

III. South African Involvement in the Colonies

In the interests of consolidating its political and economic control in all of Southern Africa, South Africa has become increasingly involved in the Portuguese territories. Economic links between South Africa and Mozambique have always been strong, yet they have been played down until recently because of theoretical differences in racial policies and a history of colonial rivalry between Portugal and South Africa. Since 1903 South African mines have used cheap migrant labor from Mozambique in exchange for hard currency payments to Portugal. South Africa also pays for the use of Mozambique's port, Lourenço Marques. In the past few years the Anglo-American Corporation of South Africa has acquired sizable oil interests along the coast.

South African involvement in Angola is more recent. The Anglo-American Corporation has participated in several consortiums financing the development of Angola's fast-growing mining industry. Angolan surplus coffee production has found a ready market in South Africa.

In 1964 Portugal and South Africa signed eight separate agreements to hasten economic development in the Portuguese colonies. In 1965 additional agreements were made to increase trade between the two regimes. In 1968 Salazar's successor Prime Minister Caetano defined his policy of alliance with South Africa:

> There is often talk in the UN General Assembly of a secret alliance between Portugal and the Union of South Africa and Rhodesia. Needless to say, there is no alliance whatsoever, either secret or open, linking these three countries. In any event, we practice different racial policies and the extent to which we are committed to pursuing and perfecting our policy of non-discrimination and good relations is well known. However, in many respects our interests in Southern Africa coincide, in that we are convinced that progress in that part of the continent requires the stable presence of the white man, who establishes roots, adapts, and becomes attached to the African land and is associated with the native there. That is why, for example, we cannot remain indifferent to the destiny of Rhodesia, whose principal outlet to the sea is Beira [a port in Mozambique].

South Africa has gone to great expense to solidify this alliance with Portugal and is already participating in the colonial wars. South African troops are active in the southern districts of Angola and in 1968 a large South African base was established there in the district of Moxico. Bases in Namibia also give logistical support to the Portuguese forces operating in southern Angola. (South West Africa is the name used by white South Africa; the United Nations has decreed the official name of the country to be Namibia —the name used by the African liberation movements.) The South African Minister of Defense announced that South Africa is setting up rocket-launching bases seventy-two miles from the Mozambican border.

In the interest of strengthening White rule in Southern Africa, Portugal and South Africa have established a symbiotic relationship: South Africa needs water, power, cheap mining labor, and oil while the Portuguese territories lack sufficient capital, know-how, organization, and military power.

IV. Cabora Bassa: Powerhouse of Southern Africa

The Cabora Bassa scheme is comprised of a huge dam and powerhouse to be built on the Zambesi River at the Cabora Bassa rapids, plus a transmission line running through Mozambique into South Africa. The first phase of the project, to be completed by 1975, includes the construction of the main dam and generating plant at the cost of $360 million. The dam will produce almost twice as much power as Egypt's Aswan Dam currently produces.

The project is being financed by an international consortium, ZAMCO, headed by the Anglo-American Corporation of South Africa. West German, French, Canadian, and South African companies are participating in the consortium. Widespread public protest in Sweden forced a Swedish electro-manufacturing combine to withdraw from the consortium. GEC-English Electric hoped to take the Swedish company's place, but backed down after being "thoroughly embarrassed" by the adverse publicity their decision caused. They were finally replaced by Siemens, a German firm already in the consortium. An Italian firm also withdrew under the pressure of protest. It was replaced by the Transmission Lines Construction Company (TLC) of South Africa. This entry of TLC into the project will bring combined (government and corporate) South African participation in the scheme up to two thirds of the total financing. The U. S. Export-Import Bank was asked to allow a loan of $55 million to enable General Electric Company of America to supply electric equipment, but GE withdrew because it appeared the loan "would not be arranged in time to meet the project's construction schedule." United States firms are still involved in smaller subcontracts. Ingersoll-Rand is supplying machinery through South Africa, and Bell Helicopter has sold five helicopters to the Zambesi Development Office for "logistical support" in the Cabora Bassa area.

The financing of the dam rests heavily on export credits to be granted by the governments of the participating firms. An additional $123 million will be provided by South African official sources. The Portuguese contribution amounts to $96 million.

One of the objectives of Cabora Bassa is to associate European economic interests with the maintenance of Portuguese control over the area. The African liberation movement FRELIMO now controls the northern third of Mozambique. This includes the area surrounding Cabora Bassa, where Portuguese and South African troops are currently fighting to regain control. In an attempt to subvert the struggle, White settlers are being introduced into the region. They will be expected to defend their privileges there and subjugate the local African population. The projected settlement of one million Europeans becomes a second crucial objective for Portugal. The South African director of the scheme said: "It will transform more than 100,000 square kilometers of jungle, swamps, and bush into fertile land for hundreds of thousands of peasant families." Over 24,000 Africans will have to move from that land to make room for the 150-mile-long lake, which will be formed by the waters backed up by the dam.

Hydroelectric power produced will be important to South Africa, which has no natural source of power. In the process of financing this project South Africa assures itself a source of power, and binds the economy of Mozambique more closely to its own. Cabora Bassa is an economic reinforcement of White minority rule in Southern Africa.

V. The Wars in the Colonies

Liberation movements in Southern Africa have forced the question of how Portugal is to maintain control over its overseas provinces. The expansion of the war effort over the past ten years has not solved Portugal's dilemma in its colonies, it has merely meant greater cost to the Portuguese. Beyond the economic crisis, the wars have cost the Portuguese popular support at home and in Africa.

The wars have become increasingly intolerable for the Portuguese people. The draft, inflation, and unemployment have forced half of Portugal's men from the age of eighteen to forty-five to emigrate over the past decade. Draft evasion and desertions from the army are now widespread. Students and sectors of the Catholic Church have organized their opposition to Portugal's colonial policy, and thousands of political prisoners are incarcerated in Portugal's jails. The war effort has been impeded by the plunging morale of troops stationed in Africa. Young soldiers do not feel that they are defending their national territory and do not know why they have been forced to risk their lives thousands of miles from their homeland.

Portugal's military presence in Africa has not curbed resistance to colonialism. Instead, it has further alienated Africans from their colonizers. The Portuguese have sacrificed a measure of political control in an attempt to consolidate their military control. In the words of a South African journalist, Al Venter, who traveled with the Portuguese in Angola, in the late 1960s:

> It is here where the Portuguese in Africa have a similar problem to the Americans in Vietnam. Both Portugal and America are trying their best to win over the bulk of the civilian populations to their respective ideals. Both nations however are encountering opposition in this field from their guerrilla opponents—the Americans from the Vietcong and the Portuguese from the MPLA.
>
> "That is why the war in Angola is so different to what it was in 1961," Captain de Campos pointed out. "You cannot kill or imprison everyone who disagrees with you—you must win their confidence for they are your future allies."

In order to win the confidence of the African people, the Portuguese have taken several measures to liberalize their colonial policy. Prime Minister Caetano has suggested the "concession of a progressive and adequate administrative autonomy" to the colonies. He was not speaking of granting independence, but of establishing a mechanism of control which would be a less overt form of colonial rule. This means the strengthening of the local administration in each of the colonies, by training a Black elite of professionals to work in conjunction with the present administration of White settlers. It means broadening a sector of the population which is allied with Portuguese interests, by offering administrative positions and professional and educational opportunities to more Africans. These measures have met with little success in terms of winning the support of the local population, for the reforms have been limited in scope and instituted at a time when the war is involving a growing portion of that population.

Caetano has also advocated large-scale settlement of Whites in the colonies. But despite the massive exodus of Portuguese from their country each year, relatively few have chosen to settle in Africa. In order to encourage emigration to the colonies, Portugal has recently offered high incentives for settlers around the projected dam sites, at Cabora Bassa in Mozambique and on the Cunene River in Angola.

In attempting to defeat the independence movements in Africa, Portugal has had to recognize its subordinate role in the capitalist world. Powerful American, British, West German, and Japanese corporations are already involved directly in metropolitan Portugal and the colonies and indirectly through their interests in South Africa. In the short run, these business interests would like to see the liberation movements suppressed by Portuguese colonialism. In the long run, they have no interest in Portugal retaining its colonial presence in Africa. Because Portugal is dependent on continued Western support for the colonial wars, it is looking for a political framework in the colonies which will form a satisfactory base for the activities of international capital but would still leave Portugal with some kind of advantageous relationship with Africa.

In light of South Africa's economic expansion in Southern Africa, the increased absorption of the territories into the South African sphere of interest appears inevitable. But Portugal is not an unwilling partner in this alliance to preserve White minority rule, and recently relations between Portugal and South Africa have improved.

Prime Minister Vorster's unprecedented visit to Lisbon in 1969 is an indication that these two regimes are anxious to co-operate for their mutual benefit. This growing integration of the Southern African economy around South Africa also serves the interests of Western business. Western corporations have long demonstrated their willingness to co-operate with apartheid and White settler regimes, as long as they are able to maintain the profitable conditions of the status quo.

As Austin Coates, a British journalist writing for the Anglo-American Corporation in South Africa, has noted:

> On the European side there is no longer the confidence in the African that there once was. Though the concept of apartheid is generally unpalatable to Portuguese, there is a perceptible veering towards what may be called South African thinking, a sense that with so much at stake Europeans in Southern Africa, in defense of their own civilization, must put themselves and their children first and never mind the outside clamor, if to do this is regarded as an admission that all men are not quite equal.

CONGO-BRAZZAVILLE

CABINDA

ZAIRE

KENYA

TANZANIA

South African oil and mining
investment. Power supplies
from Cunene River Project.

ANGOLA

MALAWI Increasingly dependent on
South African trade and aid.

Cunene River
Project

Cunene R.

ZAMBIA

Cabora Bassa Dam

Zambesi R.

RHODESIA
(Zimbabwe)

MOZAMBIQUE

RHODESIA: Almost totally
dependent on South Africa
for imports and exports.

SOUTH WEST AFRICA
(Namibia)

BOTSWANA

Cabora Bassa entrenches
South African interests
in Mozambique. Major
source of minerals for
South Africa.

Rail link between South Africa
and Rhodesia. South Africa
allocates mining and oil
concessions.

High percentage of South
African settlement. Customs
pooling.

SWAZILAND

LESOTHO

SOUTH AFRICA

Depends on sales to South
Africa. Workers need South
African jobs.

SOUTH AFRICA'S REGIONAL OFFENSIVE

South Africa hopes to secure Angola, South West Africa, Botswana,
Rhodesia, Mozambique, and Malawi as buffer states.

CHAPTER FOUR

APARTHEID TAKES THE OFFENSIVE:
THE REGIONALIZATION OF SOUTHERN AFRICA

I. Military Regionalization

A. South Africa and the Portuguese Colonies

There has never been much love lost between Portugal and South Africa during the centuries of their mutual presence in Southern Africa. White South Africans dislike Portuguese pretensions of multiracialism. South African Afrikaners in particular often speak of the Portuguese people as the "scum" of Europe and treat those Portuguese who have emigrated to South Africa accordingly. In addition, South Africa has a history of distrust for possible expansionist tendencies of Portugal in Southern Africa.

In recent years there has been a marked growth of South African military assistance to Portugal for the maintenance of Portuguese colonialism. This is a response to several changes over the last decade. The emergence of independent African states pledged to the liberation of Southern Africa, the birth of liberation movements themselves, and pressures on the South African economy to expand have all forced South Africa to play down its differences with Portugal. Their common interest in preserving White minority rule has drawn them closer together in defense of the status quo.

South Africa intends to maintain a buffer zone of friendly states in Southern Africa between itself and African-ruled states to the north. Maintenance of this zone makes it more difficult for Black South Africans trained abroad in guerrilla warfare to slip back into the country. Also, such a buffer zone keeps plenty of distance between the oppressed Black South African majority and free Africa.

Should the liberation movements in either Angola or Mozambique defeat Portugal and come to power, the area of White minority rule in Southern Africa will be substantially reduced. The very presence of African nationalist states on the borders of South Africa would provide further encouragement to the Black South African majority. And there is little doubt that an MPLA or FRELIMO government would allow South African guerrillas to cross into South Africa from Angolan or Mozambican soil. (Zambia and Tanzania now permit Mozambican, Angolan, Zimbabwean, and Namibian guerrillas to cross their frontiers.)

In the years ahead South Africa is likely to send more arms and troops to assist the Portuguese war effort. But support for Portuguese colonialism is only a strategy to achieve the goal of creating a buffer zone. Should Portugal's position seriously deteriorate in spite of South Africa's help, the strategy could change; but the goal would remain the same.

Whatever strategy South Africa pursues in the future, it is determined to use its strength to win one overriding objective—to prevent an African nationalist movement from coming to power in Portuguese Africa. If and when Portugal is finally routed by the forces of the liberation movements, the guerrillas are going to find that South Africa will intervene rather than allow an African government hostile to South Africa to come to power right on its very borders.

Already South Africa has 2,000 troops stationed in Mozambique in the area of the Cabora Bassa dam, as well as troops and advisers in Angola.

B. Settlers and Satellites

South Africa also views the White minority settler areas of Namibia/South West Africa and Zimbabwe/Rhodesia and the satellite states of Lesotho, Botswana, and Swaziland as component parts of the buffer zone.

Namibia was a German colony until after World War I. The League of Nations then declared the territory to be a mandate of the Union of South Africa. Today, despite a UN resolution in 1966 terminating the mandate and later resolutions condemning South Africa, that country rules it outright as a colony. South Africa has imposed the apartheid system wholesale, to the benefit of those White South Africans who have emigrated there. From the South African viewpoint, Namibia is the most secure area of the entire buffer zone sphere.

Zimbabwe was a British settler colony until 1965, when the small White settler minority of 220,000 defied Britain and declared unilateral independence. (Rhodesia is the name that was used by the white settlers in the nineteenth century. The official name of the country according to the United Nations and the Liberation movements is Zimbabwe.) Outnumbered about twenty to one by a subordinated African population and faced with a world trade boycott, its shaky, isolated regime relies heavily on South Africa for economic and military support. Since 1965 the Whites have rushed to imitate the South African apartheid system to consolidate their control.

Africans from both these settler territories have formed liberation movements pledged to end "Whites only" rule. These movements control no territory as yet although guerrilla fighters from both Namibia and Zimbabwe have been engaged in fighting. In Zimbabwe South African troops (called "special police") have joined Whites there in operations against the guerrillas. There have been casualties on both sides.

Zimbabwean and Namibian nationalists have come into sharp conflict with South African intentions in Southern Africa. They too will have to deal with the power of South Africa before they can win back control of their countries from settler minority rule.

The last sector of the Southern African buffer zone consists of three former British territories now governed by Africans. Lesotho is entirely within South Africa, comparable to the location of West Berlin inside of East Germany. This is almost true for Swaziland as well—it borders Mozambique on the east—while landlocked Botswana shares common borders with White minority regimes on all sides except the north.

Each of these three states has a population of less than a million. Their economies are heavily dependent upon South Africa, leaving little room for their governments to oppose the South African government. In actuality, they are "independent" in name only and have little viable basis as nation-states.

South Africa is content to leave these states under African rule, controlling their affairs only indirectly. The late Prime Minister Dr. Hendrik Verwoerd once said:

> It is in our interest to see that the people in these three territories have a sober outlook. . . . It is important that we give our friendship to such parties in these territories, especially when, as now, they are also the ruling parties.

Reduced to satellite status, they dare not challenge South African policies in Southern Africa. When the United Nations votes on resolutions to condemn apartheid, the representatives of these tiny states either abstain or discreetly stay away. Their African leaders have denounced the liberation movements in the region. They co-operate with South African police in apprehending South African guerrillas who try to travel through or seek sanctuary in their countries. With the consent of these African leaders, South Africa decides who may leave and enter these states, and planes bound for Lesotho must first land in South Africa to be searched. In light of their desperate situations, it is difficult to imagine that these states could do anything but co-operate with South Africa's buffer zone strategy.

This strategy is already paying dividends to South Africa. Minister of Information Dr. C. P. Mulder said in a 1969 speech:

> Thanks to our good relationship with our neighbors in the north, northwest, and northeast, we have been able to foil terrorist attempts and we have been able to block escape routes by terrorists to these countries.

II. Economic Regionalization

A. The Politics of Free Trade

The South African government disclaims any intentions of further territorial acquisition in Africa. Indeed, the buffer zone strategy is essentially a defense of the status quo. But while territorial conquest is not a current policy, economic expansion throughout Southern Africa and beyond certainly is.

In recent years South African imports have greatly exceeded exports. Because South Africa is buying more than it is selling, the government is anxious to change this, as South Africa is losing money. Exports must be increased.

However, South Africa has difficulty in selling its manufactured goods on European or American markets—for one thing they are far away and transportation costs are high, making the goods too expensive. The goods cannot always be sold in South Africa because under apartheid Blacks are paid low wages so they cannot afford to buy many manufactured goods. South Africa has thus been looking for new markets elsewhere.

Since 1963 South Africans have been pushing for a free trade area which would include every country in the buffer zone area. A "free trade area" means that there are no customs duties or tariffs on goods that are traded between the countries of that area. Since South Africa would be the most developed partner in such an arrangement, it would benefit the most. Highly developed South African industries would have a guaranteed market for their manufactured goods. The absence of customs and tariffs would make it difficult for newly established industries elsewhere within the region because they would have no protection from South African competition.

Trade patterns might therefore resemble a classic colonial pattern, with South Africa in the role of industrial mother country while other members produced only raw materials. Zimbabwe and Portuguese Africa are reluctant to enter a free trade scheme. A recent article in the British trade journal *African Development* helps explain why:

> For South Africa the era of economic imperialism has scarce begun. One of its paramount aims is to stabilize its neighboring states and build a firm defensive block. The well-known "outward-looking" policy also implies the desire to dominate the southern half of the continent economically.

South Africa has a favorable balance of trade only in Africa, where exports are triple imports. There is mounting pressure to expand exports further to the rest of Africa while holding down imports. In the near future, therefore, it will have to put more pressure than ever on the rest of Southern Africa, and perhaps some African states further north, to join with South Africa in a new free trade common market complex.

Nearly all nations desire trade, but when desire becomes necessity it generates tendencies for a strong nation to impose trade agreements on a weaker country, usually on terms more favorable to itself. When one nation compels another to trade and then dictates the terms, it constitutes an economic form of domination. For the weaker Southern African neighbors, membership in a common market may well become the price of continued South African protection against the liberation movements.

B. The Politics of Investment

South Africa also promotes capital investment throughout the region. Already South African public and private investment totals more than one billion dollars. South African capital is especially concentrated in Zimbabwe, where it controls six of the ten largest firms. In recent years, South African companies have been sinking capital into oil and mineral extraction in both Angola and Mozambique. They also have investments in all three satellite states.

South African capital and exports are playing a major role in the two hydroelectric dam projects currently under construction in Southern Africa. These dams will serve as a major source of both water and electric power, for which South Africa will become the principal customer.

As investments increase in the buffer zone, defense of the area becomes no longer just a military strategy to insulate apartheid—it provides protection for economic expansion as well. Should any liberation movement come to power in some part of this sphere, the new government would demand control over its own resources. This potentiality gives South Africa yet another motive to commit its strength to the destruction of the liberation movements.

C. The Politics of Migrant Labor

South Africa has long taken advantage of the severe poverty of its neighbors by employing about a million migrant workers from these countries at any given time. Most of this labor is used in the mines, where some 65 per cent of the work force is foreign. While wages are rock bottom, these jobs are the only alternative to chronic unemployment back home. Most of the workers come from Lesotho, Malawi, and Mozambique.

South Africa gets several benefits from this abundant source of cheap labor. It can pay the lowest wages because of the scarcity of jobs. Migrant competition is one more device to keep wages down within the Black South African work force (and contributes to domestic unemployment). Furthermore, the migrant workers send back badly needed foreign currency as savings, which their governments use to pay for imports. This dependency gives South Africa another lever of influence over its neighbors—it can threaten to expel or bar migrants from any neighboring area that opposes its policies. Such a measure would both cut off a source of foreign currency and swell the ranks of the unemployed back in the workers' country.

South Africa looks to Southern Africa as a vital area to increase exports and expand capital investment, as a source of cheap water and power, and as a vast labor pool. It stands to benefit most from further economic integration of the region. The more this proceeds, the greater will be South Africa's determination to preserve the political status quo throughout the area. An Afrikaner newspaper commented in 1969:

> South Africa can pack a lot of economic, technological, and cultural power into her good neighbor policy. . . . There has been no such sweeping vision of South Africa's potential role in Africa since Cecil Rhodes' old-time imperial dreams.

III. South Africa Looks Across the Buffer Zone

A. The Outward Policy

We as a small state have not only the knowledge but the experience, because we understand the soul of Africa and Africa's people, and therefore I say we have a mission to Africa and the world.

These words come not from one of Africa's many nationalist heroes of the struggle for independence, but from South Africa. From White South Africa. From no less than Prime Minister John Vorster. In 1967.

Over the last decade or so, African-ruled states replaced European colonial rule throughout most of Africa north of the Zambesi River. These new states established in 1963 the Organization of African Unity (OAU), a kind of United Nations for independent Africa. Its members pledged to work for the end of White supremacy and colonialism in Southern Africa by means of a trade boycott, vigorous international diplomacy, and support for liberation movements.

These policies obviously have not rid Africa of apartheid, but they did serve to isolate South Africa from the rest of the continent and much of the world. At first, South Africa responded to the newly independent African states with contempt and arrogance, contending that Africans were incapable of governing themselves. In recent years, however, it has toned down such attitudes in preference for what high officials call the "outward" policy. This shift is essentially a strategy to win new friends on the other side of the buffer zone with the South African version of open door diplomacy—a handshake and the rand.*

The outward policy initially developed when the satellite states of Lesotho and Botswana won independence from Britain in 1966 and Swaziland in 1968. Despite some protest from die-hard White supremacists, South Africa offered the new states friendship and assistance. The leaders of these three states accepted these gestures, promptly denounced the liberation movements, and proclaimed a policy of peaceful co-existence with apartheid. The stage was now set for expanding the outward policy to selected countries on the other side of the buffer zone.

Overtures to independent Africa since 1967 have met with some success so far. By 1970 African leaders throughout the continent were openly engaged in a bitter debate about whether or not to change their earlier posture of hostility to South Africa to a more conciliatory one. President Felix Houphouet-Boigny of the Ivory Coast urged African states to abandon the isolation strategy and called for a "dialogue" with South Africa. Some of the responses to his proposal follow.

For a Dialogue

Isolation and boycott will not solve things, we have got to start talking. You come here and see the way we live, and we can visit you to learn about your ways. This might not solve problems immediately, but I be-

---

* The South African monetary unit; R1=$1.50 (1973).

lieve, honestly and strongly, that in the end it is the only solution to our problems.

Dr. Hastings Banda, President of Malawi (in a toast to South African Prime Minister John Vorster at a Malawi state banquet given in his honor).

Against a Dialogue

It is not surprising that the Ivory Coast leader wants to surrender to South Africa even before any dialogue takes place. He is a satellite of France, and his country's economy is controlled by the French. And since the French government supplies the arms to South Africa, contrary to the resolutions of the United Nations, the French satellite can see nothing wrong with it.

Major General Yakubu Gowon, Head of Military Council, Nigeria

Our quarrel is not about frontiers, but oppression; if South Africa ceases her oppression, then her peoples will have no need of support from Free Africa. But in the meantime you cannot have a non-aggression treaty with aggression, and the whole basis of apartheid is aggression and violence against the human spirit.

Kenneth Kaunda, President of Zambia

B. South Africa's Response to Africa

1. THE CARROT

The strongest support for Houphouet-Boigny's proposal has come from Malawi, which is the only African country that has established full diplomatic relations with South Africa. It argues that this step has led to many benefits for the country: increased trade; South African tourists; over $25 million in aid; more employment for Malawian migrants; and South African private investment. In return, the South African air force will use as a base the airport now being built with South African aid. A White South African has become head of Malawi's Information Services.

Malawi's position in international politics has shifted dramatically. It systematically abstains on all United Nations and British Commonwealth resolutions against White supremacy in Southern Africa. President Hastings Kamuzu Banda is encouraging other African states to break with the OAU trade boycott and denounce the liberation movements. He refers to his White neighbors as "my friends" and argues that they have every right to be in South Africa, while calling the Arabs in North Africa the real intruders on the continent.

Elsewhere on the continent there are other breakthroughs for the outward policy. Despite the trade boycott, independent African states imported well over $100 million of South African goods in recent years. South Africa does not name specific African countries in its trade statistics so as to save its new partners embarrassment. But in a number of countries, goods with a South African label are openly sold in stores. South African fruit juices have even been served at government parties in Zaire. South African goods are much cheaper than those imported from America or Europe, which partly explains this continuing trade.

There are reports of South African capital finding its way into numerous countries which profess to have no relations with South Africa, including Kenya, Ghana, and Sierra Leone. Ghana now welcomes White South African visitors without requiring that they denounce apartheid. Gambian ports have been opened to South African ships and planes, and both trade and tourists are publicly encouraged.

A 1969 editorial in the *Rand Daily Mail*, a major South African newspaper, made this assessment of the outward policy up to then:

> Decolonization has left a vacuum in Black Africa which
> South Africa is quietly moving to fill. South Africans

are playing an important role as expatriate experts vital
to newly independent nations. Their companies are busy
in such lands as Malawi and Mozambique. Their money
is financing these projects. And their intelligence men
are building a chain of listening posts across the continent. This "outward" policy has been spectacularly successful in countries like Malawi, Swaziland, Botswana,
and Lesotho, but bridges are now being built to nations
like Malagasy, Ivory Coast, Senegal, Congo—even Kenya
and Uganda.

Those African leaders who are supporting the call for a
dialogue with South Africa argue that increased contact will
lead to modifications of the apartheid system. There is no
evidence to date that any such changes are taking place. If
anything, the reverse is true. Some critics of the dialogue
approach argue that those who favor it are simply trying to
justify the economic benefits they hope to get by establishing ties with South Africa. Comments from South Africa
itself support this argument. Prime Minister Vorster said
in 1970:

> There must be no misunderstanding about my outward
> policy. Diplomatic links with other African states would
> not in any way interfere with South Africa's policy of
> separate development. In fact, the establishment of the
> links is a guarantee towards the continuation of the
> White man's position in South Africa.

2. THE STICK

Nearly all those African leaders who have favored the
dialogue proposal have also expressed futility about the
chances of liberating Southern Africa through armed struggle. Those states which are developing closer ties with
South Africa will undoubtedly be pressured into ending
whatever support they may have given to the liberation
movements in the past. And a weakening of African

solidarity for the liberation movements is, of course, one of South Africa's principal objectives for adopting the outward policy in the first place.

The African National Congress (ANC) of South Africa viewed with dismay the support among some African countries for proposing a dialogue:

> The decision to opt for armed struggle was not taken lightly in South Africa. . . . We knew that many of us would pay a heavy penalty for daring to rise up in anger against our oppression. But the choice of how to conduct our struggle was our own and it must remain so. If some states find it difficult to support us in our course, then let them not, at least, treat with the enemy. This is our urgent plea from one African nation to another.

Most African states continue to pledge support for the uncompromising OAU position on South Africa. A few are particularly firm in their solidarity with the liberation movements, notably Tanzania and Zambia. For these states, South Africa uses the back hand of its outward policy.

In recent years South Africa has concentrated on threatening Tanzania and Zambia. Its planes regularly violate the air space of both countries. Zambia claims to have caught South African sabotage agents. South African and Portuguese troops have harassed Zambian border villages to discourage people there from helping guerrillas fighting in neighboring Zimbabwe. South African money has turned up in the coffers of the political opposition in both Tanzania and Zambia. Prime Minister Vorster has warned President Kaunda of Zambia: "If you want to try violence, as you have advised other states in Africa, we will hit you so hard that you will never forget it."

There is considerable evidence that South Africa has promoted conflict and division in free Africa, particularly within the most powerful states that are potential rivals to South African power on the continent. A good number of White South African mercenaries fought in the Congo during the turbulent years of civil war and insurgency. South Africa sent arms to both sides in the Nigerian civil war, seeing advantage in having Africa's most populous country tearing itself apart.

IV. South Africa: Savior of the Free World

A final aspect of the outward policy concerns South Africa's relations with the rest of the world, and the Western capitalist states in particular. The breakup of African unity around the issue of South Africa has significance far beyond African shores, according to Minister of Information Mulder,

> because it knocks out one of the cornerstones of the persistent attacks on South Africa in so many other countries.

And according to Foreign Minister Dr. Hilgard Muller:

> Thus when Dr. Kaunda tries to incite the West against us he does not speak on behalf of all the African states and I hope the world realizes this, if it has not already appreciated the position.
>
> As the West becomes aware of our fruitful co-operation with other African states, their attitude towards us improves. I believe that it will happen to an increasing degree because we must simply accept that our relations with the rest of the world are largely determined by our relations with the African states.

South Africa is evidently anxious to convince the West that it has good relations with its African neighbors. If African countries are willing to deal with South Africa, this will give added justification for continued contact with South Africa by countries outside the African continent. The United States, Britain, and France have all supported Houphouet-Boigny's proposal for a dialogue. Its implementation would make it easier for the major capitalist powers to continue "business as usual" in South Africa.

South African propaganda is directed especially at winning favor with the United States by appealing to the American hostility toward Communism. Again, Dr. Mulder:

> South Africa will have to do her best to prevent the spread of Communism to the north of her borders if the leaders of the West are unwilling or unable to do so. South Africa is called upon to protect Western interests in Southern Africa and as far north as she can."

A government broadcast in 1968 noted:

> We are still part of the Western culture and in essence we are Western but at the same time we are an undetachable part of Africa, and to win African states for the West in its struggle against Communism, South Africa is the key and not the fly in the ointment. The sooner the West realizes this the better it will be for all concerned.

CHAPTER FIVE

SOUTH AFRICA AND THE WEST

South Africa's claim to be an outpost of Western civilization has deep historical roots. The White supremacist regime which exists today is a legacy of the continuous expansion which has characterized Western Europe since the Renaissance.

White South Africa began as a settler society of Europeans moving into an area already occupied by a less technologically developed people, like similar intrusions into Australia, Siberia, parts of North and East Africa, and the Americas. Initially, Europeans settled along the Cape of Good Hope to set up a strategic way station at the southern tip of Africa. European ships stopped there for provisions en route to the plunder of East African city states, the exploitation of India, and the capture of the rich East Indian spice trade.

The settlement colony had originally been a Dutch venture, but passed to British control, as we have seen, during the Napoleonic Wars early in the nineteenth century. England emerged from these wars as the world's leading naval power. Its national interests consequently demanded control of the key passageway to the riches of Asia.

British concern for the South African interior rose sharply

in the 1880s after the discovery in South Africa of the richest deposits of gold and diamonds ever found anywhere in the world. Suddenly South Africa was no longer just a strategic route to Asia. British capital poured into South African mines. Englishman Cecil Rhodes urged his country into new imperialist adventures inland. The potential of this great wealth developed a second British "national interest" in South Africa. One result was the very bloody and destructive Anglo-Boer War from 1899–1902.

That war soon led to the formation of the self-governing Union of South Africa in 1910. But British capital maintained economic control of the country as before. British investment in and trade with South Africa has been a major pillar of British prosperity ever since.

During the last several decades, economic power in South Africa has become more diversified. The Great Depression and the economic aftermath of World War II reduced both trade and investment from Britain. This economic decline of Britain overseas began to open South African doors to newcomers from France, West Germany, Japan, and, above all, the United States.

During this same period, White South Africans themselves assumed a more active role in promoting the industrial growth of the country. Severe disruptions in the international economy caused by both depression and war stimulated a drive within South Africa to build a more self-sufficient economy. The government established numerous state industries to guarantee that South Africa would produce essential commodities such as steel, thereby lessening its dependence upon imports during years of crisis. For the first time, South African private entrepreneurs began investing heavily in mining and manufacturing.

Since 1652 this European settler community has occupied a strategic location for Western economic expansion into the Indian Ocean network. For a century now, this same White

1. Aerial view of Johannesburg, the largest city in South Africa, with almost 1,500,000 inhabitants in the metropolitan area. In the right foreground is the "Whites Only" air terminal; to the left is the "Whites Only" railroad station. No Blacks live in the city proper. (Photo by STER of Durban, courtesy Camera Press)

2. Kliptown, an African township outside Johannesburg. (Photo by John Seymour, courtesy Camera Press)

3. School for Africans in an old church.
(Photo by Ernest Cole, courtesy Camera
Press)

4. White South African schoolgirls at a national celebration. (Photo by
STER of Durban, courtesy Camera Press)

5 & 6. These common signs mark the extent of racial separation in South Africa. (Photo by Reed Kramer and Tami Hultman)

7. South African servant has a wide choice of American brands as she shops for her White employers. (Photo by Tim Smith)

8. More than a million Africans have been uprooted and sent to resettlement villages since 1959. This one, at Illinge, is for released political prisoners. (Photo by John Seymour, courtesy Camera Press)

9. The Angolan coffee plantation "Fazenda-Lufige" displays the heads of "unruly" Africans to serve as a reminder of the penalty paid for disobedience. (Photo courtesy Angola Comité)

10. The Church and the army are mainstays of Portuguese colonialism. (Photo courtesy Angola Comité)

This MOBIL ad was taken from the Portuguese Military journal, **Jornal do Exército**, November-December, 1964.

A translation of the ad reads:

IN THE GOOD HOURS AND IN THE BAD . . .

The wave of terrorism which treacherously attacked the North of Angola imposed heroic sacrifices on the Armed Forces and the people.

Mobil, which has served the province since 1914; which pioneered in bringing in all places the petroleum products so important for its development; which, in the good hours and the bad, always joined in the destiny of Angola and its people — Mobil could not be absent from these sacrifices.

Mobil has participated with pride in the struggle for the defense of the province, pledging itself to assure the supply of fuels and lubricants necessary for the Armed Forces and the people.

MORE THAN HALF A CENTURY AT THE SERVICE OF THE COUNTRY

11. (Photo courtesy *Africa Today*)

12 & 13. March 1960, Sharpeville. *Top:* Adults and children run to escape the bullets. *Bottom:* The scene after the shooting. Sixty-nine people were killed. (Photos courtesy of *Sechaba,* African National Congress)

14. Despite constant police harassment, Africans continue to protest in South Africa. Here demonstrators shout "Afrika!" and give the "thumbs up" sign of the African National Congress. (Photo by Ian Berry, courtesy Camera Press)

15. The pass laws are a major means of controlling the flow of population in South Africa; there are over 3,000 Africans arrested every day for pass offenses. Here Africans burn the passbooks they are made to carry at all times. (Photo by Eli Weinberg, courtesy Camera Press)

minority has acted as a broker for Western capitalist access to a cheap African labor supply and vast reserves of precious metals. Since the Great Depression, foreign investors have combined with public and private South African capital to generate one of the most rapid industrial growth rates anywhere in the world. Foreign corporate co-operation with government economic policies have helped to develop South Africa as an advanced industrialized nation: all the major capitalist countries conduct a heavy volume of trade with it. These same countries have helped it to become one of the most powerful military forces on the African continent, despite an arms embargo adopted by the United Nations.

This chapter will examine in considerable detail the nature and extent of contemporary ties between South Africa and the West. The first section surveys private Western economic interests in South Africa and the principal issues arising from this extensive involvement. The second section outlines the relationships between South Africa and the industrial capitalist world at the governmental level. As the struggle between White minority rule and African liberation intensifies, the policies of Western countries tomorrow will be shaped largely by the stakes they have in South Africa today.

Part 1. Corporate Interests and South Africa

I. A Survey of Corporate Involvement

A. Trade

Foreign corporations based in the leading capitalist countries dominate almost all of South Africa's international trade. British firms account for more than a fourth of South Africa's imports and exports. American and Western European companies account for about one half. Japanese firms have now become South Africa's most enthusiastic trading partners. In the past six years, South Africa's trade with Japan increased three times faster than its trade with other countries. To avoid discriminatory embarrassment to Japanese businessmen now in South Africa, the government has classified them as "honorary Whites" rather than as Asians.

B. Investment

Foreign investors had a total of $6.4 billion in South Africa by 1968, representing a 15 per cent increase over 1967.

Foreign corporations accounted for $5.6 billion of the 1968 total—the remainder came from governments and international financial institutions as loans. This figure represents only the "book" value of foreign investment—it does not include profits which were reinvested in South Africa nor any increase in value of the original investment due to appreciation. The *actual* value of foreign corporate investments by 1968 was therefore much higher than the $5.6 billion figure would indicate, but the statistics for book value are the only ones available.

More than 1,000 foreign firms have branches, subsidiaries, or distribution facilities in South Africa. British corporations are predominant, owning close to $3.5 billion of total foreign corporate investment. Some 375 American companies had invested over $900 million by 1968. French, West German, and other European corporations accounted for the final one billion dollars.

This large bloc of foreign money plays a major role in the South African economy. For example, foreign firms control 25 per cent of South Africa's manufacturing capacity.

FOREIGN INVESTMENT IN SOUTH AFRICA

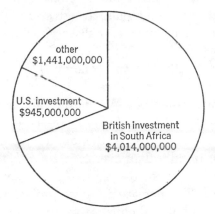

This chart represents South Africa's total foreign liabilities in 1968—that is, all the money South African business and government owed to investors in foreign countries that year.

source: UN, 1970

More than two-thirds of all foreign investment in South Africa is in British hands. The U.S. and a few West European countries dominate the other third of such investment.

To help evaluate the impact of this foreign investment in South Africa, consider the following case history of the Union Carbide Corporation.

C. Union Carbide: A Case Study

In the 1930s Union Carbide took a portion of its profits from operations in the United States and used them to buy chrome ore mines in South Africa. It sold the ore it mined to Western European nations. These sales added to South Africa's exports, bringing foreign currency into the country. The South African government took a portion of the company's profits as taxes.

Union Carbide had two choices concerning the profits it made: it could have sent them back to the United States or it could have kept them in South Africa to expand its operations in that country. Because of low labor costs and the rapid growth of the South African economy, Union Carbide decided, as many other foreign firms have done, to use its profits to start another business in South Africa.

This time it built a new factory to produce plastics and

insecticides. It relied heavily on South African labor and financing from South African banks to build its new facility. It bought South African raw materials. It advertised its products in South African magazines and distributed them to South African businesses and individuals. Its profits added new wealth to the South African economy. This new wealth is called surplus, and as it circulates in the economy, it can be used to finance other new businesses in South Africa. Thus, while adding to the absolute size of the economy, foreign investment also adds to the ability of the economy to expand more rapidly than ever.

Union Carbide's contributions to the South African economy need not stop there. To increase its own profits, the company may bring some of its administrative and technical experts to South Africa to ensure that the latest techniques of management and production are used. It may

This advertisement appeared in the South African business weekly *The Financial Mail.*

offer such expertise to other South African corporations to help them grow. This assistance could in turn create more demand for Union Carbide products or perhaps lower the cost of purchasing raw materials. It may encourage other American firms to invest in South Africa.

Like any corporation, Union Carbide has to be concerned with labor prices and policies, interest rates on financial transactions, government taxes, inflation—in general, with the outlook for economic stability and profitability. Union Carbide invested in South Africa because it had confidence in the viability of its economy.

D. Strategic Investment

Total American investment in South Africa is less than a fourth of British investment there, but it tends to have more value than the figures alone would indicate. Since 1950 Americans have invested heavily in those industries which are most crucial to a modern economy. This strategic investment has played an important part in the rapid industrialization of South Africa since World War II.

In 1958 Ford and General Motors controlled 70 per cent of the total assets of South Africa's auto industry. Automobile production is often one of the key industries in generating industrial growth because it stimulates related industries such as glass, oil, rubber, and steel production. At the insistence of the South African government, American automobile companies have helped to make the auto industry in South Africa close to self-sufficient—almost all the component parts are now produced locally. These same investments have saved South Africa millions of dollars in foreign exchange by eliminating the need to import cars. Furthermore, United States auto subsidiaries help to build up South African military potential, such as in the manufacture of trucks for troop and supply transport. A General

Motors plant has been designed specifically to allow conversion to military production if necessary.

At this point in South Africa's economic development, high technology industries such as data processing appear to be the ones that will grow most rapidly, providing the foundation for more sophisticated industrialization. American companies like IBM have a near monopoly on computer and computer-related industries in South Africa.

Despite its great wealth of natural resources, South Africa lacks oil, without which its military and industrial machinery cannot move. The government, however, has been anxious to avoid dependence on oil imports from the Middle East because of the threat of an international boycott of oil exports to South Africa. Some seventeen American companies have joined the South African government in efforts to make South Africa self-sufficient in oil production. After considerable exploratory work, they have begun drilling some off-shore sites. In addition to the search for local deposits of oil, companies like Caltex, Mobil, and Esso dominate the refining and marketing of imported crude oil. Caltex ran this advertisement in numerous South African publications:

> Ahead of Caltex lies many years of search and perhaps disappointment—or the discovery which will free South Africa for all time from dependence on outside oil supplies.

The following advertisement was run by Mobil in *The Financial Mail* of March 5, 1971:

THE POWER SEEKERS
Everyone is conscious of South Africa's need for its own supply of crude oil—and Mobil is doing something about it.

From Cape Agulhas to the Moçambique Channel, wherever off-shore drilling is taking place, Mobil is there.

As a member of a consortium, Mobil is drilling for oil in a concession stretching from Cape St. Francis to the Kei River mouth. Where other off-shore drilling is underway, as far north as Beira, Mobil is there providing fuels, lubricants and service.

Mobil is a power in the oil business in South Africa—a leader for over 70 years.

E. Technical Assistance

South Africa relies extensively on other capitalist countries to keep its industrial operations efficient and up to date. Each foreign corporation investing in South Africa brings its own expertise with it. This practice has become South Africa's major source of industrial technology. In some cases, American corporations serve South African industry without investing in the economy directly. For example, the Chemical Construction Company of New York helped construct six acid plants for the South African government-owned chemical industry.

South Africa has apparently demonstrated its ability to control its volatile political situation to the satisfaction of over 1,000 foreign firms. Mr. J. J. Palmer, representative of a group of New York and Chicago investors, put it this way in a 1964 speech:

> South Africa is the only country in Africa with a stable government. Every businessman wants a strong government to back him up and South Africa has it.

South Africa has what businessmen call a "good investment climate." Return on investment is very high. The rate at which Americans have been investing in South Africa has been steadily rising. Increasingly, United States corporations plan to use South Africa as a base from which to expand elsewhere in Africa. Consequently, there is much support from American corporate interests for South Africa's outward-looking policy. The future plans of both the United States and South Africa in regard to the rest of Africa seem to be converging.

II. Corporations and Apartheid

"What's good for General Motors is good for the country."

For years many Americans accepted the above cliché as part of the definition of the American way of life. Today, the assumptions underlying this statement are being challenged by more and more people. Numerous issues have been raised questioning the belief that corporate power necessarily serves the public welfare. Corporate pollution has ruined much of our air and water resources. Corporate tax privileges increase tax burdens on the average citizen. Corporate expansion around the globe pressures the American government to make more political and military commitments abroad.

The American people are making the challenge to corporate power in numerous ways. The investigations of crusaders like Ralph Nader are followed with widespread interest. Hard questions are being raised about the influence upon government of what the late President Dwight D. Eisenhower once called "the military-industrial complex." And some stockholders now go to annual meetings weighing their understandable concern for high profits against the social responsibility of the corporation in which they share ownership.

One of the issues in this public challenge to corporations has been the matter of extensive American corporate involvement in South Africa. Workers in companies like IBM and Polaroid have demanded that their employers stop doing business there. Students at Cornell, Princeton, Harvard, and Wisconsin have challenged their universities' role in supporting corporations that are involved in South Africa. Organizations in America's Black communities have protested American presence in Southern Africa. Church groups have challenged corporations such as Gulf, General Motors, American Metal Climax, and the Chase Manhattan Bank. The central issue in all these cases is whether American corporate presence in Southern Africa reinforces or undermines White minority rule.

Here we shall examine the conflict between private American economic interests in South Africa and that sector of the public in the United States which opposes U.S. corporate involvement there. The four principal arguments for and against this presence are summarized. It should be remembered that other foreign corporations have extensive involvement in South Africa also. In Britain, which has the largest economic stakes in South Africa, the debate over whether corporations support apartheid is far more intense than in the United States. Similar controversies are taking place in countries like Sweden, West Germany, and Italy. This discussion, however, limits itself to the debate taking place in the United States.

Argument A
American Investment Creates Jobs

Many U.S. corporations have defended investment in South Africa by pointing out that their presence provides more jobs for everyone—Black and White. It is not always true, however, that foreign investment creates more jobs. When the investing corporation uses machines instead of people to produce its product (the modern tendency), it may in fact afford fewer jobs than before.

African workers are not allowed to engage in collective

bargaining and strikes, but White workers can. African
workers are paid far less than White workers and are forbidden promotion to all sorts of jobs reserved by law for
"Whites only." American corporate profits in South Africa,
inevitably benefiting from employing an African work force
that has no right to bargain for improved conditions, are
more than double the average profits made back in the
United States. An American executive of Chrysler South
Africa recently told an interviewer:

> The African doesn't want a trade union. He isn't used
> to democracy, he is used to an authoritarian hierarchi-
> cal tribal structure. He accepts the White man as his
> guardian.

Argument B
American Corporations Undermine Apartheid

Some American corporations involved in South Africa con-
tend that their employment practices are more enlight-
ened than those of other firms. They maintain that by taking
the initiative in improving benefits for African employees,
they are quietly undermining the apartheid system.

One way of evaluating this argument is to look at the
impact of American investment in South Africa to date. In
1950 American investment there totaled $148 million. In
the last twenty years it has risen to nearly a billion dollars
—a sixfold increase. During that time, the gap between
White and African income has widened considerably. Africans lost what representation they had in Parliament before. The African press, leadership, and political parties
were banned. Laws were enacted permitting arrest and
punishment without charges, trial, or appeal. Other laws
broke up families and forcibly removed Africans from areas
where they had lived all their lives. The evidence available
so far indicates that increased American investment has
failed to "liberalize" apartheid.

In late 1970 employees at the United States headquarters of the Polaroid Corporation demanded that their employer stop doing business in South Africa. The company responded by announcing a new experimental program which would raise the salaries of Africans employed by its distributor in South Africa. In addition, it pledged to contribute funds to African educational advancement. One year after the experiment began, Polaroid decided, on the basis of this trial period, to remain in South Africa, continuing its attempts to improve conditions there.

Critics in the United States, including some Polaroid employees, have responded that Polaroid's gestures to improve conditions of its distributor's African employees clearly violate South African labor laws. A similar experiment some years ago by the Anglo-American Corporation was abruptly ended by South African government intervention. A broader criticism comes from the Reverend George Houser, executive director of the anti-apartheid American Committee on Africa:

> The fundamental danger of the Polaroid approach is that it ignores the real dynamics of the struggle in South Africa. Here is a country where 19 per cent of the population control all political, economic, and military life, a country where the great mass has no right of political expression, no political parties, no representation in Parliament, no constitutional way in which to bring about change. John F. Kennedy said, "Those who make peaceful change impossible make violent change inevitable." As concerns South Africa, it is not surprising that a violent clash is in the making.

Argument C
American Corporations Defend Apartheid

Polaroid has publicly denounced apartheid as a "repugnant" system. This action puts it in a minority position among American corporations, many of which defend their investments in South Africa by defending the apartheid system as well. A survey reviewed in *Newsweek* in early 1971 revealed that only 14 per cent of American businessmen having investments in South Africa were opposed to apartheid.

According to another survey by visiting American researchers in 1970, 63 per cent of American businessmen in South Africa would vote for either the Nationalist or the United Party, both of which strongly support the apartheid system. The managing director of Union Carbide South Africa told the researchers he opposed majority rule in South Africa because it would be bad for both the economy and Union Carbide. The great majority of American management in South Africa made similar statements in the survey.

Typifying this position, Milton P. Higgins, formerly chairman of the Norton Company of Massachusetts, told a White South African audience:

> I think South Africa is going to remain a strong country, led by White people. I think foreign countries should leave South Africa alone. If they leave you alone you will get on and do a great job.

Argument D
American Corporations are "Apolitical"

Finally, spokesmen for corporations operating in South Africa often argue that their activities are "apolitical." They claim that companies like Union Carbide are in South Africa solely to conduct business there and do not or cannot influence the political system in that country, however immoral that system may be in the view of many people. The

3M Company of Minnesota responded to an inquiry about its South African investments this way:

> In all phases of our international operations, we keep in mind, and try to instill in each of our employees, that when we do business in other countries we are guests in those countries and try to conduct ourselves accordingly. This means that we tend to follow local customs and refrain, as foreigners, from attempting to impose our views and policies—which, in our case as an American company, involve the active promotion of the equal opportunity concept.

This argument raises the important issue of defining what constitutes a "political" act. If one means making campaign contributions and voting in elections, then foreign corporations are probably correct to claim that they are apolitical in South Africa, assuming that they do not engage in such activities.

Those who argue that foreign corporations should withdraw from South Africa generally use a broader definition of politics. For example, many American corporations (Union Carbide, General Motors, International Harvester, to name a few) make contributions to the South Africa Foundation, which conducts world-wide propaganda and lobbying activities in defense of apartheid. Opponents of apartheid view such subsidies to the foundation as a clearly political act.

American corporate officials frequently express political opinions about the situation in South Africa while in that country and when they return to the United States. The evidence suggests that a great majority express support for White minority rule there. Such statements in defense of apartheid influence the South African government, executives in the home office, and American politicians, government officials, and public opinion.

Foreign corporations in South Africa often point with pride to the contributions they have made to developing a strong and viable economy there. The following quote is from a company news release:

> General Motors South Africa has made a major contribution to the growth and development of the Republic.

American corporations in particular have done much to develop both strategic industries and economic self-sufficiency in South Africa, as was discussed earlier in this chapter. Regardless of the motives of these corporations, their investments have the effect of increasing South Africa's military strength, its chances of withstanding international sanctions, and its technological capability to repress the majority African population.

Critics therefore argue that if the apartheid system is strengthened by the results of American corporate activities, it is misleading to claim that those activities are politically neutral. If Polaroid's condemnation of apartheid was a "political" act (as claimed by the South African government), then it is difficult to maintain that the far more numerous corporate statements and actions which support apartheid are "apolitical."

Perhaps the most serious accusation of all concerning the political impact of American corporate activities in South Africa revolves around a series of events which occurred in 1961. In that year South Africa experienced a severe economic crisis after the Sharpeville massacre. Fearing an outbreak of revolution and more international sanctions, foreign investors withdrew large volumes of capital. South African exports declined sharply. The South African stock market plunged. The country's foreign exchange holdings dropped to a dangerous level, and the very survival of the regime was in doubt. Many of its strongest supporters began to consider the necessity to make some changes.

During that year of panic, American corporations increased their investments by $23 million and their imports from South Africa by $50 million. American financiers made emergency loans of $85 million to the South African government, led by the Chase Manhattan and First National City Banks of New York. American corporations ran advertisements proclaiming their faith in South Africa's future. American industrialist Charles Engelhard founded the American-South African Investment Corporation to attract American capital back into South Africa.

This massive infusion of financial and moral support from American corporations during the 1961 crisis helped apartheid to survive its most serious challenge to date. The South African regime was able to weather the storm without having to make any basic changes in the society. It has been tightening the screws of repression ever since.

III. South African Views on Foreign Corporations

A. African Opinions

Those who favor the continuation or expansion of foreign corporate activities in South Africa usually assert that a boycott or economic withdrawal would hurt Africans there first and foremost.

Given the severe restrictions on African freedom of speech in South Africa, it is difficult to determine African opinion on this crucial issue. By law it is a treasonable offense, carrying a maximum penalty of death, to advocate foreign economic withdrawal from South Africa.

The two largest African political parties are the African National Congress and the Pan Africanist Congress, whose leaders have been forced underground or into exile by government repression. Both organizations are on record as favoring economic sanctions as a means to weaken apartheid. The Organization of African Unity also holds to that position, despite violations by some member states who are seeking a "dialogue" with South Africa.

The late Chief Albert J. Luthuli, Nobel peace prize winner and president-general of the African National Congress, once said:

> The economic boycott of South Africa will entail undoubted hardship for Africans. We do not doubt that. But if it is a method which shortens the day of bloodshed, the suffering to us will be a price we are willing to pay. In any case, we suffer already, our children are often undernourished, and on a small scale (so far) we die at the whim of a policeman.

B. White Opinions

The South African government strongly welcomes foreign investment, regarding it as a vote of confidence in the viability of South African society. Government officials and White political leaders often express gratitude to foreign corporations for their contributions towards making South Africa strong and self-reliant. This same government is rigidly committed to maintaining the apartheid system. If foreign investment is undermining that system, the South African government does not seem to believe it. On the contrary, White South Africa regards foreign corporations as one of its strongest allies.

The government appears confident that it can contain whatever liberalizing tendencies there might be on the part of foreign investment. In 1966 Ford's Canadian subsidiary refused, under pressure from the United States State Department, to sell the South African government four-wheel drive trucks in deference to the UN arms ban. South Africa retaliated against the Ford subsidiary in South Africa by boycotting all Ford vehicles for three years. Ford got the message and reversed its original decision. In the meantime, the original order for trucks was filled by Vauxhall, a British subsidiary of General Motors. In this instance, as in many others, South Africa backed up its frequent assertion that foreign enterprises can do business in South Africa only by co-operating with government policies.

South Africa is equally enthusiastic about expanding its extensive international trade. Beyond the strategic value of certain imports and the money value of an increased volume of business, there is a political consideration. An editorial in South Africa's *Financial Gazette* put it this way in July 1970:

> Through trade, South Africa can offer formidable resistance to any efforts to isolate her from the rest of the world. Foreign trade is in fact the means of ensuring a continued role for South Africa in world politics. Its political importance should, therefore, never be underestimated.

The South African government also values foreign corporate involvement because of its effects on the home governments of those corporations. When hundreds of major corporations in a capitalist country develop commitments in a foreign country, the government of that home country usually lends its diplomatic and even military support to the protection of these commitments. Corporate interests thus tend to become national interests. South Africa reasons that it can assure continued American, French, Japanese, and British government support if the corporations of those countries maintain a heavy economic stake in perpetuating the status quo in South and Southern Africa.

IV. Corporations and Foreign Policy

The conflict in the United States between corporations and various sectors of the public over involvement in South Africa is ultimately a fight to influence the shaping of American foreign policy. This conflict in turn raises the issue of corporate power in the American political system.

Often social studies textbooks describe political power in the American system in terms of the ballot box—each person has one vote. They claim that the citizen influences the formulation of government policy by voting for the politician whose views he agrees with.

By this definition, the political power of a Mississippi sharecropper or a waitress in Indiana would be equal to that of the president of General Motors. But the President of the United States does not call up the waitress or the sharecropper to ask advice on important decisions. In the real world of American politics, large corporations have much influence on government decision making.

One way in which corporations do this is by contributing heavily to campaign funds of politicians. Corporations themselves are not permitted by law to make political contributions. But in practice, corporate executives often make large donations to political campaigns and then get reimbursed by the company through such devices as a "bonus." In these ways, corporations have become the main source of funds for most politicians running for office. This dependency on corporate funding provides the politician with much reason to solicit and represent the views of corporate America.

Only clear-cut issues of policy formulations such as the Vietnam war usually come to public attention under this system. Foreign policy is formulated daily in decisions over trade and investments, international education programs, and labor union exchange programs, for example. Most of these questions never come to the public view and are either voted on quietly in Congress or decided in a separate commission or advisory board.

Congress's decision formally to break economic sanctions against Rhodesia by buying Rhodesian chrome ores illustrates this process. A clause affecting the importation of chrome was tacked onto a bill concerning the purchase of strategic metals. The decision about chrome ores, although couched in terms of the strategic metals question, had ramifications which went far beyond it. In effect, passage of the bill meant that the United States would not uphold economic sanctions against Rhodesia and that it gave tacit support to any British settlement with the White minority regime in Rhodesia. Corporations such as Union Carbide and Foote Mineral were among the major lobbyists for the bill in Congress. Both have sizable investments in Rhodesian chrome.

In addition to campaign funding and lobbying, there are other important corporate ties to Congress. Politicians, on a national level, tend to come from the upper middle class. In the Senate, to which the Constitution delegates the responsibility of foreign policy, nearly half the members are millionaires. The vast majority in both houses of Congress are lawyers with corporate interests of their own. Even more than elected politicians, appointed high-level government officials come from the ranks of business executives. One finds, consequently, a continuous flow of similar types of people back and forth between positions in government and the corporate world.

Congress is not the only place where corporations influence foreign policy. Corporation officials are involved in policy making before it ever gets to a vote. By sitting on Foundation boards, presidential commissions on trade and development, or advisory councils on foreign economic policy, corporate leaders participate in framing issues and making decisions before the public is ever informed. Most of these decisions never reach the Congress, the elected officials, or the public vote.

Usually, it is only when a policy has become a crisis, such as the Middle East or Indochina, that the public demands information or searches out its own, and organizes to exert pressure on decision-makers. South Africa is becoming an issue in American society today because growing sectors of public opinions are organizing just such a countervailing force to question American policy on South Africa.

Part 2. National Interests and South Africa

It would be a great oversimplification to think that foreign policy simply reflects the views of either corporations or the public on specific issues, whether in the United States or in other Western capitalist countries. While these views must be taken into account by those who actually determine and implement foreign policy, a government has considerations of its own to put forth. These considerations are usually referred to collectively by a country's leaders as "national interests."

In formulating foreign policy towards South Africa, policy makers evaluate the importance of world public opinion, military and strategic factors, relationships with allied countries, existing ties with South Africa, and the maintenance of national prosperity.

I. World Opinion

World public opinion has repeatedly condemned White minority rule in Southern Africa, and South African apartheid in particular. The principal forum for this issue has been the United Nations, which has passed resolution after resolution in opposition to apartheid.

The United States, Britain, and France have usually joined with the majority of the world's nations to vote for resolutions which condemned apartheid verbally. American foreign policy has stated its opposition to apartheid forthrightly, as in this official State Department release:

> The U.S. Government is unalterably opposed to the racial, or apartheid, policies of the South African Government. We fear that South Africa's present course, unless soon moderated, can lead only to disaster for all of its people. Our spokesmen at the United Nations and from many other platforms have repeatedly denounced the policy of apartheid.

On the matter of implementing concrete actions against South Africa, the United States and its major allies have consistently vetoed or abstained from resolutions put forth by the Afro-Asian and socialist countries. The American government says it is applying "moral pressure" on the Afrikaners to change their ways, but it opposes any measures such as trade or investment sanctions. United States ambassador to South Africa John G. Hurd said in October 1970:

> We hope to continue dialogue with this country—hopeful dialogue so that, in friendship, we understand this country, and South Africa would understand why other countries oppose its policies. Our views should be seen as friendliness, not as direct criticism.

II. Military Ties

The one UN resolution calling for action which the major capitalist countries did endorse was the 1963 embargo on sale of arms to South Africa. The ways in which these countries have circumvented the resolution in practice, however, suggest that they endorsed the embargo more to appease world opinion rather than to make a decisive impact on South African military strength.

France has openly defied the embargo since 1963 by selling to South Africa the latest jet fighter-bombers, missiles, nuclear submarines, helicopters, and other war materiel. The French government justifies these violations by claiming that the heavy armaments which it supplies are for external defense only. But there is nothing to prevent South Africa from using these same weapons for further suppression of its own African majority. The more likely explanation is that these sales are too lucrative to the French arms industry for the French government to pass up.

While France has the largest share of the South African arms market, other Western countries have made similar sales from time to time, including West Germany, Italy, and Belgium. Britain and the United States have claimed to obey the arms embargo since 1964. But in July 1970 the newly elected Tory government in Britain announced its intention to resume open shipments of arms to South Africa. Meanwhile, some doubts have been raised about the truth of American compliance. The British newspaper the *Guardian* declared editorially on March 30, 1970:

> In spite of the arms embargo, Mr. Vorster still receives about 35 million dollars' worth of military supplies from the United States annually, mostly in Lockheed transport aircraft.

Nearly all the NATO countries permit their corporations to invest in the South African armaments industry. They place no restrictions on the transfer of military know-how, including the sale to South Africa of blueprints and patents for military production. For example, the entire South

African army and police force are equipped with NATO
FN rifles, manufactured in South Africa under license from
NATO. All these governments permit their citizens to accept jobs in the South African arms industry. Both Britain
and the United States continue to export spare parts for
the large quantities of British and American military hardware sold to South Africa before 1964. Every one of these
activities is explicitly forbidden by the July 1970 UN Security Council amendment to the Arms Embargo Act of 1963.
Both Britain and the United States abstained in that vote.

Furthermore, the American definition of "military item"
is a narrow one. For example, the Beech Aircraft Corporation is permitted to export light aircraft to South Africa on
the grounds that they will be used for civilian transportation. But some of the same models in question were used
by the American military for counterinsurgency in Vietnam.
They can easily be adapted for internal military maneu-
vers in South Africa as well. Similar loopholes exist for other
American exports to South Africa, such as Ford trucks and
American Motors Jeeps. Some American investment in
South Africa also has military potential, such as the con-
vertibility of General Motors and Ford plants to the production of weapons.

In 1965 an American corporation, Allis-Chalmers, erected
South Africa's first nuclear facility with the encouragement
of the United States government. The U. S. Atomic Energy
Commission (AEC) trained South African staff members
at the government's nuclear complex in Oak Ridge, Ten-
nessee. The AEC also supplied both consultants and the enriched uranium necessary for the new reactor.

While the South African government is interested in nuclear power as an energy source to overcome its shortage
of petroleum, South African scientists have recently per-
fected a new process for creating isotopes of enriched
uranium similar to those necessary for explosive warheads.

Should South Africa convert its nuclear development to military purposes, American assistance will have helped make that country the only nuclear power south of the equator.

III. Strategic Considerations

The historically strategic value of South Africa to European expansion still figures in Western intentions to maintain its presence in the Indian Ocean. South Africa rarely loses an opportunity to remind the Western powers that it is a willing and necessary ally because of its crucial location at the juncture of the Atlantic and Indian Oceans. To maximize its appeal to the West, South Africa portrays itself as a bastion against communism in the Southern Hemisphere.

A friendly South Africa means protection of Western Europe's critical sea route to Middle Eastern oil. In addition to the value of South African ports as stopovers for commercial shipping, South Africa's location is also of military value. Both Britain and the United States have free access to South Africa's Simonstown Naval Base. The United States also maintains missile tracking stations on South African soil. Commenting on the increased importance of South Africa because of the closure of the Suez Canal and the build-up of the Soviet navy, British Foreign Minister Sir Alec Douglas-Home wrote in 1969:

> The policing of the South Atlantic and of the west of the Indian Ocean becomes important both to Britain and to Western Europe. These areas are in effect (although they may not formally be made so) an extension of NATO's responsibility for the security of Europe.

As British commitments east of the Suez are reduced, the United States is taking on more of the defense of Western interests in the Indian Ocean sphere than ever before. The strategic value of South Africa, long a principal "national interest" of British foreign policy, is becoming of equal importance in the calculations of American global strategy. Perhaps these considerations help to explain why the United States and its principal allies have not enforced the UN arms embargo more effectively.

IV. Economic National Interests

Extensive foreign corporate interests in South Africa constitute a major consideration of each home government in its formulation of foreign policy towards that country. A trade volume of nearly $5 billion, investments of well over $6 billion, and the rich natural resources of South Africa have a direct effect on the prosperity of the Western world. Since these governments are pledged to maintain that prosperity, national interests tend to coincide with corporate interests.

A. Trade

Trade regulations are an important instrument of foreign policy. The United States does not buy sugar from Cuba, for example, because it disapproves of Cuba's policies and hopes to disrupt its economy by imposing a trade boycott. On the other hand, preferential trade agreements are usually extended between countries which enjoy friendly relations.

Like its major allies, the United States government places no restrictions on American trade with South Africa, except for the ban on the export of more obvious types of military hardware. Since exports to South Africa exceed imports by more than three times, trade with South Africa helps to ease the chronic American balance-of-payments deficit caused in part by a surplus of imports over exports. When the United States revoked Cuba's sugar quota after the 1959 revolution there, it reassigned part of it to South Africa. The quota guarantees South African sugar producers a constant volume of American business at a fixed price, above the average world market price. In effect, the American taxpayer subsidizes South African sugar growers.

Western governments are anxious to maintain access to South Africa's vast reserves of mineral resources. These countries import large quantities of antimony, chromium, uranium, corundum, lithium, vanadium, platinum, asbestos, manganese, and diamonds, all of which are strategic raw materials for industrial production. The United States government has a policy of buying raw materials abroad in order to conserve resources at home. To help large American corporations plan far in advance, the government keeps stockpiles of nearly 100 minerals in case of a future shortage. In a sophisticated industrial society, a shortage of any one basic raw material could disrupt large segments of the economy.

The most important raw material historically in South Africa has been gold. South Africa based its rapid economic growth in the twentieth century on the wealth generated by the sale of billions of dollars worth of this most precious of all metals. South Africa accounts for 75 per cent of gold production for the capitalist world's monetary needs. For decades, its gold backed up the major currencies of the international monetary system—the dollar, the pound, the mark, and the franc.

B. Investments

Every country in the world has to weigh strategic and military considerations in the formulation of its foreign policy. Similarly, every country has at least some foreign trade to take into account. But unlike the socialist and underdeveloped states, the industrial capitalist nations alone export large volumes of capital for investment in other countries.

American investment abroad has increased at a staggering pace since World War II. Today American-owned companies in foreign countries produce a total of at least $200 billion dollars a year in goods and services. If the operations of these companies abroad were considered as a separate economy, they would have a higher Gross National Product than any other country in the world except for the domestic American and Soviet economies.

American economic growth abroad is increasing twice as fast as at home. Nearly every major American corporation depends on its foreign operations for 10 to 50 per cent of its total sales. American economic expansion abroad has now reached a point where events all over the world influence whether there is prosperity or depression in the United States. Corporate interests abroad have become, more than ever before, vital national interests in order to protect the affluent American standard of living.

American corporations have more investments in South Africa than in any other country in Africa. In 1967 the average profit on all United States corporate investments there averaged 19.2 per cent, compared to 10 per cent elsewhere and still less on domestic American investment. Similar investments in the other White minority-ruled countries of Southern Africa are rising sharply. Many American companies want to expand elsewhere in Africa from a solid industrial base in South Africa. All of these factors provide ample reason for the American government to support American corporate activities in South and Southern Africa.

Still, were American corporations to withdraw or be forced out of South Africa, the effects on the American economy would not be substantial. The government might

oppose such changes to prevent setting a precedent for elsewhere, but not because it would plunge this country into
another depression. United States corporate investments in
South Africa are only 1.2 per cent of total American investment abroad.

The British situation is a different story. Britain is an
island poorly endowed with natural resources. Its prosperity has always depended upon vigorous economic expansion, which was the fundamental reason for the creation
of the British Empire. Adjusting for the difference in size
of economy, Britain exports four times more goods and
twice as much capital as does the United States.

Total British investment in South Africa—worth about $4
billion counting both corporate and public interests—is 10
per cent of total British foreign investment. While British
investments in Canada and Australia are even greater, investments in South Africa bring home the most earnings
because profits are so high there. British profits from South
Africa, averaging about $240 million a year, contribute
much to offset Britain's balance-of-payment deficit.

The British have invested four times more than the
Americans in South Africa. Since the British economy is
only one tenth the size of America's, British investments in
South Africa are forty times more important to its economy
than American investments in South Africa are to the
United States.

British economic interests in South Africa are therefore
enormous. In contrast to the United States, the loss of
British investments in and trade with South Africa would
bring catastrophe to the British economy.

Britain is one of America's oldest allies. Since World War
II, support for a healthy British economy has been a principal tenet of American foreign policy. American corporations are more involved in the British economy than in any
other country in the world except Canada. A depression

in Britain would in turn have serious economic repercussions in the United States.

Directly to some extent, but indirectly through Britain to a far greater extent, American national interests have a substantial stake in the South African economy.

PART TWO

BUILDING FREEDOM: LIBERATION IN THE PORTUGUESE COLONIES

INTRODUCTION

The White supremacist regimes in Southern Africa represent only one side of the struggle for the area. Part Two of *Race to Power* considers the Africans' side of the struggle —the fight to regain control of their lives and lands. In each of the major countries of the Southern Africa bloc there are militant African resistance organizations which oppose the regimes in power and the capitalist interests supporting them.

Resistance is not new to Southern Africa. It took the Portuguese four centuries to penetrate beyond the coasts of the colonies, and South Africa's history is marked by continuous struggle against European domination. Although the forms of resistance have changed, the struggle of Africans to maintain and win back control over their land has remained constant. At various times this struggle has been primarily military, at others it has assumed a predominantly political or cultural form. Repression has been the constant response of the minority rulers. Today, resistance in Southern Africa takes many forms. Because of conditions outlined in Part One, resistance in South Africa, Namibia, and Zimbabwe has taken the form of clandestine organization, workers' and students' strikes, sabotage, and continued preparation for armed struggle.

Resistance in the Portuguese colonies reached the level of protracted warfare in the 1960s. In Mozambique, Angola, and Guinea-Bissau, the African people have won control of sizable areas of their homelands and now have self-government in these liberated zones. Chapters Six, Seven, and Eight each contain a detailed history of the development of the movement toward liberation and a description of the new life in Mozambique, Angola, and Guinea-Bissau. The chapter on Mozambique presents an overview of various aspects of the liberation struggle there. The chapter on Angola examines the role of racism in Portuguese colonialism as well as presenting an in-depth description of life in Angola's liberated areas. The chapter on Guinea-Bissau emphasizes the relationship between theory and practice in the revolution in that country.

Much of what follows is told from the inside—by people actually engaged in the movements for national liberation. It is told in their words, sometimes directly in English, sometimes translated from Portuguese, but always with the force of political commitment. Each chapter focuses on one political movement, the movement which in that colony, has taken the forefront in organizing the struggle.

At different points in the development of each resistance struggle there has been more than one nationalist party. Particularly in the initial phases of struggle, differing interests or political orientations and lack of communication usually have resulted in the formation of a multiplicity of groups committed to different strategies. Because the struggle has been based entirely on popular support, the group or groups who best understand the situation in their country and who are the most successful in responding to people's needs gradually have become predominant.

Today in Guinea-Bissau there is only one movement, the

PAIGC (African Party for the Independence of Guinea and the Cape Verde Islands). In Mozambique, although an organization called COREMO (Revolutionary Committee of Mozambique) exists, only FRELIMO (Front for the Liberation of Mozambique) can be said to hold substantial territory. The situation in Angola is less clear: three parties —GRAE (Revolutionary Government of Angola in Exile), UNITA (National Union for Total Independence of Angola), and MPLA (Popular Movement for the Liberation of Angola)—claim leadership in the struggle there. All evidence available to us, however, indicates that the MPLA controls the most territory and has the soundest base of popular support, the strongest military development, and the most refined governmental structure. The OAU (Organization of African Unity) has given its support to PAIGC, FRELIMO, and MPLA.

Although Chapters Six, Seven, and Eight consider FRELIMO, MPLA, and PAIGC separately, it is important to point out that they have strong ties to each other. As the White regimes in Southern Africa work together to ensure their continued control, so the liberation movements in the Portuguese colonies have regionalized their opposition to White domination. The movements have common historical roots, common political philosophies, and a common inter-movement organization. Many of the leaders of these movements studied together at the university in Lisbon in the 1950s, where they began to develop their political philosophies. Through the years the movements have worked closely together, learning from each other's experiences, exchanging information, and dealing with common problems. In the early 1960s they entered into a formal alliance called CONCP (Conference of the Nationalist Organizations of the Portuguese Colonies). Although each movement works out the strategy for its own territory separately, CONCP assumes some of the common functions of publicizing and winning support for the wars.

Each of the movements in Southern Africa starts from the fact that the revolution in its territory can only come from within. At the same time, they see that the struggle in any one territory is of crucial importance to all the others. Together, they make up a network that puts independence for African peoples as the most important issue in Southern Africa today.

> We never accepted
>
> We were as tall trees
> bending when the strong wind blows
> but who know
> submission is just for a time
>
> We stowed anxiety in our hearts
> courage in our hands
> bullets in our homes
>
> Tenderness and hatred impelled us
>
> Our sons measured their height
> by the length of guns
>
> The anguish of waiting weighed on us
> like an endless yearning
>
>   .   .   .   .   .
>
> Happy those who live in our time
> in freedom
> building freedom

FRELIMO New Year's Greeting, 1970

CHAPTER SIX

MOZAMBIQUE

In Mozambique, it was FRELIMO that organized the resistance to Portuguese domination in the 1960s. In the following chapter Mozambicans will describe how they organized a party, why they decided to use arms against the Portuguese and how they run a people's army. They will talk about problems they have faced since the struggle began and their hopes for a new Mozambique.

WHAT DO WE WANT?

We want to free our country, Mozambique. We want to reconstruct our land, we are fighting in order to have a *free Nation*.

A free Nation means: to have no more slaves, to have schools for all, health services for all, work for all, land for all to cultivate and produce food.

FREE NATION is doing away with hunger;

FREE NATION is to end misery;

FREE NATION is to do away with illiteracy;

FREE NATION means doing away with the exploitation of the black man by the white man, of the national by the foreigner, of *man* by *man;*

FREE NATION means the elimination of all the concessionary monopolies dealing in cotton, sugar, sisal, tea, which benefit only one person or a small number of people;

FREE NATION means to have justice and respect for human beings.

Mozambique Revolution, 1965

I. Prelude to Armed Struggle

The Mozambicans had resisted Portuguese oppression in a number of ways. They formed political and cultural groups, some composed of students and others of workers and peasants. Wherever these groups formed, they were swiftly suppressed.* By the late 1950s it had become clear that local pockets of resistance would only meet with violent repression. In Mozambique the most horrifying example of this was the massacre at Mueda on June 16, 1960, in which about 600 people were killed.

> Enough of these massacres
> I have suffered for five hundred years
> I can bear it no longer
> this forced labor
>
> I suffered on the railways
> in the fields of cotton
> in the timber mills and on the sisal plantations
> I can bear it no longer
>
> I can bear it no longer
> this was the cry of the people
> of those who have suffered
> since the first day of the invasion
> The people say: Enough.

D. S. MAGUNI

After this massacre, things in the north could never return to normal. Throughout the region it had aroused the most bitter hatred against the Portuguese and showed once and for all that peaceful resistance was futile.

Thus, everywhere it was the very severity of repres-

* See above, pp. 52–60 for a detailed account of this.

sion that created the necessary conditions for the development of a strong militant nationalist movement.
The tight police state drove all political action underground . . . the excesses of the regime destroyed all
possibility of reforms which, by improving conditions
a little, might have secured the main interests of colonial
rule from a serious attack for some time to come.

The first attempts to create a nationwide . . . movement were made by Mozambicans working in neighboring countries, where they were beyond the immediate
reach of PIDE, the [Portuguese] secret police. At first
the old problem of inadequate communications led to
the establishment of three separate movements . . .

The accession of many former colonies to independence in the late fifties and early sixties favored the formation of "exile" movements and for Mozambique,
Tanganyika's independence, gained in 1961, seemed to
offer new scope. All three movements established separate headquarters in Dar es Salaam [the capital of
Tanzania] soon afterwards.

Eduardo Mondlane, The Struggle for Mozambique, 1970

In June 1962 three separate groups of Mozambican nationalists—UDENAMO (National Democratic Union of
Mozambique), MANU (Mozambique African National
Union), and UNAMI (African Union for an Independent
Mozambique)—combined to form the Mozambique liberation front, FRELIMO, under the presidency of Eduardo
Mondlane. Two years later, after much hard work and planning, FRELIMO held its first congress, where the aims of
the party were defined. Some of these are

—to further the unity of Mozambicans;
—to employ directly every effort to promote the rapid
  access of Mozambique to independence;
—to promote by every method the social and cultural
  development of the Mozambican woman;

—to promote at once the literacy of the Mozambican people, creating schools wherever possible;

—to encourage and support the formation and consolidation of trade union, student, youth and women's organizations;

—to cooperate with the nationalist organizations of the other Portuguese colonies;

—to procure all requirements for self-defense and resistance of the Mozambican people;

—to procure diplomatic, moral and material help for the cause of the Mozambican people from the African states and from all peace and freedom loving people.

Mondlane, *The Struggle for Mozambique*

It was only after the formation of FRELIMO that the decision was made to wage a military struggle against the Portuguese.

THE NECESSITY FOR ARMED STRUGGLE

The historic meeting of the FRELIMO Central Committee in July 1964 made a decision of vital importance to our people. That decision concerned the form which our struggle should assume. Basically, the option was between resorting to armed struggle for the liberation of Mozambique or continuing the path followed up till then—namely, attempted negotiations with the Portuguese government and petitions to the United Nations.

The general feeling in FRELIMO was that we should have recourse to armed struggle. In this connection, about 200 militants had already received military training in Algeria and had returned to Mozambique, where they were awaiting the instructions of our Organization. However, the final decision was still to be made: and it was one which could not be made lightly. Because of its importance and gravity it required serious consideration and a complete analysis of the situation.

There were several problems to take into account. Obviously, the first one was to determine whether armed struggle was really the only way left open for us to achieve independence. After all, from a theoretical point of view it could be argued that several African colonies had achieved their independence through peaceful means—by Parliamentary, political and legal struggle. So why should not those means be valid for Mozambique?

. . . Perhaps the most weighty consideration in approaching the decision of armed struggle was the awareness of the sufferings war would bring our people. Would armed struggle be worth the cost? Would it not be better to continue with the known evils of exploitation and oppression so as to avoid the horrors and uncertainties of war?

The pros and cons were exhaustively weighed, and all doubts were successively eliminated. The position of the Portuguese government was clear—to all attempts at negotiation on the part of FRELIMO it reiterated that Mozambique was part of Portugal and that the Portuguese constitution does not allow the alienation of any parcel of Portuguese territory. The Portuguese government accused us of being "bandits," and it increased its repression. It was clear therefore that only by force would we be able to win our independence.

The suffering inherent in the war was not beyond our people's endurance. The will to be free was a guarantee of that. Colonialism and all it represented had to be eradicated from our country—whatever the cost. In making this decision, the Central Committee of FRELIMO felt that it was correctly interpreting the will of our people as a whole.

Mozambique Revolution, September 1970

The Call to Arms

MOZAMBICAN PEOPLE, workers and peasants, workers on the plantations, in the timber mills and in the concessions, workers in the mines, on the railways, in the harbours and in the factories, intellectuals, civil servants, Mozambican soldiers in the Portuguese army, students, men, women and young people, patriots,

IN THE NAME OF ALL OF YOU

FRELIMO TODAY SOLEMNLY PROCLAIMS THE GENERAL ARMED INSURRECTION OF THE MOZAMBICAN PEOPLE AGAINST PORTUGUESE COLONIALISM FOR THE ATTAINMENT OF THE COMPLETE INDEPENDENCE OF MOZAMBIQUE.

Our fight must not cease before the total liquidation of Portuguese colonialism.

MOZAMBICAN PEOPLE,

The Mozambican revolution, the work of the Mozambican people, is an integral part of the struggle of the people of Africa and of the whole world for the victory of the ideals of Liberty and Justice.

The armed struggle which we announce today for the destruction of Portuguese colonialism and of imperialism will allow us to install in our country a new and popular social order. The Mozambican people will thus be making a great historical contribution toward the total liberation of our Continent and the progress of Africa and of the world.

Mozambique Revolution, February 1965

A. The Story of Chipande

On September 25, 1964, the first military operation of FRELIMO was launched. The story of Alberto-Joachim Chipande shows how the movement developed to this point through the eyes of one person, Chipande himself:

I myself decided to join the struggle because every man should be free, or if he has to, should fight to be free . . .

II. The War

If you ask me
who I am,
with that face you see, you others,
branded with marks of evil
and with a sinister smile,

I will tell you nothing
I will tell you nothing

I will show you the scars of centuries
which furrow my black back
I will look at you with hateful eyes
red with blood spilled through the years
I will show you my grass hut
collapsed
I will take you into the plantations where
from dawn to after night-fall
I am bent over the ground
while the labor
tortures my body with red-hot pliers

I will lead you to the fields full of people
breathing misery hour after hour

I will tell you nothing
I will only show you this

And then
I will show you the sprawled bodies
of *my* people
treacherously shot
their huts burned by *your* people

I will say nothing to you
but you will know why I fight.

ARMANDO GUEBUZA

I first heard about a certain organization for liberation in 1960. That was MANU. Certain leaders worked among us. Some of them were taken by the Portuguese at the massacre at Mueda on 16 June 1960 . . . After that experience I had a still stronger feeling for the need to get our liberty. And when everyone else considered what had happened they began to act as well, and they supported MANU.

And then in 1962, when FRELIMO was formed in Dar es Salaam, its leaders invited some delegates from inside Delgado to go and talk with them. People who had previously supported MANU began supporting FRELIMO . . .

After the formation of FRELIMO I became an organizer inside Delgado [Cabo Delgado, a district in northern Mozambique]. This is how we worked. We had formed an agricultural cooperative at Mueda, and when FRELIMO's leaders knew of this they sent delegates inside Delgado to ask the leaders of our cooperative . . . to support FRELIMO. They . . . agreed that they would use the cooperative as long as possible as a means of political organization. We had only a few people in the first year, and then in the second year we cultivated cotton . . . And our cooperative developed. Many joined; and so the Portuguese company [in Mueda] got short of labour, and we began selling our cotton even to that company. We leaders worked hard and voluntarily; we took no percentage of the crop, we had no profit in money . . . Then that Portuguese company complained to the authorities that our cooperative was really anti-Portuguese . . .

The authorities said they would allow no organization with many members in it—30 was the most they would allow. We agreed to that and founded a cooperative with 25 members to grow rice. In the first year we produced a good harvest, we had money in the savings bank, enough to pay wages and we also bought a tractor . . . In 1962, after the formation of FRELIMO,

people began giving active support. We had many contacts with Dar through secret messengers, and we began
issuing membership cards. We started organizing people. Some of them were arrested, and again we came
under Government suspicion.

This time it was different. Now the Portuguese wanted
our groups to work for the destruction of FRELIMO.
They said that we should send men to Dar to create
confusion. We sent our vice-chairman, and the Portuguese gave him money for his journey. But we gave him
a different task. We gave him a letter to the leaders
in Dar to explain why he had the money, and this money
we told him to give to FRELIMO and we found the
necessary money, ourselves. So really this man went
to Dar as a delegate to the First Congress of FRELIMO
while pretending to the Portuguese to be their agent.
He came back after the Congress and told the Portuguese that there were conflicts in Dar between the various groupings in FRELIMO . . .

Then he went again in September as our delegate. But
this time it went wrong. The Portuguese weren't so
simple as to accept what he said just like that. They
sent our comrade again, but they also sent another
man to spy on him . . . When our comrade came back,
he went again to the Portuguese and told them nothing
had changed—the groups in Dar still couldn't agree with
each other; but the real spy had meanwhile given the
Portuguese a very different and real report. So after our
comrade came back the second time, the Portuguese
started arresting and interrogating our comrades—that
was in January 1963. In February they arrested Lazaro,
the chairman of FRELIMO in our region, and the next
day they arrested our comrade who'd been the delegate . . .

After that there were many arrests, and PIDE agents
were all over the place. Many died in prison; others
came back with broken health. We had a comrade working in the administrator's office at Mueda. He warned

us by letter about those who were going to be arrested . . . On 13 February, early in the morning, the
administrator of Mueda came with armed police to
the Catholic mission where I was a teacher . . . But
we—Lourenço Raimundo, also a secretary of our cooperative, and I—had decided not to sleep there. We made
off when we heard the noise of the trucks coming. We
stayed all day in the bush, and when night fell we
walked to Tanzania. We walked from the thirteenth to
the eighteenth and then that night we crossed the
Rovuma into Tanzania.

We got to Lindi and there we were met by a representative of FRELIMO. We told him what had happened. Many refugees came too at that time, because of
the Portuguese repression. We held a meeting and decided that some members of our cooperative should go
back into Mozambique, because we knew it was our
duty to mobilize the people, and that without us the
people would not have leaders. We decided that the
partly educated younger men should go to Dar for
further training, while the older men should go back into
Mozambique and hide there to go on with mobilization . . .

In Dar the leaders asked us what we wanted to do.
We said, to join the army. They asked us, didn't we
want scholarships? No, we said, to fight. So our leaders made contacts with countries ready to help, and
the first was Algeria. In June 1963 we went to Algeria
and trained there until the spring of 1964. On 4 June we
got orders, 24 of us, to meet the President of FRELIMO,
and he told us we were chosen for a mission. Next day
we went down to Mtwara. On 15 August we were ordered by the representative of FRELIMO to leave that
night. We crossed the frontier, and there inside Delgado
we found waiting for us the arms and equipments for
my group, six French rifles, twelve pistols, five cases of
hand grenades . . . We took these and started for the
South, through the forest, but with orders not to begin

till we had the word from our leaders . . . We were not
to attack Portuguese civilians, not to maltreat prisoners,
not to steal, to pay for what we ate . . .

My group had orders to go towards Porto Amélia . . .
We found it hard, because the enemy was patrolling
day and night along the roads and even the bush paths.
At one point my group had to wait a couple of days
before we could get past. We had good contacts, but
because of the Portuguese patrols, it was arranged that
at dangerous points only one man should receive us.
We suffered from food shortage. And we had to take
off our boots for fear of leaving tracks for the Portuguese to follow; we walked barefoot.

We advanced to Macomia. From there we couldn't
get on to Porto Amélia, because the Portuguese had set
up a blockade and they'd mobilized the people against
the bandits . . . The bandits used to pillage Asian shops,
and the Portuguese said we were like that. This held
us back. The Asians informed the Portuguese of our
tracks. We came to the conclusion that we should start
the struggle. We were already fifteen day's walk from
the frontier with Tanzania. So while there in Macomia,
not able to get any further and wanting to start, we sent
messengers to Dar to tell them the details of the situation and explain the dangers of delaying while the armed
bandits were around . . .

On 16 September we got our orders from Dar to begin on 25 September; that was at a meeting of our
group leaders. We decided that each should go to his
own area and begin. Through organizers we planned
that the people should rise at the same time—a real
national insurrection. To defend the people after that,
each group should form militias and explain things to
the villagers, while also sabotaging the roads, and, of
course, attacking the Portuguese soldiers and administration. That was the outline of the plan we made.

Quoted in Mondlane, *The Struggle for Mozambique*

B. Military Chronology

1964   September 25: First military offensive. Several administrative and military posts in Cabo Delgado attacked. November: Attacks extended to Niassa, Zambezia, and Tete [districts]. FRELIMO consolidates positions in Cabo Delgado and Niassa.

1965   No major FRELIMO offensives. Period of apthrough   parent stalemate, in which FRELIMO con-
1966   trols most of the bush and village areas, continuing to mine roads, conduct ambushes, etc. Portuguese retain the towns and a few fortified bases. Approximately 9,000 Portuguese soldiers are killed in Mozambique during the first 3 years of the war.

1967   Fighting extended to all northern regions. FRELIMO gains extensive control of Cabo Delgado. Advance in Niassa towards the frontiers of Mozambique and Zambezia provinces. Control of Catur zone. Further operations begun in Tete and Zambezia.

1968   Operations in Tete continued. Fighting extends to the Zambesi River, and approaches site of the Cabora Bassa Dam.

1969   FRELIMO ambushes, mining and sabotage continue.

1970   Heaviest fighting of the war in a series of Portuguese offensives in all three provinces. Fighting concentrated around Cabora Bassa. Struggle for control of the roads in Tete province. Portuguese equipment and materials for the Dam site transported by air.

1971   Brutal but ineffective Portuguese offensive in Niassa. 7 Portuguese posts abandoned in a

few months. FRELIMO attacks railroad that
runs from the coast to Tete. Guerrillas within
5 miles of the Cabora Bassa site. Portuguese
army obliged to escort all traffic through Tete.
June: FRELIMO soldiers cross the Zambesi.
Rhodesian soldiers killed. Cadres operating in
the south. 2,900 Portuguese troops killed in
this year.

Mozambique Revolution, 1964-71

C. How FRELIMO Fights

Today about one third of Mozambique is freed from
Portuguese control. FRELIMO successes do not come because of advanced technology. FRELIMO has no aircraft;
it uses arms retrieved from the enemy or supplied by
friendly foreign nations. Guns are scarce. FRELIMO success is based on a combination of good organization, knowledge of the land, support by the general population, and
determination. Below we will examine some of these
factors.

1. CHARACTER AND ORGANIZATION OF THE ARMY

The army is representative of the population at large,
in that the vast majority of the guerrillas are peasants
initially uneducated, illiterate and often unable to speak
any Portuguese; but there is also a scattering of those
who have had some education within the Portuguese
system. The majority naturally come from the areas at
present affected by the fighting, because it is there that
widespread campaigns of political education and training programmes are possible. There is, however, a continual stream of people from further south, from all over
Mozambique, who escape in order to join the struggle;
and at the beginning, many people from refugee camps,
who had fled from every district of Mozambique to es-

cape repression, joined in as soon as a structure to contain them had been created. In the army, people from different areas accordingly mingle, so that each unit contains representatives from different tribes and different areas fighting together. In this way, tribalism is being effectively combated within the forces, and an example is being set to the rest of the population.

This is not the only way in which the army leads the way to social change. By accepting women into its ranks, it has revolutionized their social position. Women now play a very active part in running popular militias, and there are also many guerrilla units composed of women. Through the army, women have started to take responsibility in many areas; they have learned to stand up and speak at public meetings, to take an active part in politics . . . When a women's unit first visits a village which is not yet sufficiently involved with FRELIMO, the sight of armed women who get up and talk in front of a large audience causes great amusement, even incredulity; when the villagers are convinced that the soldiers in front of them really are women, the effect on the astonished men is often so forceful that the rush on recruits is very much greater than the army can cope with or than the area can afford to lose.

The army is helping to raise the standard of education as well as of general political consciousness. Recruits are taught wherever possible to read and write, and to speak Portuguese, and even where an organized teaching programme cannot be arranged, they are encouraged to help each other to learn these basic skills. Indeed, the Portuguese authorities are increasingly suspicious of ordinary peasants who speak Portuguese, because they know that these are more likely to have learned it in the FRELIMO army than in a Portuguese school. The army also organizes various specific training programmes such as radio work, accounting, typing, as well as in subjects more narrowly orientated to the war . . .

It is clear from these comments that the role of the army goes far beyond simply fighting the Portuguese. Like the party, it is a nation-making force. It prepares not just soldiers but future citizens, who pass on what they learn to the people among whom they work.

Leadership is not based on rank but on the concept of responsibility; the leader of a certain body is referred to as the man "responsible" for it. There were some leaders who had had a little schooling; but very few of these, even among those in the most important positions today, had gone beyond primary school . . .

After fighting began, the army was enlarged dramatically with new recruits from the areas of action; and in order to use this growing force efficiently, the organization had to be rapidly improved. The army itself was organized into battalions subdivided into detachments, companies and units. This has meant that, while small-scale operations can still be carried on over a very wide area of country, we also have available much larger forces for more important actions, such as attacks on Portuguese bases or against the Mueda air-base . . .

Mondlane, *The Struggle for Mozambique*

2. THE ARMY AND THE PEOPLE

A visitor to Mozambique commented on the closeness between FRELIMO soldiers and the people:

We saw many examples of the complete unison between the army and the civilian peasant farmers. At one of their meetings, for instance, an army commander asked the Youth League to assign some of its members for a patrol, as the army was occupied elsewhere. This they did—and the group included both boys and girls. On another occasion, in one of the camps, the peasants arrested two soldiers who had left the camp without permission. Civilians actually *arrested* the military. Their subsequent treatment was extremely interesting. For they were not punished, but given an ideological lecture before the whole camp, including reprimands by the local people. The commander invited general opinion and everyone was allowed to speak. Some months earlier three Portuguese deserters had been found wandering in the bush by some peasants who immediately brought them to the army.

Mozambique Revolution, 1967

In addition to the guerrillas, the people's militias help carry out the war:

. . . While there is fighting in an area, they [the militias] coordinate their activities with the guerrillas, reinforce them when necessary, and supply them with information about the particular locality. When the guerrilla forces have liberated an area, the militia can then take over the organization of defence, of production and supply, leaving the main forces free to move on to a new fighting area. In regions where there is not yet an active armed struggle, militias are formed in secret whose task is to prepare the ground for guerrilla fighting; to mobilize the people; to observe the Portuguese forces; to arrange supplies and assistance for the guerrillas as they move into the region.

In a sense, these people's militias are the backbone of the armed struggle. The guerrillas carry the main offensive and do most of the direct fighting, but it is the work of the militias which makes it possible for them to operate . . .

Miguel Ambrosio, company commander from Cabo Delgado: I have fought in Zambezia and Niassa, far from my own region and my own tribe. I have fought in the country of the Chuabos and the Lomes . . . The Chuabos, the Nyanjas and the Lomes received me even more warmly than if I had been from their own region. In Western Niassa, for example, I came across Comrade

Panguene, and although he is from the south, you couldn't distinguish him from the people of the region: he is like a son of the region. The people understand that we are all Mozambicans . . . The people are united and help us. Otherwise, for instance, we couldn't go into enemy areas; it is the people who give us all our information about the movements of the enemy, their strength and their position. Also, when we start working in an area where we have no food, because we have not yet had the opportunity to grow any, the people supply us and feed us. We also help the people. Until militias have been formed in a region, we protect the people in their fields against the action and reprisals of the colonialists; we organize new villages when we have to evacuate the people from a zone because of the war; we protect them against the enemy.

Mondlane, *The Struggle for Mozambique*

There are vital differences between an army such as that which FRELIMO has and the Portuguese forces. The FRELIMO army is based on the support of the people for whom it is fighting and moves closely among them. The Portuguese soldiers, on the other hand, are invaders fighting far from home and in the services of a government that cannot offer them, in their own country, basic opportunities, welfare, or education in return. The attitude of FRELIMO towards these soldiers is described here by Samora Machel:

Our struggle is an armed struggle—it is characterized by violence. This violence is directed against foreign oppression, against Portuguese colonialism and its regime. Our struggle is never directed against the Portuguese people. We first had to define against whom we were fighting. We asked ourselves, against whom is Portuguese aggression directed, and the answer to that was: it is directed against our people. So what we did

to begin with was to organize the people who were exploited and oppressed to react against that oppression.
It was then that we were forced to take up weapons and
fight the Portuguese. We don't like war. We don't like
killing. We feel sad that we have to kill other human
beings, but it has to be done for us to win our dignity
and liberate our country.

We know that the soldiers who fight against the Mozambicans are themselves the sons of poor people. We
know that they are conscripted and forced to fight.
They are the instruments of colonialism, they are not
fighting for the good of the people of Portugal. They
appear before us, as the first wall in the defence of the
imperialists. So we are *forced* to kill the Portuguese
soldiers: to get to the real colonialists and imperialists,
we have to destroy that wall. That's why, when we capture a soldier, we have a policy of clemency. Those who
surrender, we consider our allies. Those who desert from
the Portuguese are of course our friends. And even those
that we take prisoner during the war, we are aware that
they were forced to fight. Our own soldiers defend the
interests of the people and are children of the people.
Without the people, there are no soldiers. In FRELIMO
the soldiers are the people with guns, the people are
armies against Portuguese colonialism.

Interview with Samora Machel, August 1971

FRELIMO fighters not only fight, they also share in the
planting and harvesting of crops and contribute in other
ways to the daily life of the villagers:

Today in the national liberation struggle we have one
essential aspect which is armed warfare, but another
aspect just as fundamental is production. It is necessary
that each of us understands the absolute necessity of
involving ourselves in this task. For instance, the principal duty of the guerrilla is to fight, but a guerrilla must

also produce. The duty of the peasant is to work in agricultural production, but the peasant must also fight, must be prepared to engage in armed village defence . . . We must always bear in mind that our goal is the liberation of the people, and that it is important for us to shape human relationships which will mirror what we want Mozambique society to become later. We have to create relationships of perfect identification between the fighters and the population, and between the leaders and the guerrillas. All this constitutes the reality of our work.

Marcelino dos Santos, interviewed
by Boubaker Adjali, June 1970

III. The New Mozambique

A mango does not become a great tree in its first day, but like a growing mango tree, we are deeply rooted in the soil that is our people, and the masses are now tasting the first fruits.

Machel, September 25, 1970

A. The Relationship Between Armed Struggle and Nation-building

One of the chief lessons to be drawn from nearly four years of war in Mozambique is that liberation does not consist merely of driving out the Portuguese authority, but also of constructing a new country; and that this construction must be undertaken even while the colonial state is in the process of being destroyed. We realized this in principle before we began fighting, but it is only in the development of the struggle that we have learned quite how rapid and comprehensive civil reconstruction must be. There is no question of making a few provisional arrangements and waiting until we control our whole country before deciding how to govern it.

We are having now to evolve structures and make decisions which will set the pattern for the future national
government.

Mondlane, *The Struggle for Mozambique*

B. Political Structure

In the liberated areas, the political structure is the party.
In the villages, people's militias are created which are
dependent on the local party organization and on the
military leadership of the zone; their power rests on the
nationalist and revolutionary forces. Besides this, economic life is organized so that the producers work in
cooperatives under the direction of the local party; this
takes away from the chief his traditional role as organizer of the economic life and at the same time puts an
end to the exploitations of the peasant by any privileged
group. It should also be stressed that this process is not
a "dictatorship of the party"; the party is an open organization, and its members are drawn from the whole
population, with the majority being, as is the majority
of the population, peasants; its role is to provide a political framework above the local level. There is no deep
distinction between party and population: *the party is
the population engaged in political action.*

Public meetings, held through the local party, are an
important part of life in the liberated areas. At these,
non-party members can hear more about FRELIMO and
about the struggle, can voice their opinions, ask questions and enter into discussion. At the present time the
administrative life of villages is being reorganized on
the basis of people's committees elected by the whole
population, and the way is being prepared for the extension of this system to the district level.

The void left by the destruction of the colonial state
posed a practical problem which had not been clearly
envisaged by the leadership; a series of services disap-
peared along with Portuguese rule, particularly services

of a commercial nature, while the people continued to exist and to require such services. The inadequacy of the colonial administration meant that there were also many social needs that had never been met but which were nevertheless strongly felt by the population. Thus, from the time of the first victories in the war, a great variety of administrative responsibilities fell on FRELIMO. A population of some 800,000 had to be served. First and foremost, their material needs had to be satisfied, an adequate food supply assured, and other important articles such as clothes, soap or matches provided; then medical and educational services had to be established, and administrative and judicial systems organized.

For a time the problem was acute. We had been unprepared for the extent of the work before us, and we lacked experience in most of the fields where we needed it. In some areas, shortages were very serious; and where the peasants did not understand the reasons, they were withdrawing their support from the struggle and in some instances leaving the region altogether. During the two years after the struggle began, the battle to build up services was at least as important as the military one. By 1966 the crisis was past. The worst shortages had been overcome, and embryonic structures had been formed for commerce, administration, health and education. The New Mozambique was beginning to take shape.

Mondlane, *The Struggle for Mozambique*

Samora Machel describes the ideals behind the political organization:

The People divide the tasks between them. One group will be directly engaged in armed struggle against the invaders. Another group will be involved in production to allow the struggle to go on. Others will be concerned with transporting materials—for the war, for people's shops, for the schools. Some will take care of the sick and wounded. Others look after children. All these groups are engaged in direct struggle—their task is to destroy the Portuguese forces. It is necessary to destroy the whole structure, so that the new structure can take its place. The old society was characterized by the fact that it took initiative away from the people, as if society was controlled by a series of miracles. With our structures we are trying to make people understand that everything that is done or undertaken depends upon each man himself.

We encourage our people to share, to learn from each other, to be with people of all ethnic groups. For example, in the field of agriculture, there are certain regions that have experience of producing rice, while another will know how to produce maize, or manioc, or cassava, or beans. This knowledge from different places must be generalized and made available to everybody everywhere. The same is true with culture: with dances, for example. Those from the North and those from the South will all be dances from Mozambique, so that our people feel that they are the people of Mozambique. We still have the remains of colonialism, the problems of religion and tribalism and differing traditional cultures . . . this was aimed at weakening and dividing the people, so that colonialism could continue to oppress us, to exploit the peasant. These are the kinds of problems that we have in our regions. Our struggle is not simply an armed struggle: it is a revolutionary struggle, a fight to create a new society and a new man, free from the weight of superstition, which takes away a man's initiative. Our concern is not only against Portuguese colonialism, but to free our people from the inheritance of colonialism, to restore the dignity and freedom of the Mozambican people.

This work of revolution can only proceed successfully if the leadership is in contact with the rank and file, and if the people have a direct channel to the leadership. This is the characteristic of a revolutionary society. The capitalists are not concerned with the problems of the people; they are not leaders because they want to serve the people. In a capitalist society, the more education you get, the more you become cut off from the people. You are taught to ignore your origins. In revolution, the more education that someone has, the more aware he should be of the interest of the people. Even if you get to be a university professor, you should not forget that you come from the people.

In the enemy zones, the Portuguese encourage individualism and individual production. In our zones there is no such thing. We organize cooperatives, and ensure the equal distribution of produce. The produce is divided into that which is needed for consumption by the cooperative, and that which will be sold or exchanged for other basic needs. It is FRELIMO that supervises this system in such a way that there is no surplus. We have to destroy individual production, which enables and encourages people to make profit and accumulate capital, and create collective production, destroy the profit mentality. It's no easy task. That's why we stress that our struggle is not against a color or a race, because exploiters need not only be white. They can come from America, Europe, Asia, but he can also come from Africa, even from Mozambique. There are no black and white parasites. All parasites feed from blood and therefore have to be fought.

Some of our exports, such as cotton, we don't have the machines to convert to cloth, and we can't at the moment establish this system. But there are some products which could be produced in large quantities in the present system—such as ground nuts, cashew nuts and sesame seeds—and these could be exchanged for clothing and other needs.

Interview with Machel, August 1971

C. The Role of Women

It was in October, 1966, in a meeting of the Central Committee, that FRELIMO decided that the Mozambican woman should take a more active part in the struggle for national liberation, at all levels. It was decided that she should receive political and military training in order to make her more capable of fulfilling whatever tasks the revolution might demand of her. Thus, a few months later, in the beginning of 1967, the first group of women from Cabo Delgado and Niassa began their training. At first this was merely an experiment to discover just what contribution women could make to the revolution—how they would use their initiative, whether they were in fact capable of fulfilling certain tasks. The "experiment" proved highly successful and this first group of women became the founder members of the women's detachment, and were scattered throughout the interior each with her specific assignment. It was soon discovered that they could play a very important role both in the military and political fields, but especially in the latter.

One of the prime functions of a women's army is, quite naturally, just like the men's army, participation in combat. In Mozambique the women's military activities are usually concentrated in the defence of the liberated areas, thus freeing the men for the offensive actions in the zones of advance. However, many of the women prefer the more active combats in the advance zones, and choose to fight alongside the men in ambushes, and mining operations, where they have proved themselves as capable and courageous as any of their male comrades. As another aspect of this function, we have also women working in the Department of Security constantly on the look-out for enemy infiltration.

Although highly effective in the field of combat, their contribution has been less noticeable (just because of their relatively small numbers compared with the men) than their activities in the political field, where their impact has been far out of proportion to their numbers. Since 1967 the women have demonstrated that they have a key role in the mobilization and political education of both the people and the soldiers themselves. In this work we explain to the people the need to fight, what kind of struggle we are waging, with whom we fight, and against whom, what are the reasons for our struggle, what are our aims, and why we chose an armed struggle as the only means to independence. We explain the work we are doing and the results we have achieved so far. We explain how we are dependent to a certain extent on foreign aid and which countries and organizations are helping us, and that, despite this help, we must be as self-reliant as possible.

In this connection, it is stressed that the success of the revolution depends on the combined efforts of everyone such that no one can be omitted, and thus the traditional rather "passive" role of women must be changed so that their abilities are used to the full. Women are encouraged to give their opinions in meetings, to participate in the various committees, etc. Here we have the rather difficult task of fighting old prejudices that women's functions should be confined to cooking, rearing children, etc. It has been proved that we women can perform this task of mobilization and education better than the men for two reasons. Firstly, it is easier for us to approach other women, and secondly, the men are more easily convinced of the important role of women when confronted with the unusual sight of confident and capable female militants who are themselves the best examples of what they are propounding . . .

Mozambique Revolution, 1970

Maria Nganje discusses the woman's role:

When I was 17 years old my parents forced me to marry. This is the custom here—women marry very young. I would prefer to study rather than to marry, but as I did not see any possibility of being able to continue studying, and as tradition is very strong, I married. I have a son. When FRELIMO arrived my husband joined the guerrillas. He is a FRELIMO fighter. I showed a willingness to study and so FRELIMO placed me in a school. Before that I was in a FRELIMO base— as I already had first grade, I taught the comrades at the base how to read and write. In my class I had 141 students. Then after that I studied second [grade] and at the end of last year I was transferred here to the pilot school where I am studying third grade.

The Portuguese troops, when they arrive in a village, steal chickens, pigs, cattle, from the people. The guerrillas never take anything from the people. When the Portuguese soldiers find girls on the roads they violate them. In FRELIMO we women are very much respected— and this impresses our sisters who come from the enemy zone, as I did. We are accustomed to something quite different. Under the colonialists, when a man in uniform appeared, it usually meant ill-treatment. We are so surprised at first when we see the guerrillas treating us as sisters, not as objects of pleasure.

The problem of participation of women in our education program is serious in this province. We must change the traditions which force us to marry when we are very young. I myself am engaged in a campaign aimed at the families in this region to explain to them the need to change this custom: it is harmful to us and to the revolution . . .

. . . In this province girls traditionally marry very young, sometimes when they are ten years old—and that is just the age when they should go to school. And when this happens, of course, the husbands do not allow them to go and study. We have launched a big campaign aimed at the parents and now many of them understand that they should not permit their daughters to marry so young. Since the revolution started, this kind of marriage has diminished very much. And the proof of our success can be seen by the attendance of girls in our schools—in five schools we have more girls than boys. But this does not happen everywhere; women's participation in schools is still a problem.

IV. Mozambique Today

A. Eduardo Mondlane

Eduardo Mondlane was the founder and first president of FRELIMO. Here is his own account of how he became involved in the struggle:

> I myself am from the Gaza district of southern Mozambique, and, like many of us, my involvement with resistance of one form or another goes back to my childhood. I began life, as most Mozambican children do, in a village, and until the age of ten I spent my days herding the family livestock with my brothers and absorbing the traditions of my tribe and family. That I went to school at all I owe to the far-sightedness of my mother, who was my father's third and last wife, and a woman of considerable character and intelligence. In trying to continue my education after primary school, I experienced all the frustrations and difficulties in store for an African child attempting to enter the Portuguese system. Eventually I managed to reach South Africa, and with the help of some of my teachers I continued studying on scholarships to college level. It was during this period that my work with NESAM, and so my serious troubles with the police, began. When I was offered a scholarship to America, the Portuguese authorities decided to send me to Lisbon instead. During my brief stay there, however, I was harassed so constantly by the police that it interfered with my studies,

and I made efforts to take up my scholarships in the
United States. Succeeding, I studied sociology and an-
thropology at Oberlin and Northwestern Universities,
and then worked for the United Nations as a research
officer in the Trusteeship section.

Meanwhile I kept in touch as far as possible with
developments in Mozambique, and I became increasingly convinced from what I saw and from my occasional contacts through the UN with the Portuguese
diplomats that normal political pressure and agitation
would not affect the Portuguese stand. In 1961 I was
able to visit Mozambique on leave from the UN, and
travelling widely saw for myself how conditions had
changed, or not changed, since I had left. On my return I left the United Nations to engage openly in the
liberation struggle, and took a job lecturing at Syracuse
University which left me the time and opportunity to
study the situation further. I had established contacts
with all the separate liberation parties, but I had refused to join any of them separately, and was among
those campaigning strongly for unity in 1961 and 1962.

Mondlane, *The Struggle for Mozambique*

On February 3, 1969, Mondlane was killed by a bomb
sent to him through the post in Dar es Salaam, Tanzania.
One year after the assassination FRELIMO published this
testament to the role Mondlane played in the movement:

A great sadness enveloped our people. Confused, they
wondered how it could have happened; disconcerted,
they remembered the lessons learned in battle—look
for the cause of defeats in our own weakness—and
wondered if the organization itself might have some
weak points. The militants understood that suddenly
a heavier load had fallen on their shoulders; the people demanded explanations and clarification. For a few
weeks the military offensive slowed down, the militia

stopped cultivating and the people stopped transporting material. Each of us asked ourselves about the future of the organization and of our struggle. And there were many among us who thought that with Mondlane a whole heritage of possibilities had been lost.

His presence was the guarantee and the symbol of our efforts: the efforts to determine the nature of our struggle; the efforts to define the nature of the enemy, not by the color of his skin but by his activities against the interests of the people; the effort to give FRELIMO a base solid enough to ensure that the organization could survive and the revolution continue without depending on the physical presence of one individual; the effort to make FRELIMO independent in its relations with other countries, accepting only aid which was given with absolute respect for our struggle and our people.

In all of these efforts he was at the forefront. In particular, he was the first and most enthusiastic in the effort to educate, to prepare politically, to give to the largest number of people the weapon of knowledge, even when they showed doubt or indifference. His death appeared to us (and this was the intention of our enemies) as a threat to all of that. And, in fact, it did unleash dangers, hatred and other minor upsets. We had always been conscious of how such an event could be used as a weapon against the Front. Mistrust and suspicion set in around us.

And nevertheless, during this period, discipline was maintained. The militants showed calm and strength and exhorted the people not to despair. They reminded the people of the causes and the aims of our struggle, why Mondlane had died, and why he had lived. They recalled his teachings—that for Mozambicans the choice was not between living and dying, but between living freely and living in slavery. The people and the soldiers understood that this was a bigger political test, harder than a battle against armed Portuguese, demanding

more courage than resisting daily bombings, being a
part of the effort towards self-sufficiency. In this way
they confronted this new challenge and pledged that
this heritage would be saved by all means.

Today, one year after the death of Mondlane, we can
say that this pledge has been kept. We have achieved a
greater unity. We have opened new schools for our
children, and new medical centers for the wounded and
sick. We have increased production so that most of the
regions are self-sufficient in food. We have learned much
—we learn every day. The heritage was not only saved
but developed even more.

FRELIMO Information, 1970

Mondlane's death revealed a number of differences
among the leaders of FRELIMO. These became apparent
at the first Central Committee meeting after his assassination, held in April 1969:

. . . Something completely new happened at this meeting, distinguishing it as an historical landmark in the
development of FRELIMO: like a fresh wind there appeared a completely new element of criticism and
self-criticism. . . . confidence had been prejudiced by
differences among the leadership. We were not very
clear about where the basis of these differences lay, but
we perceived that when important decisions had to be
taken there was a clash of standpoints, revealing the
existence of two lines, each represented by a certain
number of comrades, defending different positions.

All of us were conscious of this division—but, because
we thought we would aggravate the situation if we
brought the question into the open, because we were
convinced that it was necessary and convenient to present at least an appearance of unity in the FRELIMO
leadership, we never discussed the problem.

Mozambique Revolution, April 1969

A provisional Council of the Presidency was set up. This consisted of Uria Simango, Samora Machel, and Marcelino dos Santos. In November 1969 Simango published a pamphlet against FRELIMO. In it he aligned himself with, among others, Lazaro Kavandame, who had been expelled from FRELIMO for making private profit out of trading in Cabo Delgado. Simango was at once suspended from the Council of the Presidency and severely criticized for choosing to publish his criticisms of FRELIMO rather than bringing them to a general meeting to have them discussed. At a meeting of the Central Committee in May 1970 Simango was expelled from the party, and Samora Machel was elected acting president, and Marcelino dos Santos became acting vice president. Looking back on the events since Mondlane's death, Dos Santos had this to say:

> It is precisely from that moment, an important moment in the history of our fight, that there clearly appeared the fundamental contradiction which existed—not in the Mozambican population, but within the governing leadership of FRELIMO and between a faction of the leadership and the people as a whole. . . .
> Our goal from the beginning has been to achieve victory in the struggle for national liberation, a victory which would allow for the realization of our people's aspirations but which at the same time would enable us to create a really new society. This means that we have to fight against Portuguese colonialism and imperialism, but that we also have to fight those Mozambicans who want to maintain the same system based on man's exploitation of man. Even more, we are convinced that the building of a new society in Mozambique demands a full scale war against all those negative aspects, all the vices and corruption which, as we know, characterize the colonial society from which we come. This involves, among other things, a strong individual

effort, a continual self-criticism. The transformation of man himself will only be achieved if each of us understands clearly that genuine liberation means liquidation of all the inequalities which exist among the many different groups in our country. (This can only be accomplished, in the present phase of the struggle, if we accept an identification of everyone, a unity, in defence of the interests of the people.) And only if each one of us commits himself completely to revolutionary action; that is, assumes a complete involvement in the everyday struggle, in real concrete practice—which cannot be done spontaneously or at random, but needs to be defined and disciplined . . .

Dos Santos, interviewed by Adjali

B. Report from the Front, 1970

The Portuguese appear to have some difficulty in deciding on a consistent approach to their problems in Mozambique. Only a little over 18 months ago the Governor General told the Legislative Assembly that in Cabo Delgado and Niassa districts guerrilla infiltration had been "progressively eliminated." Later at the opening session of the Governing Council he said that the situation in Cabo Delgado and Tete was "gradually returning to normal." Yet only a year later they felt compelled to launch the largest offensive they have ever undertaken since the start of the war six years ago. It seems that they try to compensate for what they cannot achieve militarily by interminable propaganda about the end of the war being in sight.

In fact, however, our military reports indicate exactly the opposite. A comparison between our activities in the twelve month period July 1968–June 1969 and the following year July 1969–June 1970 is surely overwhelming proof that our forces are progressing from strength to strength.

Apart from this increase in the scale of our operations, there have been no spectacular changes in our strategy or programmes. The last military review a year ago traced the gradual evolution of the struggle through the early days of isolated mines and sabotage, then more and more ambushes and regular attacks against fortified posts culminating in highly organized offensives using all these tactics to their best advantage. This we continue to do.

Our fighters are concentrating on intensifying their activities in the areas where they are currently operating and firmly consolidating their position. The enemy continues to hold out in isolated encampments with their land communications severed. Our people characterize our military situation and define our strategy by referring to the African saying: "To kill a snake in a hole, don't put your hand inside it; pour in hot water and the snake will come out—then kill it." The Portuguese are isolated in their posts, their "holes." We create conditions that force them out—by cutting their communications and hence their supplies and by constant harassment. Once they are out, more vulnerable, then we attack. The isolation, both in terms of the physical aspects of the war terrain and of the freedom of movement, coupled with the insecurity of never knowing when or from where the next attack will take place, has very adverse effects on the morale of the Portuguese troops, particularly the conscripted men who form the vast majority. Our forces have always been aware of this fact, both from their conversations with prisoners and deserters and from their observation of the enemy in action . . .

Following the American and British examples of using "strategic villages" to better control the activities of the local population, Portugal has been spending vast sums of money (reportedly $2.5 million in 1968) on the establishment of these "strategic villages" (*aldeamentos*). During October 1969 the *Notícias* of Lourenço Marques published a series of articles on the

new *aldeamentos*. It described one, Marere in Cabo
Delgado, as being under 24-hour vigil from all sides,
with sentinels posted openly or in trenches and defended by the army, the militia, the Public Security
Police (PSP) and the Fiscal Guard. It is a significant
indication of life in these settlements that more and
more people are fleeing from them into the liberated
zones.

The reason for this seems to be that the Portuguese
are caught in an insoluble dilemma. They have observed from the experience of FRELIMO that with
the support of the people anything can be achieved, even
against overwhelming odds. They therefore try to se-
duce the populations with their "development programmes," not realizing that this will achieve nothing
as they will not give the one thing the people really
want—their freedom. Moreover, any positive effects that
these measures might have are far outweighed by the
necessity to resort to more and more repressive actions
in order to stay in control.

A recent UN report based on studies by an Ad Hoc
Working Group of experts established by the United
Nations Commission on Human Rights states that:

"Evidence as a whole revealed that with the intensification of guerrilla activities, the Portuguese military
and police are indiscriminate in their methods of capture and more often than not of innocent men, women
and children who are herded into concentration camps
there to suffer beatings and humiliations. A witness
likened the treatment of African prisoners to 'tortures
reminiscent of Nazi heydays.'

"Portuguese reprisals, in the form of taking hostages,
following a scorched earth policy, massive and continuous aerial bombardments and indiscriminate killing,
are a normal feature of the war in the three Portuguese
colonies of Angola, Mozambique and Guinea (Bissau).

"The general pattern of evidence reveals severe conditions of torture by the use of such instruments as

palmatória—a flail or paddle which inflicts severe pain on hands and feet—electric shock appliances and outright beatings. Inflicting torture is one of the most common features in the Portuguese territories applied by police, prison and military authorities."

By far the most important means of control and repression in the colonies is the armed forces themselves, who now number more than 60,000 in Mozambique. Over the past 18 months there has been considerable reorganization of the military to cope with the deteriorating position overseas. The Portuguese Ministries of the Army and Defense were merged in order to effect closer integration of military and logistic operations. Parallel measures in the colonies were intended to deal more efficiently with "subversion" by bringing about a closer collaboration between military commanders and administrative authorities. Changes in regulations governing military service have become a regular feature of the Portuguese scene as the manpower demands of the wars continue to rise. Latest amendments in September 1969 and February 1970 concerned compulsory extensions of certain officers in the reserve and certain classes of demobilized troops, provision for the recall of officers of certain classes, and the annual training of reserves.

All these measures hardly conform with official statements about guerrillas being "progressively eliminated," but then neither does the latest huge offensive mounted by the Portuguese in Mozambique.

Operation Gordian Knot: Beginning in May 1970, the Portuguese began a huge offensive against FRELIMO forces, designed to "put an end to the war once and for all." Events in the previous few months had led it to be expected. In January the arrival of two ships in the same month with a total of 3,000 new troops was an early sign that a major effort was about to take place. In addition, the civilian governor-general was replaced by a military man, major-engineer Arantes e Oliveira, and the Commander-in-Chief of the Armed Forces was replaced by Portugal's "top expert" in guerrilla warfare, General Kaulza de Arriaga. He was previously one of the advisers of the Portuguese Military General Staff and was one of the founders of the colonial regime. Soon after his appointment, the General paid a visit to the USA where he had lengthy talks with General Westmoreland on the American tactics used in South Vietnam. He then arrived in Mozambique to put into practice his new-found knowledge, announcing that "in a few weeks FRELIMO forces will have been liquidated."

According to the communiqué issued by the Portuguese High Command, they deployed in this offensive 35,000 troops supplied with 15,000 tons of military equipment. In addition to the regular troops they used a special corps rather like the marines, called "special hunters" (caçadores especiais) and also commandos. Much new war material was brought in—such as jets (which were being used in Tete and Niassa but which appeared for the first time in Cabo Delgado on 29th May 1970), and increased numbers of bombers and helicopters, armoured cars and anti-mine cars. For the two weeks following May 20th, the Portuguese carried out daily bombing raids with squadrons of 164-40 planes, including jets, bombers, reconnaissance planes, propaganda planes (equipped with loudspeakers) and helicopters. They then attempted to attack three of our bases with air-lifted and artillery forces, but all they succeeded in doing was to burn a few huts—the bases had already been moved elsewhere some time previously: the nature of our war determines that we do not have fixed bases. Yet despite this they issued almost daily communiqués about the destruction of "dozens" of FRELIMO bases, the capture of "many tons" of equipment, death of "hundreds of terrorists." In fact they did not cause us any serious losses, either in men or materiel, nor did the offensive in any way affect our control over the area . . .

This offensive was extremely important to FRELIMO, but not in the way the Portuguese anticipated. It was important because it constituted the first real test for us, and we were able to face up to that test. It revealed the level of development of our struggle, how solid our organization is, how high is the fighting spirit of our fighters and our people. The fact that we were able to confront victoriously, in one operation, 35,000 Portuguese soldiers (more than half the Portuguese army in Mozambique) equipped with the most modern weapons and with the constant support of a strong air force, demonstrates . . . that our people are absolutely determined to defend at all costs our revolutionary achievements and march on to new fronts. What was wrong with the Portuguese "show of force" was that it completely ignored the determination of our people, our determination to be free.

Mozambique Revolution, 1970

C. Building Up Victory, 1972

FRELIMO's great successes during the past few months represent not merely the continued effectiveness of strategies and tactics developed over a much longer period; equally important, they demonstrate a qualitative advance in the nature of our struggle. For these recent achievements have sprung from the consolidation of a feeling of confidence among our people and our fighters in *the certainty of final victory.* This is a subjective element, to be sure, but it is an increasingly crucial one. Moreover, such confidence finds its basis in objective reality, in the concrete situation of our struggle.

One aspect of this reality is the great victories which we achieved in 1971, the most dramatic of which can be readily seen in the military field. Thus, during 1971, we killed about 2,900 enemy soldiers, destroyed 27 bridges, attacked and destroyed 49 posts and camps, 6 trains and 14 boats. These are statistical data of great importance, since they indicate a substantial reduction in the human and material forces of the enemy. If we then combine these losses in Mozambique with the decrease in the population in Portugal itself, especially of those who emigrate to other countries to escape the colonial wars abroad and misery at home, and combine these also with other losses suffered by the colonial forces in Angola and Guiné, it becomes evident that Portugal approaches a point where her human reserves will be exhausted. This at a time when our own forces grow constantly as we liberate new zones.

By the end of 1970 we had already taken the war south of the Zambezi River in Tete Province. But 1971 saw the struggle spread, within a few months, like wildfire so that today it covers the whole of the Province. As a result we are now attacking the enemy at his most sensitive point—we are vitally affecting his economy! Tete is our richest province in minerals, yet a South African mining company, Comocmin, has already withdrawn its workers from certain zones of that province simply because it considered the Portuguese authorities incapable of ensuring the physical security of the workers against the guerrillas. Others will withdraw. And the confidence of foreign investors will be even more badly shaken.

Linked to this, and even more crucial, is a growing failure of nerve on the part of the Portuguese themselves. Witness the complete failure in 1971 of the colonialist plan of "building roads to win the war." The Portuguese rested great hopes on this scheme, even to the extent of appointing in 1971 an expert in road-building to be governor-general of Mozambique. Yet a few months later the Portuguese themselves lost faith in the plan, finally admitting to themselves a fact that had been apparent for many months. Of course our own experience had taught us, as the enemy came belatedly to see, that roads, like pipe lines and rail lines, are the most vulnerable of targets; today we are certain that such roads will not be constructed.

Moreover, the disarray in the Portuguese camp has been reinforced by those anti-colonial and anti-fascist forces who are organising themselves within Portugal itself and who have begun to launch heavy blows against the colonial war machine. And this in turn is merely one among a number of external factors which is contributing to our sense that victory is merely a matter of time. The African countries, the socialist countries, and indeed all the world's progressive forces declare, and increasingly put into practice, their support for our cause.

But the most important factor which inspires our vigourous sense of confidence lies closer to home, with the Mozambican people themselves. For we have succeeded, once and for all, in engaging the whole of the population in our common struggle. As a Tanzanian journalist who visited our country last April has written: "The question is sometimes asked whether FRELIMO has the support of the people of Mozambique. It is not a question of support. Everybody is involved . . . [at the meetings] none of those speeches about the need to rally around FRELIMO and drive out the Portuguese were heard. Everybody understood why. It is the 'how' that they talk about." And even in those provinces where the armed struggle has not yet begun the people look to FRELIMO as their organisation, their guide. An analogy may help to clarify this point: the situation is reminiscent of Europe under Nazi occupation. Then the dominated people did not consider the Nazi authorities to be their leaders, but instead waited for orders and directives from their *real* government, which operated clandestinely or in exile. Such is the situation with those parts of Mozambique which still lie behind enemy lines.

One key to such results has been the work of the po-

litical commissars, of course—constantly at work raising
the level of political consciousness of the people and
the fighters in our country. Everybody becomes clearer
by this means as to the ideological orientation, the targets and the objectives, of FRELIMO. And this in turn
enhances their fighting spirit.

Another key lies in an even more fundamental reshap-
ing of social and economic relations. In the liberated
areas, even while the war rages on, a new society, a new
nation, is being constructed; the process reflects itself in
the spheres of production and distribution, of education
and health, of defence and participation. This dramatic
reality affects fundamentally the people who live the
new life of a free Mozambique; its message and its promise permeate the consciousness of those who still live
beyond the forward line of our successful battle. National reconstruction and national self-confidence go
hand in hand, and to this rule liberated Mozambique is
no exception.

The sum total of these various developments is an
impressive one. Their significance is also clear: as stated
at the outset, they have granted us the certainty that
victory, ultimately, is ours. The revolutionary process
thus becomes a cumulative one. Our successes reinforce our confidence in a final victory; this confidence,
in turn, makes us fight with increased ardour and determination, and helps us to achieve new successes. In this
way a dialectic has been established which is fatal to
Portuguese hopes; its forward momentum cannot be
halted short of the independence of Mozambique.

Mozambique Revolution, 1972

D. "Our Life Is the War"

Our life is the war. If we sleep two or three days without
hearing of the war it seems that we have no life. Food,
clothes, etc., do not matter to us . . . We know how to
distinguish the whizzing of the weapons of the enemy.

Where there is a fight we are able to tell: "Now that was our fighters who fired. Now it was the enemy who fired." When our weapons sing, our hearts become filled with joy, because that means that the enemy is feeling our force, our children are teaching them that our country wants to be free and *will* be free.

> Kapingo Numumbi, chairman of a local FRELIMO branch

It is beautiful to see an ideal cherished intensively for a long time take shape and be converted into reality. Especially when that ideal means freedom, peace, progress—in short, happiness—for a whole people. Moreover, when the realization of that ideal is not accidental, does not come haphazardly but is the fruit of a common work, of the conscious efforts of thousands and thousands of men, women and children, who accept suffering sacrifices, animated by a firm will to see that dream, that they have dreamed for a long time, become concrete. It is beautiful to see the liberation of our country, Mozambique, take shape.

Life in the liberated areas is a simple life, marked and inspired by the Revolution. The morning starts at about 5 A.M. The people go out for their work—to the shambas, to carry water, to pound maize, to peel off the cassava, to build storehouses, to cut wood, to chop timber to build houses, etc. The guerrillas and the militias go to patrol work. The children go to schools.

The conscience of the Revolution is present in all the work, and manifests itself in the force put into all activities by the people. There is an immense number of cultivated fields in the liberated areas. In some areas, as in Manachude (Cabo Delgado) and Ngazelo (Niassa) about 80 per cent of the land is cultivated. In some other areas production is less, due mainly to the lack of rains and to the monkeys, which devastate the fields, as for example in Cuero. But the people work with intensity, with perseverance. We know we are producing for our-

selves, and not for the Portuguese colonialist "boss."
And this gives us a new spirit.

There is, it is true, the problem of air-bombings. The
Portuguese, unable to conquer our guerrilla forces, take
revenge on the civilian population, bombing all the villages they can spot. However, the harm caused by those
air-bombings is now less than at the beginning of the
war, because the people know how to build anti-aircraft
shelters and to camouflage themselves. The crops were
destroyed by air-bombings in some areas. Our people accept this situation with a revolutionary spirit and op-
timism. One peasant told how last year an aircraft
dropped one bomb in his field, drying up the earth in an
area twenty meters in diameter. "That place where the
bomb fell was the one which produced the most," he
said.

In the field of education, there are more than 20,000
students in Mozambique in the FRELIMO schools.
There are only primary schools as yet, many of them in
the open air. There is lack of teachers—in many zones,
for example, in Namkaba-Chinde, there is only one
teacher for more than 120 students. Material for teaching
is almost non-existent; the students have to write on a
blackboard with dry cassava as chalk. Instead of paper
or slates they use a piece of wood, which they later
scrape with a knife to erase what they wrote. Many of
the students have to walk several miles to the nearest
school. On the way they often have to hide themselves
from aircraft. However, the number of students increases, in spite of all difficulties, and the progress they
make is considerable.

In every Province, District, Locality and Circle, there
are committees entrusted with the administration of
that zone, responsible for the maintenance of order, the
supervision of production, organization of the schools,
direction of the militias, etc.

Every day the guerrillas make reconnaissance, to prevent surprise attacks. When they locate the enemy, the

guerrillas take the necessary steps; to assure the protection of the population in hideouts or to prepare defences; to inform the military base in order to prepare the intervention of a stronger guerrilla force if necessary. Other guerrillas watch the movements of the enemy. And at the right moment, the ambush takes place.

This is the reality that is today liberated Mozambique. We have reason to be satisfied with the results we have already achieved in the struggle for the liberation of our country. Of course we shall not sleep over our successes. On the contrary, these successes encourage us to continue the struggle with even greater determination. Because they prove that, in spite of all difficulties—and they are many—the final victory is certain. Our country, our people want to be free and *will* be free.

Editorial, *Mozambique Revolution*

How can we tell you the size of our Dream?

During centuries
we waited
that a Messiah might free us . . .

Until we understood.

Today
our Revolution
is a great flower
to which each day
new petals are added.

The petals are the land
reconquered,
the people freed,
the fields cultivated
schools and hospitals.

Our Dream has the size
of Freedom.

FRELIMO, 1969

CHAPTER SEVEN

ANGOLA

Portugal, the poorest country in Europe, allocates over 50 per cent of its budget for military expenditures (more than any country in the world except the United States). Portugal is forced to do so in order to fight three wars in Africa in a last-ditch effort to hold onto the remnants of its once vast empire. Angola, where one of the wars has been fought since 1961, is larger than France, Spain, and Portugal combined. It is the largest and richest of the Portuguese colonies, having an estimated 1971 population of 5,500,000 Africans and 300,000 White settlers.

Angola has extraordinary mineral and agricultural wealth and abundant hydroelectric potential. These resources include diamonds, iron and manganese ore, bauxite, copper, potash, platinum, coffee, sugar, tobacco, cotton, sisal, and one of the largest reserves of oil on the African continent.

Despite this wealth, the Africans in Angola live in poverty, deprived of economic, political, and social rights. They live predominantly in the rural areas, where, before the war of liberation, there were practically no medical or educational facilities. The country's resources, land, and

economy are administered, owned, and exploited by
the Portuguese with the participation of South Africa,
Britain, the United States, and other Western nations.
Portuguese-owned plantations produce cash crops for export while foreign-owned mines extract and export diamonds, iron, and oil. Production for internal consumption
plays a small part in Portuguese development plans.

Life for the Africans in Angola is marked by a system of
forced labor, political repression, and social and economic
discrimination. All public demonstrations and gatherings of
Africans as well as all African political associations and organizations are outlawed. Portugal's secret police and army
have long enforced rigid surveillance and control of African
political behavior.

This oppressive system has not gone unchallenged. Many
groups have formed to resist the Portuguese colonial presence. One response was the formation in 1956 of the MPLA
(Popular Movement for the Liberation of Angola). The
MPLA is a coalition of political groups and individuals who
joined together to rid Angola of its Portuguese oppressors
and in the process to create a new society.

> Our aim is not only to free the country, but also to make
> a revolution. That is to say, not only to wipe out the
> Portuguese, but also to change all the existing structures
> in Angolan society. Today our fight is at the stage of a
> national liberation struggle; we think we'll go further
> when we have independence. But we'll have to continue
> our revolution, continue to change the structure of An-
> golan society thoroughly. We must start building toward
> that now. Let's say that it is in the liberated zones that
> we are trying to create the embryo of the Angolan so-
> ciety of tomorrow.
>
> The Angolan people, a colonized people, like all the
> colonized people in the world, are a people who have
> had their minds distorted by colonization itself. In our

particular case it's been even worse, because we've been colonized for five centuries. So it's rather hard to change the minds of a people who have been colonized that long. It's hard, and we often feel it, but it's possible.

Humberto Traca, MPLA representative,
interview in Liberation News Service, March 6, 1971

In 1972 the struggle to build a new Angola reached its eleventh year of continuous fighting. To understand more fully why the Angolan people are at war today, it is necessary to look back in history.

1. Prelude to Armed Struggle

A. The Background of Resistance

In 1482 the Portuguese first landed at the mouth of the Congo River and soon afterward came in contact with the vast kingdom of the Mani-Congo, the inhabitants of what is today Angola. For four hundred years this colony, which for a century had been a highly respected trading partner, would become the source of a pillage that resulted in more than 5,000,000 slaves for Brazil, the Caribbean, and the Portuguese court. Under a charter granted in 1452 by the Pope to the King of Portugal, "full rights to capture the saracens, pagans, and other infidels in your properties . . . to subjugate them and reduce them to perpetual slavery" were bestowed on the future colonialists, launching the slave trade.

The Portuguese, however, were not able to simply subdue Angola with a more advanced form of warfare. In the words of Angola's liberation leader, Agostinho Neto:

> Our people's resistance against the Portuguese occupation isn't just beginning. This isn't the first time our people are rebelling against the Portuguese colonial

domination. Always, ever since the Portuguese first
landed on the African coast, our people have been determined to fight them, especially when the colonial
occupation took on extremely cruel aspects with the
military repression that the Portuguese carried out to
force the Angolan people to submit to their authority.

There are magnificent examples of this resistance
against the Portuguese, such as that put up by Queen
N'Zinga for many long years, and those that were carried out in the south and north of the country. But the
people were not united, the wars were led by certain
ethnic groups, and the Portuguese had a chance to pit
some groups against the others, thus frustrating the results expected from these struggles.

It was only after the 1920s that Portugal was able to
completely dominate the country. However the resistance did not end, it simply took on new forms—especially in the cities, where the population was more in
contact with the settler, suffered from the racial segregation and economic exploitation more directly, and hence
felt the injustice of colonial occupation more keenly.
Several movements were born there, some of them in-
tellectual, which sought to mobilize the people against
the foreign rulers.

I should mention the Let Us Discover Angola Movement, which was started in Luanda; the African Studies
Center, founded in Lisbon; and other groups that utilized literature, music, and other forms of popular culture, with a great catalyzing effect among the population.

Agostinho Neto, *Tricontinental*, No. 12, 1969

B. The Birth of the MPLA

By the early 1950s, realizing that unorganized resistance by
itself was not enough, Angolans began to form political
groups. However, because all trade unions and political

activity were prohibited in the Portuguese colonies, the new organizations were forced to develop in a clandestine manner and began to spread throughout Angola.

> . . . action which began in the cities spread to the rural areas and it became evident that it was necessary to create political organizations which began to emerge as completely differentiated from the previous regional or tribal groups, assuming a national character. The militants of the political groups were by now talking on behalf of Angola rather than of specific ethnic groups. That was around 1950, and with increasing political awareness and the appearance of pamphlets and signs on the walls against the settlers, police (PIDE) repression began. Various comrades in our movement were arrested, many of whom are still imprisoned.
>
> At the beginning, in view of the police repression, we formed several political groups that pursued a common objective. Most of them operated in Luanda, the capital, the most important being Movement for the National Independence of Angola (MINA) and the Party for the United Struggle of the Angolan Africans (PLUA). From the unification of these and other organizations the Popular Movement for the Liberation of Angola (MPLA) was born in December 1956 . . .

> Neto, *Tricontinental*, No. 12, 1969

The manifesto which called for the unification of the nationalist movements and the formation of the MPLA declared:

> The objectives of imperialism's exploitation and oppression of the Angolan people are now, and will continue to be, the obtainment of maximum profits.
>
> The entire administration of Angola is in the hands of the colonialist State. All aspects of Angolan social existence have been disorganized and annihilated. Our

history has been reduced to silence, deformed and, distorted.

We have been humiliated both as individuals and as
people.

Colonialism has injected the germs of destruction,
hatred, backwardness, poverty, obscurantism, reaction,
into the Angolan body. The road we have been thrust
upon is contrary to the higher interests of the Angolan
people, to our survival, to our freedom, to rapid and
free economic progress, to our well being, our bread,
our earth, peace and culture for all.

MPLA, December 1956

The manifesto emphasized the international dimensions
of Portuguese colonialism. It saw European, American,
South African, and other financial and military support as
an essential prop to the Portuguese colonial empire. It went
on to condemn the penetration of Angola by foreign capital and stated:

Because of this, Portuguese colonialism can disappear
only through struggle. As a result, the only path to freedom for the Angolan people is through revolutionary
struggle. In order to achieve victory, however, this struggle can only come about through a united front of all
anti-imperialist forces of Angola—regardless of political
groups, social positions of individuals, religious beliefs
and philosophies—within a vast Popular Movement for
the Liberation of Angola.

In the years following the manifesto, political activity
increased sharply.

In 1958, the underground activities had reached a high
level of efficiency: leaflets, proclamations, creation of
underground schools. They instigated movements of
mass uprisings particularly in the rural areas. The people
refused to pay taxes and to work in what the Portu-

guese called the *contrato* (the forced labor system).

Portugal, in its usual manner, reacted with force. From March to July of 1959, PIDE arrested more than 160 Angolan patriots and nationalist leaders. In April the Portuguese Air Force took position in Angola in an attempt to intimidate the population. In the air over the main Angolan cities the airforce conducted war manoeuvers which included the dropping of napalm bombs. The colonialists also armed the settlers and built shooting ranges for their training.

Despite the Portuguese show of arms, MPLA issued on June 13, 1960, a Declaration to the Portuguese Government which set out conditions for a peaceful solution to the colonial problem. Portugal rejected the propositions and continued to make mass arrests and strengthen its military potential.

One of those arrested in June was Dr. Agostinho Neto, [then] honorary president of the MPLA. Following his arrest, the Portuguese government transferred Neto to Lisbon; from there he was deported, without trial, to the Cape Verde Islands. In protest, the people of Icolo-E-Ibengo, Dr. Neto's birthplace, staged a peaceful demonstration in the streets. The Portuguese soldiers opened fire on the peaceful crowds killing 30 and wounding 300 people. This event is now known as the "Massacre of Icolo-E-Ibengo."

Six months later the MPLA with other anti-Portuguese movements including the PAIGC from Guinea [Bissau] and the Cape Verde Islands and the Goan League, made the following statement in a press conference at the House of Commons in London:

"Instead of considering the propositions made toward the peaceful solution to the colonial problem, the Portuguese government is intensifying war preparations. This government's attitude leaves the nationalist movements only one alternative: resort to force."

Kapiassa N. Husseini, journalist
who visited liberated areas of Angola,
Motive, February 1971

C. The Beginning of Armed Struggle

On February 4, 1961, the armed struggle began with an action aimed at releasing political leaders from imprisonment and the accompanying threats of exile or death.

When the repression had reached its peak and many comrades had been arrested for their patriotic activities, several MPLA members in Luanda decided to attack the prisons and police posts in order to free those arrested.

First they attacked a patrol and seized its weapons, then, so armed, they proceeded to attack the police posts and prisons. The operation was not altogether successful, as they did not succeed in setting the prisoners free, but it helped to awaken the people to the imperative need to fight, and the Portuguese were faced with an unexpected situation, the prelude to the difficulties they would begin to confront in maintaining their rule.

Neto, *Tricontinental*, No. 12, 1969

Realization

Fear in the air!
On each street corner
Vigilant sentries light incendiary glances
in each house
hasty replacement of the old bolts
of the doors
and in each conscience
seethes the fear of listening to itself
History is to be told
anew
Fear in the air!

It happens that I
humble man

still more humble in my black skin
come back to Africa
to myself
with dry eyes.

NETO

The Portuguese responded with the most savage ferocity
and on 5 and 6 February, 3,000 people were machine-
gunned in Luanda. A few days later, a further massacre
of 5,000 people took place at Baixa de Cassange, a region in the interior bordering on the districts of Malange
and Lunda.

The best militants took refuge in the forests in the
north-west of Angola in order to carry on the war, which
took on such proportions that within three months that
vast region, apart from the towns, was liberated from
the colonialists.

Angola in Arms

While Angolan nationalist parties were consolidating
themselves in 1956, a new political party that did not join
the MPLA was formed by royalists of the Bakongo tribe
on the Zaire-Angola border. This party, which wanted to
secede from Angola to form its own state, soon developed
into the UPA (Popular Union of Angola) under the
leadership of Holden Roberto. The UPA claimed to be a
national party, but it was tightly controlled by a Bakongo
elite. The MPLA has been interested in gaining independence for, and developing, the entire country in a non-elitist
and ethnically impartial way.

When the MPLA initiated armed struggle in 1961, the
UPA quickly followed suit. However, the UPA had done no
mass political organizing or education. The UPA did not attempt to identify the capitalist basis of Portuguese colonial
exploitation. Rather, the UPA encouraged indiscriminate

racial and ethnic hatred as a tactic to mobilize people to fight the Portuguese and even other Angolans.

> As can be imagined, the results were absolutely cata-strophic. People killed Angolans for no other reason than that they did not belong to their tribe, or were of mixed origin, or literate.
>
> Commenting on this situation, President Agostinho Neto recently said: "In this way, we lost thousands of men, women and children who were almost all sincere patriots and ardent fighters for our cause of national liberation."
>
> The colonial army [in the confusion] was therefore able to regain control of the situation and to launch the big offensive of August–September 1961, with a degree of cruelty far exceeding that of the Nazis during the Second World War.
>
> The genocide carried out by the Portuguese fascist hordes resulted in 50,000 dead and 300,000 refugees.
>
> *Angola in Arms*

D. The Development of Slavery and Racism: Background to the Portuguese Massacres

The Portuguese response to the initiation of armed struggle cannot be seen as a simple reaction to Angolan demands and initiatives. Portuguese troops and settlers, outnumbered and in a foreign country, responded out of fear combined with the desire to "restore control." However, fear and the need for control alone do not explain the lightning-like massacre of 50,000 Angolans. In order to understand the background of the massacres it is necessary to examine the development of Portuguese racism.

When the Portuguese first landed in Angola, Portuguese culture was not more "developed" than the various Angolan cultures they found. As James Boggs has written in *Racism and the Class Struggle*, "[the Portuguese] found African cus-

ANGOLA 193

toms strange and exotic but also found much to admire in
their social and political organization, craftsmanship, archi-
tecture and so on. At this point the chief technological advantages enjoyed by the Europeans were their navigational
skills and firepower (both, by the way, originally learned
from the Chinese)."

The Portuguese

> ran into many amazing beliefs and superstitions, but
> few or none that seemed more disconcerting than others
> they could find at home. Victorious Congolese armies
> tended to see signs and ghostly symbols in the sky, yet
> there was nothing out of the way in that. The Portu-
> guese themselves regularly saw angels, and so of course
> did other Europeans. More often than not they found
> it easy to accept the people . . . as natural friends and
> allies.

Basil Davidson, *The African Slave Trade*, 1961

This is not to say that the Portuguese saw the Angolans
as absolute equals. Angolans were viewed as heathens (non-
Christians), and there was certainly mutual suspicion. There
is also evidence of some degree of racial prejudice among
both the Angolans and the Portuguese.

The earliest Portuguese expeditions took small numbers
of Angolans of the Bakongo tribe to the royal court in Lisbon. These men were treated with great courtesy, educated
as to the ways of the Portuguese kingdom, and then returned to the Bakongo as interpreters. Later a few Angolans
were traded to the Portuguese as slaves by the king of the
Bakongo. These men and women had been captured in warfare against other Angolan tribes.

As the years passed, the Portuguese mission changed
from one of exploring and trade to one of slaving. The reason for this change was that the Portuguese had begun to

expand their colonial empire in the Caribbean and Brazil and now needed agricultural laborers on a large scale. The slave trade, as it began to develop a century after the Portuguese first landed in Angola, started to tear apart the social and economic fabric of Angolan society. This new form of slavery, chattel slavery, was hereditary and the slaves were treated as work animals or possessions rather than as human beings.

By 1575 the slave trade was carrying off approximately 3,000 Angolans per year. This trade in human life was to increase to at least 25,000 Angolans per year in the period of 1826–36. And even as late as 1913 Portugal was charged with shipping out 20–40,000 slaves per year to the plantations on the Portuguese island of São Tomé.

During this 350 year slaving period, 5–7,000,000 Angolans were shipped off to Portuguese colonies. The Portuguese, in order to insure a steady flow of slaves, continually provoked tribal wars and supported those chiefs who were their suppliers. This process, according to Basil Davidson,

> repeatedly confirmed the conservative element in African feudalism and at the same time distorted the influence and power which this element could wield. Generally the relationship tended to petrify African institutions within traditional forms that grew ever more brittle and inflexible. It played into the hands of those who had the most to gain from obstructing social change. It paralyzed the will to evolve new and more effective—more modern—political institutions.

Not only was Angolan political development stunted and distorted by the slave trade; economically, the country was forced to follow a path towards "underdevelopment." By exporting human beings the Portuguese were sending away the very people who would otherwise be producing wealth at home. Furthermore, the Portuguese paid for slaves only in non-durable consumer goods, mostly guns and whiskey. According to James Boggs:

> . . . as the slave trade expanded, its enormous profits concentrated capital in Europe and America for the expansion of commerce, industry, and invention. . . . In the Americas the blood and sweat of Africa's slaves produced the sugar, tobacco, and later cotton to feed the refineries, distilleries, and textile mills, first of Western Europe and then of the Northern United States.

In order to justify the slave trade, the Portuguese (among others) began to develop the theories of superiority which accompany the rise of racism. The Portuguese theories were not unlike the rationalizations for slavery developed in the Americas, described by Boggs:

> The more instrumental the slave trade in destroying African culture, the more those involved directly and indirectly in the slave traffic tried to convince themselves and others that there had never been any African culture in the first place. The more brutal the methods needed to enforce slavery against rebellious blacks, the more the brutalizers insisted that the submissiveness of slavery was the natural state of black people. The more valuable the labor of blacks to . . . agriculture, precisely because of the relatively advanced stage of agriculture in their African homeland, the more white Americans began to insist that they had done the African savage a favor by bringing him to a land where he could be civilized by agricultural labor. Thus, step by step, in order to justify their mutually reinforcing economic exploitation and forceful subjugation of blacks, living, breathing white Americans created a scientifically cloaked theory of white superiority and black inferiority.

The racism that underlies the rationalization of this slavery is not an individual idiosyncrasy; Boggs continues:

> The first thing we have to understand is that racism is not a "mental quirk" or a "psychological flaw" on an individual's part. Racism is the systematized oppression by one race of another. In other words, the various forms of oppression within every sphere of social relations—economic exploitation, military subjugation, political subordination, cultural devaluation, abuse—together make up a whole of interacting and developing processes which operate so normally and naturally and are so much a part of the existing institutions of the society that the individuals involved are barely conscious of their operation. As Fanon says, "The racist in a culture with racism is therefore normal."
>
> This kind of systematic oppression of one race by another was unknown to mankind in the thousands of years of recorded history before the emergence of capitalism four hundred years ago—although racial prejudice was not unknown. . . .
>
> Slave oppression had also existed in earlier times, but this was on the basis of military conquest and the conquerors—the ancient Greeks and Romans—did not develop a theory of racial superiority to rationalize their right to exploit their slaves.
>
> Just as mankind, prior to the rise of capitalism, had not previously experienced an economic system which naturally and normally pursues the expansion of material productive forces at the expense of human forces, so it had never known a society which naturally and normally pursues the systematic exploitation and dehumanization of one race of people by another. An organic link between capitalism and racism is therefore certainly suggested.

Racism in Angola was encouraged by the Portuguese traders, settlers, and ruling class. Today this racism has become firmly institutionalized both in the social structures and minds of the Portuguese. The Portuguese have never called their policy in Africa one of racial superiority. Instead they have invoked the criteria of "civilization" or assimilation. In practice, however, this distinction has made little difference. All of the Whites in Angola, from the governmental elite and bankers to the poorest farmers, benefit from the racism in Angolan society. There is always at least one group of people, Black Angolans, who earn less and own less than the White settlers. Following directly from such institutionalized and continually encouraged hate and fear is the mentality of racial superiority, of animal-like tortures, of forced labor and migration, and of disregard for the life of individual Angolans. The following story, told after the outbreak of violence in 1961, illustrates what racism means:

> Ariteine Tunga is a school teacher, thirty years old. His village, Nsalambongi, was near Damba in Northern Angola. He has a special status among the refugees: he can read and write. In the course of their punitive expeditions the Portuguese always looked first for those who could read and write, assuming they must be leaders of the revolt. Anyone having a pencil in his hut was shot out of hand. Tunga escaped in time. In exile, he does the village's writing. Around him gather all those who are left from Nsalambongi village. They live in huts and sheds near the Catholic hospital in Kimpangu.
>
> Tunga told his story:
>
> "The [Portuguese] soldiers collected the young men of the village. They tied their hands behind their backs. And they tied their feet.
>
> "To save space they bent their knees and bound their thighs and shins together. Trussed up like chickens they packed them tightly together, till they filled the lorry.
>
> "To stop them from becoming restive the soldiers said

they were going off to forced labour. The usual thing.
They had just come to fetch labourers.

"And many allowed themselves to be reassured."

Then the lorry drove out of the village, into the jungle. When it came back, later the same day, to fetch the
soldiers, it was empty.

What had happened?

The school teacher has two others from the village
with him: the carpenter João Minigiedi, twenty-one
years, and the farmer João Paiva, forty-five years. We
are sitting in a whitewashed room in Kimpangu, and in
the open doorway swarm children from the refugee
camp. When the question has been translated into Kikongo, everyone answers in chorus:

"*Zenga*"

Ariteine Tunga passed his hand like a salute across
his throat, to show me. *Zenga* means beheading.

The young men who were tied up like chickens
were tipped off in a glade in the jungle. With machete
knives and axes the Portuguese chopped off their heads.
The villagers found their corpses—still tied up.

Anders Ehnmark, a journalist who visited
Congo-Angola border in 1961 in
Transition Magazine, 1968

In 1961, after the outbreak of violence, White settlers in
all parts of Angola quickly armed themselves:

. . . throughout wide reaches of "innocent" central Angola [where there had been less rebellion], the hysteria
was not controlled. Indeed the lives of . . . [the few]
white officials who tried to stem the tide of mad human
passion appears to have been in real danger at the hands
of their fellow white-trader, planters, labour recruiters,
etc. . . .

Many reports have been told by observers of the bodies of Africans, remote from the site of revolution . . .
buried by the hundreds in the ground by bulldozers,

and thrown into the Quanza River until it stank so that
chains were placed across it to catch the rotting corpses.
Eyewitnesses tell of the inconceivable atrocities practiced on these people who were rounded up and slaugh-
tered without trial, without a chance to say a word in
their own defence, and with an almost complete lack of
tho most rudimentary human compassion.

> Rev. S. Gilchrist, Canadian missionary and
> medical doctor, "Angola Awake,"
> *Transition Magazine,* 1968

II. The War

A. MPLA Military Development

In December 1962 Agostinho Neto escaped from prison. The
leadership of the MPLA then began sending militants out
of Angola for training in an attempt to rebuild its nucleus
after the Portuguese rampage of the preceding year. This
rebuilding was an extremely difficult task: the Portuguese
had shown their utter disregard for Angolan life and their
willingness to kill anyone and everyone who demonstrated
any objections to their rule. People's fear of the Portuguese made it difficult for the MPLA to establish bases outside the country (in Congo-Brazzaville) while at the same
time supporting and expanding the pockets of resistance
inside Angola.

In early 1962 the MPLA had suffered setbacks outside
the country. Their bases in Zaire (then Congo-Kinshasa),
an independent African country which had come under the
influence of American investment and military pressure,
were closed down and MPLA militants who were training
there were expelled. Also, the Organization of African Unity
(OAU), under the prompting of the (then) Congo-Kinshasa
government, recognized the UPA as the official organization of Angolan liberation.

The MPLA spent the years 1962–64 organizing, reanalyzing, and developing its strategy of self-reliance.

> One of the major principles which we must rigorously follow is to utilize our own forces in resolving the problems of the revolution. This is not to depreciate in any sense the importance of international solidarity or sympathetic movements which are now emerging in all the capitalist countries of Europe and America, including the United States itself. Nor, of course, do we depreciate in any way the political and material support given by socialist and African countries—support which has greatly facilitated our struggle. But we must recognize that all of this is secondary. What is primary and essential is our action within the country, for it is through this action that we will achieve real independence.
>
> To utilize our own forces in military activity means to arm our guerrillas with the weapons of the enemy: it means to regain the food, clothing, medicine, money, and other means necessary for the guerrilla's existence. And we have the right to do this, not only the necessity. Because everything the colonialists possess in our land, the arms, the food, the clothes, the medicines, the money and other material goods, all of this is the product of the labor of our people. It is the result of the exploitation of our people. It all belongs to our people and must be used in the legitimate interest of our people.
>
> Daniel Chipenda, quoted in Donald L. Barnett and
> Roy Harvey, *The Revolution in Angola,* 1972

In 1964, after careful preparation, the MPLA opened a new front. Cabinda, a small, densely forested, oil-rich district of Angola, became the next scene of MPLA organizing and fighting.

The war in Cabinda had an enormous psychological impact on the entire population of Angola. It restored the confidence of old militants who, in the towns and countryside of Angola, had kept alive their faith in the Movement.

The Cabinda guerrilla area was not only a laboratory where the MPLA put into practice its concept of guerrilla war and trained very able cadres, *but it was also the first nucleus of a national and popular armed struggle to be organised in the history of the Angolan people.*

Angola in Arms

By 1964 the MPLA had solidified its strength inside Angola, reopened guerrilla action in Cabinda and was becoming an influence outside the country. In July 1964 . . . the Organization of African Unity reexamined the MPLA and found it to be a "serious nationalist movement deserving the OAU's support."

Husseini, *Motive*

Later on, in March 1965, the chiefs of state of the OAU, at a meeting in Ghana, pledged military and technical assistance to the MPLA. Thus the MPLA became widely recognized as the major liberation movement in Angola.

However, the major developments in the struggle were not going on outside the country but within Angola itself.

Thanks to its perseverance, on 16 May 1966 the MPLA succeeded in opening a new combat front, the eastern front, or Third Region, which included the districts of Moxico and Cuando-Cubango.

The Third Region . . . is four times as large as Portugal, [or] as vast as the whole of Vietnam (both north and south). . . . Simply stating the size of this region is enough to render absolutely absurd the colonialist propaganda claim that "the terrorists have bases outside the country and infiltrate into Angola to carry out an ambush and then run away again."

Iko Carreira, interview in
Tanzania Standard, April 23, 1971

By late 1970 the military situation of the MPLA had advanced dramatically. Iko Carreira, member of the executive body of the MPLA, outlined the situation up to that time:

> In 1967 a new front was opened in the district of Luanda and in 1969 in the district of Bié . . . Now, a year later, one third of the country is involved in guerrilla war.
>
> At this time, the five politico-military fronts led by the MPLA extend over six districts of the country, that is, about 400,000 square kilometers, where an estimated population of 500,000 live.
>
> In the north we have reactivated two war zones in the regions of Cumbos and Nambuargongo about 200 kilometers from the capital.
>
> In Cabinda, despite the inherent difficulties of the terrain (rain forest) our combatants still harass the enemy and have thus succeeded to hold in this little enclave an important portion of the Portuguese army.
>
> The third region (Moxico and Cuando-Cubango) [eastern region] is completely in the control of the forces of liberation. Our columns freely cultivate this region of 300,000 square kilometers. The Portuguese armed forces have entrenched themselves in several isolated outposts, linked to each other only by air flights.
>
> The fourth region—Luanda and Malange—to the north of the Benguela railway, which transports the copper of Zambia and Congo-Kinshasa, is only partially under control.
>
> In their advance towards the rich regions of cotton and diamonds, the guerrillas are engaged in hard combat not only against the colonialist forces but also against the Katangan ex-police and South African commandos.
>
> Finally the fifth region—districts of Bié and Huambo —is the heart of the country because of its human and economic importance. Our columns reached this region in 1970 after the Portuguese built a strategic dam in this region of high plateaus.

But the war is not limited to rural areas. Popular mobilisation is developing in the urban areas. Commandos of the MPLA have moved to action in Luanda [the capital] and have carried out sabotage against oil installations and armories.

Carreira, *Tanzania Standard*

B. Portuguese Tactics

The type of war we are currently waging is a guerrilla war; this means we use mostly small units. We encircle the Portuguese, if possible we crush them. If it's not possible, we retreat before they have time to react. So it's a deadly type of war for the Portuguese. It's ambushes, raids, surprise attacks on barracks, on stationed troops. If troops are stationed, we harass them; when they withdraw, we pursue them, when they are on the move we fall upon them. We always keep the initiative. Of course the Portuguese also try to launch counter-offensives but this requires well-trained troops with high morale. What the Portuguese lack most is morale. Even before, having been only harassed, and not yet defeated, they didn't believe in the fight they were waging and that's what is most important. So they aren't very efficient.

But when it comes to attacking the population, then they are efficient indeed! And they often do it because they say that they haven't succeeded yet in removing the guerrilla from the population. They figure, since one cannot catch a fish out of the water, one takes the water out of the fish. They have built a lot of fortified camps, strategic posts like those which the Americans build in Vietnam: this has the effect of isolating populations, of taking them away from guerrilla centers. But people keep escaping from these camps, and we, on our behalf, have often attacked those camps in order to liberate the populations.

Traca, *Liberation News Service*

These camps are part of the Portuguese reform measures which goes back to the psychosocial programs of 1962–63. During these years the Portuguese army built some 150 resettlement villages for the Bakongo in order to entice them back to Angola from their refuge in Zaire (then Congo-Kinshasa). This rural resettlement plan was then

> applied to other districts where country folk were corralled into strategic hamlets known as *senzalas do pais,* so as to deny cultivators to guerrilla infection, while also intending to give these people a few elementary social services for the first time. The policy was applied to Moxico late in 1968 and has largely failed of its effect.
>
> There have been two main reasons for this failure. In the first place, country people greatly dislike being rounded up into camps behind barbed wire, and escape to guerrilla protection in the forests whenever they can. Secondly, guerrilla activity around these camps makes it hard for the Portuguese army to allow people to go out to cultivate without at the same time allowing them to escape. The consequence is that food has become extremely short in the camps, for the Portuguese can do little more than supply their own garrisons. The heavy hand of Portuguese military repression is a dreaded reality, no matter what Lisbon may intend. "Their 'psycho-social,'" said an MPLA commander, "cannot save the Portuguese. They should have tried it long ago. Now the war has become a people's war, and the 'psycho-social' fails." This is certainly true of the Mbundu and their neighbors; the evidence suggests that it is also true elsewhere.
>
> Basil Davidson, "Angola in the Tenth Year: A Report and an Analysis May–July 1970," *African Affairs,* January 1971

Because the MPLA soldiers control most of the land of the liberated territories, the Portuguese are forced to re-

main in their heavily guarded camps. From these camps
they make occasional forays and then quickly return to their
fortified settlements. In addition, the Portuguese rely
heavily on their air power.

Indeed, the colonialists' greatest trump card is still their
control of the air, and they take advantage of this to
bomb the peaceful population. The main victims are of
course the women, children and old people, who have
more difficulty in protecting themselves from air attacks.

Angola in Arms

. . . the air force . . . is more of a psychological weapon
than a really effective one. They often bomb with great
intensity. Some regions have been under bombing for
months but never has there been great damage on the
fighter's side. Very few of us happened to be killed.

On the other hand, whenever they bomb not only do
they aim at the population but also at the food crops,
because we must have some kind of agriculture for supplies. We cannot expect supplies from the outside; it's
impossible, especially in the inland zones. Some of these
zones are located 400 to 500 miles from the border of
Zambia to the east in the center of the country. One can
hardly travel 400 miles on foot with ammunition
[though this is part of the way the MPLA does supply
itself with ammunition], let alone if one wants to bring
food. And lately, this is to say, since May [1970], the
Portuguese have started using defoliants, which are
chemical products. These chemical products, as we have
been able to verify, are the same as those which are being used in Vietnam.

Traca, *Liberation News Service*

Now they are using the last weapon they have—famine.
The destruction is continuing. The bush has lost most
of its leaves.

They are throwing chemicals into the river to kill the fish. From helicopters they are shooting wild game, which is the source of meat for our guerrillas.

Carreira, *Tanzania Standard*

The MPLA Denounces the Criminal Use of Chemical Defoliants and Herbicides by the Portuguese Colonialists

We want to bring this matter to the attention of international organisations, world public opinion, and all people of good will who treasure peace and liberty.

Beginning May 1, 1970, the Portuguese colonial army began spraying chemical products, herbicides, and defoliants on the cultivated fields in the liberated regions in Eastern Angola.

An MPLA doctor, who happened to be in the area on May 21, sent us the following report:

It was 10 o'clock. Five enemy planes flew low over the banks of the Luena River. Two of the bombers circled the area trying to detect signs of human life. The three other planes started to spray the fields with chemical poisons. From time to time the bombers dropped incendiary bombs on the gardens and camouflaged houses in the forest.

The chemical agents acted very quickly on the cassava leaves and branches* and on sweet potatoes, causing them to become completely dry in less than two days. The toxic poisons were also attested to by the badly burned trees in the forest, which looked as if they had suffered a violent fire.

These chemicals, deposited on the leaves (and perhaps those deposited on the soil), penetrated quickly the roots and tubers causing a progressive deterioration from the exterior to the heart of the plants. Soon the cassava plants and sweet potatoes became soft

* Cassava (also called manioc) is the staple of the Angolan diet. Similar to a sweet potato, it provides the people with a nutritious starch.

and mushy; they turned black, as if they had been
soaked in water for several days.

The results begin to appear about 24 hours after the
poison touches the plants—the result being the total
destruction of all crops affected.

Tuber eaten in this poisoned condition causes severe
abdominal colics and diarrhea.

The MPLA is now alerting world public opinion and
asks all international organisations, all people of good
will, to condemn this monstrous crime, to bring pressure
on the Portuguese colonialists to renounce this inhuman
practice, to reinforce their support of the Angolan people who are fighting only to become free in their own
country.

> The Steering Committee of the MPLA,
> Angola, July 10, 1970

The MPLA has been able to verify that the chemical
defoliants and poisons used by the Portuguese are the same
as those being used in Vietnam. This finding has been further documented through United States Senate Foreign Relations Committee investigations. While the United States
is not officially supplying any military equipment to
Portugal for use in Africa, Portugal is a member of NATO.
As such, the United States has supplied her with a great
deal of military equipment, always with the stipulation that
the material be used only in Portugal or for the defense of
Portugal itself. Although this aid is used in Angola, Mozambique, and Guinea-Bissau, the United States government has taken no steps to curtail or restrict its use (see
Portugal and NATO, 1967).

In 1969 the United States exported $57,330 worth of these
chemicals to Portugal. By 1970, the year chemical sprayings
were resumed in Angola, the figure had risen to $229,320.
The American companies that manufacture this type of
chemical have been identified as Dow Chemical (manufac-
turers of the most dangerous of the chemicals, poisonous to

humans as well as plants), Agrisect Chemical, Hercules, Monsanto, and U. S. Rubber (see *U. S. Export-Foreign Trade,* No. 410, November 1970; National Action Research on the Military Industrial Complex).

. . . Defoliants had been used in 1961 (during the initial uprising) near the capital, Luanda, in the Catete district. At that time a method had been devised that enabled the people to save at least part of their crops. In 1970, in the third region, where defoliants were again used, there was a very small minority of people who had seen and could recognize defoliants. They tried to explain to the people that immediately after spraying ceased, the cassava crops must be cut down to their roots. The population did not initially accept their advice. They could not accept the idea that something falling like rain from above could jeopardize the crops in the earth. They could not accept that this vapor—like liquid falling from small civilian airplanes—was harmful. For more than a week they refused to take the measures prescribed by the MPLA and the crops were killed, roots and all.

. . . after suffering the effects of defoliants in the first region near Luanda, one very old man had thought of cutting the cassava trunk as fast as he could and as near to the roots as possible, thus stopping the defoliants from penetrating to the roots. This became the MPLA's way of fighting defoliants. In 1970, in the fourth region, they have adopted this way of fighting back. As a matter of fact, out of ten fields they can save seven or eight by cutting down the cassava plants as fast as they can after the defoliants have been dropped. This means they have to cut the cassava plant down to the level of the earth before the defoliants can enter the roots. This has to be done one half hour after the defoliants have been dropped and not much later than an hour and a half.

> Boubaker Adjali, Algerian journalist
> in Angola in mid-1970, interviewed by
> the Africa Research Group, 1971

The people of Angola suffer for the war, but it is their war: they supply the food, information, moral support, recruits, and the people's militia in liberated Angola. Why have they exchanged the hardships of life under the Portuguese for the hardships of an extended war of liberation? A look at the life they are building in the liberated zones of Angola can begin to answer this question.

III. The New Angola

For the Angolan people, armed struggle means more than eliminating Portuguese rule and substituting Angolans for Portuguese rulers. It means changing the structure of Angola's colonial society and creating "the embryo of the Angolan society of tomorrow."

> Fortunately, for those who fight on the side of justice and against tyranny, for those who desire freedom, armed action is not only a sacrifice; it is above all a *force*. It is not only the irrigation of our battlefields with the blood of the best sons of our peoples. It is also a school —a means by which the people continue this struggle in the future, after political independence, in order to be completely free—politically, economically, and socially independent . . .
>
> Our contribution must be made not only for the liquidation of the colonial system but also for the liquidation of ignorance, disease, and primitive forms of social organization—it is in the literacy campaigns, in the clinics, in the Centres of Revolutionary Instruction, in agricultural and industrial production that each Angolan must make his contribution . . . beneath the bombs that periodically fall over the forests . . .
>
> Organization of the masses, trade unions, organization of youth, women, and others are now having their first experience inside the country. Institutions of medi-

cal assistance, education and commercial exchange, and
of cooperation in labor are making their appearance in
the liberated zones.

Agostinho Neto, quoted in Barnett and Harvey,
The Revolution in Angola, 1972

A. Village Life and Production

The majority of the Angolan population lives in villages in
the hinterlands of the northern tropical rain forest and
savanna or in the central plateau (or *planalto*) of west-
central Angola.

Economic life in the villages centers around agricultural
production. Most villages consist of a number of household
compounds (sleeping, storage, and cooking huts and pens
for domestic animals). The number of people living in a
village ranges from twenty to one hundred.

Since the war for liberation began, the life and production of much of the rural population has been uprooted.
The Portuguese continue to bomb villages. They try to
capture villagers and resettle them in "strategic hamlets."
A villager describes the arrival of guerrillas in this setting:

> One day in early September 1967, ten guerrillas entered
> our village. The people were very frightened. They had
> never seen Angolans carrying such guns. Most of us ran
> and hid in the forest or fields. The guerrillas called us
> out, saying they only wanted to talk to us. But the peo-
> ple were still very frightened. Slowly, one or two at a
> time, we started drifting back to the village. But we re-
> mained a good distance from the guerrillas as they
> started speaking to us.
>
> "Don't run away," the leader of the guerrilla group
> told us. "Don't believe what the Portuguese told you
> about the guerrillas. They gave you nothing but lies.
> They say we are foreigners come from other countries

to chase them out and take their place, but you can see this is a lie. We are your own sons. Some of us went to foreign countries, but only to be trained so we could come back to Angola and fight the Portuguese tyranny. We have come back to fight because, as you well know, the Portuguese came to our country long ago and treated us worse than monkeys for centuries. That is why there is now war in Angola against the Portuguese. But this war is not only our war, the guerrillas', it is a war that must be made by all of us, the guerrillas and the people together . . ." The guerrillas went on speaking for a long time. The people drew a little closer but still kept their distance . . .

The guerrillas came to the village about once a week. Each time they would gather the people together and talk to us about why they were fighting and why it was necessary for all Angolans to unite in the struggle against Portuguese tyranny. They told us it was not just the guerrillas who would be fighting for the liberation of our country; the whole people would be fighting, including us. But everyone would not fight in the same way as the guerrillas, with guns . . .

Slowly but surely the guerrillas won the confidence of the people. When they came to the village, they never touched the young girls or the belongings of the people. When they wanted a chicken or some eggs, they always paid a fair price. They told us they were guerrillas, sons of the people, soldiers of the people, who were fighting to liberate the country.

Neto, in Barnett and Harvey, The Revolution in Angola

Two Finnish reporters, who visited Angola in 1971, describe what life is like in the villages in the liberated zones.

The struggle has affected the life of the villages not only in regard to traditional ties [women are now engaged in combat], but also in everyday duties—the work in the field and the cooking—for the villagers now have important tasks to do to help the struggle. They provide food for the guerrilla units in the area as well as for the near-by bases. They are organizing medical aid by caring for and feeding the sick. They often carry goods, generally part of the way to the next village, where others continue with the carrying. The intelligence work *done by the villagers* is very important. They report everything they see to the guerrillas and thus enable them to keep up to the situation. The Portuguese cannot much affect the life of the liberated areas. They have no administration in the east of Angola outside their bases, nor do they dare to move from them by land. The only way to affect the life of the villagers is by air-raids and bombardments.

> Mikko Lohikoski and Börje J. Mattsson,
> *Report of a Trip to Angola,* Helsinki,
> February 4, 1971

Traditional governing patterns have changed:

Many of the village leaders are men who have been much respected even before, but in order to be elected today they must actively participate in the struggle for liberation. Where the traditional village elders have not actively supported the struggle, the villagers have elected a new leader.

> Lohikoski and Mattsson, *Report of a Trip to Angola*

The villagers of the liberated areas have organized themselves so that they are able to both increase and diversify agricultural production. The most important crops grown are rice, cassava, potatoes, and maize.

When the struggle started in this region [Moxico] we began teaching them [the villagers] about collective farms, but at first they didn't understand and didn't want to follow our advice. Later they came to understand better and began working on the collective farms, but even now they still continue to cultivate family plots in addition to the collective ones controlled by the action committees. They are coming to learn, though, that collective farms are better, or at least necessary. The militia, for example, must patrol and guard those working in the fields, but they couldn't do this if they weren't given a share of the harvest. Then, before the revolution, when they had only private family plots, some faced problems of hunger and were forced to exchange what few things they had for some cassava or millet or maize. In the past they couldn't just take things from another's fields, but now they all have a share in the harvest of the collective plots and are more secure against hungry periods. And it is also easier to help the guerrillas with food from the collective fields; people don't worry and say that they don't have enough for the guerrillas. In some cases the villagers have decided to cultivate all their land collectively. They have found that they can produce more and in better ways on the collective plots, so they have done away with family fields altogether. Most villagers, however, have not yet come this far.

Setta Likambuila, Sixth Regional
Commander, quoted in Barnett and Harvey,
The Revolution in Angola

Some of the food grown in the collective plots (also called "people's plantations") goes to the people's stores. Each people's store serves between 80 and 125 villagers.

People's stores have now been organized in every zone. Before the struggle began the people lived in their villages by the rivers and sold some of their products to the Portuguese merchants. With the few escudos they received they bought some salt, matches, soap and other things. Once the struggle started, people in the liberated areas could no longer go to the Portuguese shops, so our movement started organizing people's stores. At first, these were run by the guerrillas under zone commanders; but later, when the action committees were formed, the people's stores were put under their control. The people now have no money, but they take their crops, skins, beeswax, honey and other products to the stores and exchange them for cloth, clothing, cooking fat, salt or other things they need. The prices of all the goods are established by the Steering Committee and are the same throughout the liberated areas. So if a man brings in some fish they are weighed and their price determined; he can then purchase an equal value in cloth, soap, etc. But sometimes, since not all the stores are well-stocked and the supplies are usually low, a person will not get all the things he wants when he brings in his goods. He will be credited for the amount he doesn't receive in other goods and will come back later.

Likambuila, quoted in Barnett and Harvey,
in The Revolution in Angola

B. The Role of Women

The young woman of Angola is making important progress in a struggle which belongs to the whole Angolan people and which requires her participation. We see her engaged in all the tasks of our movements, constantly raising the level of her consciousness and advancing together with the men in each of the victories won by our people . . .

The young woman of Angola has said YES to sacrifices, YES to the emancipation of women, showing her growth of consciousness over the nine years of our people's armed struggle. She does so in the knowledge that in the future she will have equal rights and duties in society.

Unpublished statement by Eugenia Neto, 1969

Women in the liberated zones are no longer bound to their traditional roles. There is a concerted effort not to allot tasks by sex, but rather to have all people participate in all the work that must be done: agriculture, combat, teaching, learning, and medical aid. Angola now has women technicians, radio operators, teachers, medics, and political commissars. The Organization of Angolan Women (OMA), founded in 1961, supports and represents women of Angola. OMA operates at all levels of the liberated territory government, from the villages to the regions. OMA members travel from village to village meeting with women to discuss the difficulties of women in traditional society, what liberation means, and the ways in which they can help the struggle. Ruth Neto, member of OMA, describes the role of women in the war for liberation:

In the ten years of the Angolan people's armed struggle against Portuguese colonialism, Angolan women have made an outstanding contribution. They have become tremendously important to the work of mobilization, carrying out one of the aims of the Organization of Angolan Women, which is to mobilize all the capacities of women within the revolution, so that the Angolan woman can bring a higher consciousness to her work for the rights and interests of women and children and create favorable conditions for her total emancipation. What is more, the Angolan woman is taking an active part in all activities related to the guerrilla war. She participates in armed combat and as a political commissar. She treats the sick and the war wounded. She teaches the people literacy. Since the regular daily bombing raids, she has been cultivating the fields, defying the barbarities of the Portuguese colonialists. She is also to be found as a liaison agent, infiltrating into the areas still under enemy control, exposing herself to capture, if discovered, and braving every danger.

In our traditional society, as in all traditional societies of that time, the Angolan woman's role was primarily that of a mother, educator, and adviser. Often even a political adviser. We have one famous case, that of Queen Ginga Mbandi, in the seventeenth century, who for many years, led a large army against the Portuguese, winning brilliant victories over the colonialist invaders. After the time of colonialist penetration, like all Angolans, the Angolan woman started to be exploited, but more so because she was discriminated against as a woman. For centuries she was condemned to a life of poverty and ignorance. If the Angolan people are exploited in the colonial society, the women are even more so. In addition to racial discrimination, they suffer from wage discrimination in relation to the Angolan men themselves. Since female labor is cheaper, the colonialists try, whenever they can, to employ women in all branches of agriculture in order to make more profit. Coffee picking, for example, is generally done by women who get half the pay given to men, although this is already very low. But their output is the same and they work the same hours. This is why women are usually involved in agriculture.

Women are actively participating in the armed struggle on an equal footing with men, their only limitation being the difficulties related to their physical condition as women. Special mention should be made of the activity of women in the civil defense of the population.

Women are playing a vital role as teachers in the Centers of Revolutionary Instruction, where they are carrying out an important literacy and political education campaign . . . OMA militants are playing an outstanding part in this work as nurses, first aid assistants, and doctors.

Ruth Neto, interviewed in Tanzania by the
Africa Research Group, summer 1972

OMA has been working to change many of the traditional customs of marriage which formerly meant the subjugation of women. In the spring of 1971, for example, OMA called for the abolition of bride price in the liberated areas. Bride price is a traditional practice which involves the prospective husband giving money, goods, or property to the bride's family "in exchange" and "as insurance" for their daughter.

In addition, the practice of polygamy is being gradually replaced in the liberated areas by monogamy.

> At first the men had two or three wives, and the chiefs had even more—ten or fifteen, according to the custom of the tribe. We used to ask them why they had so many women. They told us that if you had many women you wouldn't suffer. If one was sick, you could go to the house of another, or if one goes on a mission or for a visit, the others who remain can take care of you; and if visitors come, plenty of food can be prepared. When the struggle began we started teaching people that it was wrong to have more than one wife. We explained that when a man had many women only one was really his wife; that the others were treated just like servants. After a time, the movement passed a rule that guerrillas could marry only one wife. Some of the villagers follow this, but some still marry several women . . .
>
> Likambuila, quoted in Barnett and Harvey,
> *The Revolution in Angola*

Women participate in all activities, as Likambuila describes:

> We have learned that women are extremely good at intelligence and reconnaissance work; they are able to remain unnoticed among the enemy for several weeks or months. At first many guerrillas thought the women were useless, but this was because the women were so badly

oppressed by the men. Now we have come to understand that the women are very important to the revolution. There are many women and girls in the guerrilla units and in the militias; they are learning at the CIR [Centers of Revolutionary Instruction] and some have been sent to other countries for advanced training in many fields.

There are many cases of courage and heroism by the women . . . One of our women guerrillas was captured by the Portuguese, and after two months of interrogation and torture they persuaded her to lead them to the Command Post of Zone D. As they were approaching the base she asked if she could go relieve herself in the forest, as she was suffering from severe stomach pains. They allowed her to go and she managed to escape, running to inform the guerrillas that the Portuguese were near. The commander prepared an immediate attack on the Portuguese column and managed to ambush them before they reached the base. In the meantime, the other comrades had a chance to prepare their things and move off to a different place.

C. Health Care

Before the war for liberation there were no permanent medical facilities for the African population living in the rural areas. All hospitals and the majority of doctors and nurses were located in the European urban centers. Missionary doctors and nurses would pass only sporadically through villages to provide first-aid care.

The majority of the African population has been plagued by a high incidence of infant mortality, hypermalnutrition, and other diseases.

Nineteen sixty was also a year which saw many people die of epidemic diseases such as smallpox and grippe. Deaths were so many that the Portuguese sent medical

assistants into the villages to inoculate people against
smallpox. This was only the fourth time in memory that
such a thing had happened.

Economia do País, quoted in Barnett and Harvey,
The Revolution in Angola

Before the war was initiated, there was no degree
granting medical school in Angola, so that medical training
was only available to the White population and a few
assimilados who were selected to study abroad. Very few
Africans could thus learn any medical skills to aid their
people.

In 1961 the MPLA's medico-social organization was established. SAM, Medical Assistance Services, now operates
at all levels in the liberated territory. SAM has a hospital
in Dolisi in the People's Republic of Congo (formerly
Congo-Brazzaville) and medical stations along the Cabinda
and Zambian borders. In all the liberated regions of Angola,
there are medical centers and one doctor who is responsible
for co-ordinating the medical activities throughout that
region.

The "central hospital" of the Eastern Region is located
in the main base of that region. The head of the hospital was a young man who had received his education abroad. There are only eight doctors altogether in
the liberated areas, the rest of the staff has been taught
by the MPLA itself, more precisely by . . . SAM.

The hospital was divided into two sections. The first
one was for the guerrillas inside the base, the other
part for the villagers outside of it. The latter was much
better constructed. It was made of twigs and straw,
comprising three separate rooms: the "waiting room,"
the "reception room" of the doctor, and the "treatment
room," where the assistants of the doctor may give
injections, for example.

The guerrilla infirmary, inside the base, is practically nothing but a straw-mat and a small shed made of straw. A part of the medicine supply is kept here but most of it is hidden so that the Portuguese will not be able to find it if there is an air-raid or if the enemy attacks by land, which is very unlikely.

Lohikoski and Mattsson, *Report of a Trip to Angola*

In the sectors there are dispensaries or first-aid posts staffed by qualified nurses and medical assistants. Many of the dispensaries are mobile so they can reach the people throughout the regions and escape Portuguese bombing. These mobile units provide free health and hygiene programs for the population.

In 1969 a school for elementary medical care in the Eastern Region was opened to meet the needs of the people living in the liberated areas.

The course of the school lasts about 3 months during which time the students learn not only the elementaries of medical treatment (i.e., the most common diseases of the region, their symptoms and their treatment—the SAM published a special book for this), but also mathematics, history, geography, etc. It is wished that the students acquire a certain degree of general knowledge at the same time. When these students have finished the course they will go to some other village or base where there is no medical staff yet. When they consider their knowledge and experience to be sufficient they will, on their turn, take apprentices from the surrounding area. In this way the training is handed down, and the amount of trained staff continuously increases.

The circumstances in which the hospitals function are naturally very primitive. Yet surprisingly demanding operations were performed. For example, we saw a wounded guerrilla soldier who had been hit by a bullet. The bullet had pierced the side of his body and stopped in the back, two or three centimeters under the skin.

The doctor of the hospital had removed the bullet and the wound was now healing well.

It is obvious, however, that there is a great shortage or even total lack of many kinds of medicines as well as of other necessary hospital equipment. For instance, adhesive bandages would be very handy on many occasions—the bushes are often thorny and marching makes blisters and cuts on the feet. There was not enough medicine for eye, ear and nose infections, which are common among children. These infections spread through flies, and can be very painful, even dangerous, especially for eye-sight. Also venereal diseases occur, but not very extensively. Penicillin is badly needed; intestine diseases are among the most common because of the poor diet. The coldness of the nights and the exhaustion from marching add to their effect. There are some sort of pills available for curing them, but not nearly enough since so many suffer from them.

Lohikoski and Mattsson, *Report of a Trip to Angola*

With the aim of improving and extending medical care in the areas under the political and military influence of the MPLA, SAM introduced the following program in 1971:

1. A mass vaccination campaign.
2. Expanding the school and training cadres.
3. Building a thirty-bed hospital.
4. Increasing the number of field dispensaries.

Despite all its difficulties, from lack of medical staff to inadequate medical facilities, SAM extends care to more and more Angolans. In an interview at the MPLA's Department of Information in Tanzania, Dr. Mwambaka Videira, Regional Director of the Fourth Region, discussed the value of blending traditional and modern medicine:

Traditional medicine—so stupidly disparaged during the colonial occupation and unknown to many of us—is

highly developed and of great value in that region.
This kind of medicine, which is generally practiced by
tribal elders or specialized healers, has nothing to do
with magic or fetishism and is of great social value. One
need only mention that in an area which is now having
to struggle against tremendous difficulties as far as products for personal cleanliness, like soap, are concerned,
the venereal diseases which plague some so-called civi-
lised areas are non-existent here, because they are
treated by ingestion, baths or irrigation with products
made from certain roots.

Like all rural people, [Angolans'] initial reaction to
anything new is a distrustful and circumspect attitude,
but they are profoundly pragmatic. They only believe
in things they can see with their own eyes, in spectacular results. So, in general, when care has been taken
to administer the [modern] treatment correctly, they
flock to us without any hesitation. The people appreciate scientific medicine, especially for infectious and
febrile diseases, where the effects of medicines, and
especially of injections, are spectacular and immediate.
They appreciate everything having to do with surgery,
but they still rely on traditional treatment for diseases
which involve a complicated, protracted and repeated
cure . . .

Quoted in Barnett and Harvey, *The Revolution in Angola*

D. Education

The educational process in liberated Angola is an integral
part of transforming the society. Angolans realize that education, under any social system, is education *for* a particular
kind of life. It is much more than a transfer of information.
It is a process of making sense of the world and learning how
to affect it for the better.

Under Portuguese colonialism, the education of Africans
was education for servitide. As one Portuguese official
stated, "The raw native has to be looked at as an adult with

16. Schoolroom in liberated Mozambique. (Photo courtesy FRELIMO)

17. Collective agricultural project in liberated Mozambique. (Photo courtesy FRELIMO)

18. Thanks to FRELIMO, medical services are available in the interior of Mozambique for the first time. (Photo courtesy FRELIMO)

19. Men and women militants transport supplies to the interior of Mozambique. (Photo courtesy FRELIMO)

20. The struggle involves everyone in the liberated areas. Here villagers join the guerrillas in a salute to the liberation of Mozambique. (Photo courtesy FRELIMO)

21. Remains of a helicopter used by the Portuguese which was shot down by FRELIMO over Cabo Delgado district in July 1971. (Photo courtesy FRELIMO)

22. Education is a high priority for each of the liberation movements. Here students in liberated Angola work from the MPLA's literacy manual. (Photo courtesy Angola Comité)

23. The liberation struggle draws from the cultural life of the people. Here militants in Angola find time for dancing. (Photo by Börje Mattsson)

24. Like the PAIGC and FRELIMO, the MPLA has established clinics and trained medical aides in its liberated areas. Here an Angolan guerrilla is treated for bullet wounds. (Photo by Börje Mattsson)

25. NATO weaponry plays a major role in the Portuguese colonial wars. Here is a section from a French helicopter shot down by FRELIMO over Mozambique. (Photo courtesy FRELIMO)

26. The "NAPALM" marking on this bomb casing recovered by the PAIGC in Guinea-Bissau indicates that it was supplied to the Portuguese by the United States (probably through NATO). (Photo courtesy PAIGC)

27. Villagers in the liberated area of Guinea-Bissau. The PAIGC is concerned with building on the cultural life of the Guinean people while breaking down old injustices such as hierarchical social structures and the social inferiority of women. (Photo by Mike Shuster)

28. A "schoolroom" in liberated Guinea-Bissau. (Photo by Mike Shuster)

29. (Photo by Mike Shuster)

a child's mentality . . . He needs to be tutored . . . guided in the choice of the work suited to his abilities. . . ." There were few schools and most were located in cities, beyond the reach of the vast majority of the African population. Those Africans who did go to school were trained in Portuguese history and geography. They were taught that their African culture was inferior to Portuguese culture and that being civilized meant being like the Portuguese. In short, they were instructed in a manner which would assure that they could never change their social and economic status. Lisbon dictated colonial educational policy, including curriculum content, textbooks, and the examination system. As a result, 98 per cent of the African population was illiterate under Portuguese colonialism.

Education in liberated Angola is education for a better way of life. Education is seen not just as training, but as a process of gaining self-reliance, of understanding the situation of Angola, and of creating new relationships between people which will enable them together to change their lives. In 1965 the Center for Revolutionary Instruction (CIR) was established by the MPLA to co-ordinate education at every level.

Today, the MPLA has separate divisions for primary and secondary education. Already more than 3,000 children have gone through MPLA schools. For the first time in the immense regions where there was never any school under colonialism, people see the possibility of having children educated, in the midst of the forest and the war.

A narrow straight glade has been cut into the thick undergrowth. The huge tree-tops high above filter green sunlight.

Between two trees, one and a half meters above the ground, a wooden board has been suspended with a sheet of paper pinned to it on which it says: "Angola é a nossa terra"—"Angola is our country." Below a child is busy with a green felt-pen doing arithmetic: 12—4 = 8.

A dozen other children between seven and fifteen years of age watch the blackboard—all of them barefoot, most of them without a shirt, with a book in blue and yellow entitled *Handbook of Literacy* and a thin exercise book for arithmetic on their knees.

Der Spiegel (West Germany), February 8, 1971

The MPLA places heavy emphasis on adult education, both for political workers and for the general population. Angolans study the history, geography, and economy of Angola. In addition, cadres study philosophy and economic theory so that they will be in a better position to evaluate their own struggle in the broader perspective of world history. At each level, education is related to the everyday realities of the students to their economic conditions, to their experience with the Portuguese, to their own history, and to the war of which they are a part.

Tchiweka, a member of the CIR, describes the political training of MPLA cadres:

In the courses on political training, we try to give simple courses about current events in the world today. We talk about imperialism, colonialism, neo-colonialism, and the solidarity between peoples. Naturally, we talk about our friends, our allies, the reasons for these alliances, of our motivations, of their motivations, about international organizations and their goals, or their limitations. I am speaking of a United Nations or an Organization of African Unity, which are present organizations. People hear about these organizations, for example, on the radio, when the Organization of African Unity declares something about Angola, or when the UN condemns or does not condemn Portugal, etc. We explain the value or lack of value of such and such an organization, of such and such a resolution, and with a half a dozen concepts, ideas, or examples drawn from the actual situation, we manage to give our militants an over-all view and political understanding.

But we insist on one thing. That is a knowledge of our country, of our movement, and our struggle. We explain the history of the movement, its birth, the errors committed by its leaders, the different stages of our struggle, and the positions that our movement took at each stage. We explain counterrevolution, its objectives, how it is sustained and by whom. It is important that people understand the structures in which they work or are going to work. For example, it is in understanding the structures of the movement that we were able to explain the structures of popular self-government, such as the germinating of popular power through the creation of action committees. We also talk about Portuguese colonialism, what it represents, what it intends to do, its methods, the exploitation which it perpetuates, how it attempts to promulgate reforms which achieve nothing and which only attempt to perpetuate the domination of our country. We speak about our brothers in Mozambique, in Guinea, in São Tomé. This is part of the general training for all militants, no matter what their responsibility. The content of each subject is more or less developed depending upon the level of those studying.

                    Tchiweka, interviewed by B. Adjali

It is not only the content of the education which gives Angolans a new perspective on their situation, but also the way it is carried out. Angolans learn from each other. All teachers are fellow Angolans. They teach because, as they see it, they have been especially lucky in gaining some knowledge which they can share with others. The MPLA literacy manual opens with a preliminary word for teachers, outlining this philosophy:

Comrade teacher, you know how to read and write, but in our country, out of 100 people, 99 do not . . . You

are not a professor nor are your comrades students.
You are only someone who has had the opportunities,
for various reasons, of learning that which your comrades have not learned, and who, at this moment, fulfills
the revolutionary task of communicating this knowledge to others.

New relationships of openness and cooperation are
worked out through learning together. At the same time,
collective education encourages mutual criticism between
teachers and students.

We hold general weekly meetings which usually lead to
criticisms, to problems between guerrillas, between students and teachers, problems of organization. These
meetings not only permit us to ameliorate our work in
our organization, but also human relationships. For
example, when our comrades have committed certain
faults (because we have weaknesses like people everywhere), then they submit to the criticisms of others.
They defend themselves as well, or they recognize their
faults, and where there is tension between different
relations, between different members of the collective,
it disappears when the dialogue begins between those
who have committed the faults and those who were the
victims.

Tchiweka, interviewed by Adjali

Education is closely integrated with the other tasks of
daily life. As one CIR member put it, "You might say that
the symbols of the CIR are the book, the weapon, and the
hoe." Students participate in agricultural work and fighting.
The general population helps out with setting up schools.
CIR students prepare textbooks and teach primary school
as part of their training. When their programs are over, they
return to their sectors, zones, and villages to continue the
work of building a new Angola.

LITERACY

Being able to read can be a powerful tool in today's world. It allows people to relate their own lives to a much broader context and thus gain a perspective on it which might help them to change their situation. Colonized people throughout the world have been denied this tool. Like anything else in education, however, learning to read does not, in itself, give power to the learner; it depends on the conditions for learning, who is teaching, how it is being done and why. For example, a literacy program designed by factory owners to teach workers how to read just enough to fill different work positions does not give the workers any more control over their work situation. The owners still decide what kinds of labor are needed and what literacy level is required for that work. Factory literacy programs do not give workers the tools for critically evaluating their employment in its local, national, and international context. While this type of program may improve the immediate material condition of the workers (e.g., in salary increases), ultimately it maintains the status quo of power relations in the factory.

In liberated Angola, the process of learning to read is seen as part of the process of putting control back in the hands of Angolans. Both by the content of the reading material and by the method of teaching reading, the literacy program in liberated Angola helps students gain a new image of their daily reality and their own ability to change it. The MPLA has developed its own literacy manual for this purpose. It opens with basic guidelines for the teacher which reflect the principles of collective education: Angolans teaching each other, non-hierarchical relations between students and teachers, mutual respect and concern, and constant consciousness of the political nature of learning.

You and your illiterate comrades form a group in the service of the revolution.

–You must maintain relations of comradeship, of equality, of mutual respect for and with your illiterate brothers and sisters. You must not feel that you are doing them a personal favor, but that you and they together are fulfilling a duty: that of teaching and that of learning.

–You must always concern yourself with their problems, with their work and with their lives.

–You must constantly pay attention to their difficulties and worries.

–Notice that some illiterate comrades may have defects of vision or of hearing. Help them particularly.

–Never give orders during a lesson, nor lose your patience.

–Never forget that the work in a literacy group is collective.

–Change the exercise whenever you feel that the comrades are tired.

–Don't forget that you learn as much from the comrades as they learn from you.

–Avoid any act on the part of the comrades that might embarrass or hurt another less gifted comrade. Only in this way will there be able to be a good spirit of comraderie within the group.

–Whenever possible, especially in the first lessons, have yourself pass unnoticed in the midst of the group so that all will freely express their opinions.

–Before giving each lesson, study it attentively, making use of the explanations contained in this guide.

–Do not begin even one lesson without studying the *Political Themes* that come at the end of this guide.

–Each teacher must teach only twelve comrades.

–Have the comrades take care of their manual. Read them the instructions that come on the cover of the manual.

MPLA literacy manual

The lessons are designed to teach reading by relating it to the daily reality of the learners. The first pages of the manual consist of drawings and photographs of Angola and Angolan people. The class members discuss these pictures; as soon as the students and teachers are familiar with each other and have built up trust, the first lesson begins. It emphasizes the notion of belonging to a group called Angolans and a country called Angola.

From the concepts of *our country* and *our people* comes the concept of a *united people.*

QUARTA LIÇÃO (4)

MPLA literacy manual: *Victory Is Certain*

Out of the concepts of *one country* and *one people* dominated by *colonialism* but *united* in their fight against it comes the notion of Angolans making Angola truly their own country.

MPLA literacy manual: *Victory Is Certain*

As the vowels and consonants are learned, sentence concepts become more elaborated. Historical facts are introduced. All through the manual, each vowel, each consonant, each picture, and each review lesson is related to the political context in which the students live. One of the last lessons of the manual presents the letter "X," a complicated sound in Portuguese which has varied pronunciations and tonal values depending on its context. It is compared with imperialism:

VIGÉSIMA SÉTIMA LIÇÃO (27)

1. Vamos ler:

X	Xa	Xe	Xi	Xo	Xu
x	xa	xe	xi	xo	xu

2. Vamos ler sòzinho:

O _X_ é como o imperialismo. O imperialismo esconde-se sempre dos olhos dos povos e aparece de muitas maneiras diferentes. Umas vezes é o colonialismo, depois muda de aspecto e aparece o néo-colonialismo. O néo-colonialismo é uma maneira mais manhosa de enganar os povos de Africa, da Ásia e da América Latina. O _X_ também muda muitas vezes. É como o camaleão.

MPLA literacy manual. _Victory Is Certain_

A discussion follows with explanations of the parallels between X and imperialism: "Sometimes X is read sh, sometimes ks, sometimes s, and finally eis. But the people always manage to discover and conquer imperialism, by struggling a lot. We too will be careful. We will study and we will discover the values of X."

The learners see their own experience on the pages of the book. They see it as part of an experience shared by many people. Through discussion both of themselves and their place in the larger picture, they begin to understand the importance of their work and the possibilities for creating change. But the concept of working together as Angolans to attain a common goal is not just an abstract concept: it is being realized in the very process of learning to read. The goal of becoming literate is achieved by working together as Angolans with a common purpose. Achieving literacy is living proof for the students that they can gain control of their own lives and history.

The war in Angola is not only a war between the Angolan people and the Portuguese government. It is a war which involves multinational interests ranging from South Africa to the United States, encompassing both corporate and government involvement. As in Mozambique, Portugal has expanded its efforts to attract foreign investment and with it foreign military support.

The Gulf Oil Corporation takes a primary role in sustaining the Portuguese war effort in Angola. Gulf produced 7.5 million tons in 1970; an annual production of 15 million tons was predicted for 1973. Its $150 million investment in Angola (as of 1970) provided jobs for a total of thirty-three African Angolans, while the $16 million Gulf paid Portugal in 1970 represented 30 per cent of Angola's military budget for that year. Gulf Oil also paid two years' advance taxes (an extraordinary action) to the Portuguese in 1970 at the time of a Portuguese financial crisis. For 1972 Gulf's projected payments to Portugal were $33–50 million—47–71 per cent of Angola's colonial military budget.

The Cunene River project in Southern Angola is a joint project of Portugal and South Africa. It will include a series of twenty-seven dams and hydroelectric plants which will irrigate land to encourage White settlement in the region and at the same time produce electricity for the mining schemes in Namibia, Southwest Angola, and South Africa.

Portugal continues to receive increasing military support from Britain, France, West Germany, and the United States through NATO. South Africa supplies helicopters and troops. The United States provides military advisers. At the end of 1971 the United States also authorized Export-Import Bank loans to Portugal of $436 million, a total equivalent to four times all the Export-Import Bank's assistance to Portugal from 1946 to 1970. These are only a few of the ways that Portugal has internationalized its wars.

Despite all the Portuguese efforts, the liberation forces of Angola are expanding on many fronts. They have specifically targeted the sites of foreign involvement for new offensives: in February 1972, they opened up a new military front, in the south of the country near the Cunene River hydroelectric and irrigation project. This offensive signifies the opening of the sixth region, which is part of the MPLA's strategy to generalize the struggle. The MPLA sees its war as a fight not only against Portugal but against the powers that buttress it. Agostinho Neto talks about the strategies and prospects of the MPLA:

> We have learned not to expect an easy, short war, because the Portuguese are receiving aid from many imperialist powers. We know that it will last a while longer and that we must do our best to make it as brief as possible.

We also know that we must concentrate on relying on our own forces rather than on foreign aid, which is always limited—aid that sometimes does not reach us on time or in sufficient amounts. Our decision, however, is not based solely on this argument. The use of our own forces is also a means of educating the people—educating them for work, for the reconstruction of the country. This will, of course, demand great popular awareness so as to fight underdevelopment and advance toward the progressive development of the country . . .

This is our road. We must step up the struggle against imperialism and win genuine independence so as to have true progress and so that the people may be free.

Neto, *Tricontinental,* No. 12, 1969

CHAPTER EIGHT

GUINEA-BISSAU

We have liberated more than 80 per cent of our national territory. We shall liberate the rest. We shall liberate the Cape Verde Islands. Step by step, we construct our State. Our present position is that of an independent nation with a part of its national territory, notably the urban centers and the islands, still under foreign occupation. Through this struggle, we have conquered the right to our own personality in the international field.

> Amilcar Cabral, late Secretary General of the PAIGC

Operating freely throughout the bush, swamp, and forest of their own country, the people of Guinea-Bissau continue their struggle to free themselves from Portuguese colonialism. But their fight goes far beyond the expulsion of the Portuguese:

The greatest success of our struggle is not to have been capable of defeating the Portuguese, but that of creating, in our land, a new social and cultural life, at the same time that we fight.

> Cabral, *Actualités*, August 1969

We are trying to build something new and unique. We
are trying to give a voice to the peasant, to the people,
which has been denied them for five centuries. And that
is the only way we can really understand a revolution.
You must change the life of the peasant . . . We tried
to let the peasants take a part in government; we tried
to give them the vote, to show them that they will be
running their country, Guinea . . . We are trying to
avoid the trap which many African countries have fallen
into. They are independent but nothing has changed in
the villages. We are avoiding having the elites doing
everything; the masses will. We think we can do it in
Guinea. We can make the so-called elites to go into the
fields and plow for a while. Maybe it would be better
for them than sitting at a desk. When you switch roles,
you learn the value of the work someone else is doing.

Gil Fernandes, foreign representative
of the PAIGC, in *Ufahamu*, Vol. I, No. 1, 1970

I. Armed Struggle

A. Prelude to Armed Struggle

Clearly, if the Portuguese government persists in refusing to reconsider its position—ignoring as it does the
interests of our people—nothing will stop our Party from
accomplishing its historic mission: the mission of developing our struggle for national liberation, of replying
by violence to the violence of the Portuguese colonialist
forces; of completely eliminating, and by every means,
the colonist domination of "Portuguese" Guinea and the
Cape Verde Islands.

Cabral, in Basil Davidson, *The Liberation of Guiné*, 1969

The above warning by Amilcar Cabral, in an "open letter" to the Portuguese government on October 13, 1961,

came just a few months before the Guinean people began to respond with violence to the violence of the Portuguese colonial forces. Commenting on the "open letter" as one of the final attempts to seek a peaceful resolution, the PAIGC leaders stated:

> Seeking a peaceful solution to its conflicts with the Portuguese colonialist, the PAIGC took specific steps to try to persuade the Portuguese government to recognize the right of the people of Guinea and the Cabo Verde Islands to self-determination and national independence and by so doing to enhance the possibilities of cooperation between them and the Portuguese people. These steps which at the same time promoted the interest of international peace and security included the dispatch of a "memorandum" and an "open letter" to the Portuguese government dated 1 December 1960 and 13 October 1961 respectively. In this way specific proposals were submitted to the Portuguese government for the peaceful elimination of colonial rule in Guinea and the Cabo Verde Islands.

> Cabral, *Revolution in Guinea*, 1971

Ignoring all such efforts to seek a peaceful solution, Portuguese dictator Salazar responded,

> We will not sell: we will not cede: we will not surrender: we will not quit one fragment of our sovereignty. . . . Our constitutional laws forbid it and even if they did not, our national conscience would do so.

> Quoted in Davidson, *The Liberation of Guiné*

The next few months saw increased air traffic at the Portuguese airstrips in the Cape Verde Islands and at Bissau, the capital of "Portuguese" Guinea. The Portuguese raised the number of colonial troops to 6,000 and sent in European special agents from the Portuguese secret political police (PIDE). They also increased military equipment which included numerous tanks and jeeps, and also five jet fighters and two bombers. The Portuguese had no plans to seek a peaceful solution, but rather they sought to reinforce their authority by increasing the repression of the nationalists.

The centuries-old failure of Europeans to regard Africans as human beings had become even more apparent in 1961. Machine-gun and mortar fire could be heard in the villages and in the countryside daily. Any nationalist, or suspected nationalist, was arrested and imprisoned without trial. But by the end of 1961 and the beginning of 1962, the repression had grown even more severe. All African organizations, political or not, were declared illegal. Any village which was suspected of any type of involvement with the PAIGC was destroyed. In a communiqué dated March 24, 1962, the PAIGC leaders stated that the "situation is more tense than ever in Bissau, and protest and revolt have swept into various other regions. Thousands of lives are under threat from the modern arms of the troops and police of Salazar, ready to drown in blood the liberation of our people. . . ." The Portuguese were determined to crush the rebellion before it started. It became increasingly clear to the people of Guinea-Bissau that they were faced with but one alternative.

B. PAIGC Military Development

The guerrilla walks proudly on the land, while the little Portuguese commands the clouds. . . .

From a song quoted in Davidson, *The Liberation of Guiné*

By the middle of 1962 small but well-organized bands of guerrillas were operating out of strategically located bases in the southern and central regions. From these bases, initial activity was limited to sabotage of Portuguese communication and transportation routes. Bridges, roads, and railways were the early targets of attacks. But as the guerrillas gained more experience, Portuguese patrols and small garrisons increasingly became the objects of ambush and attack. The attacks were designed not only to put Portuguese troops out of action, but also to capture badly needed weapons and supplies. Village members accompanied the party members on ambushes so they could see for themselves that the Portuguese were not invincible. After seeing the Portuguese patrol destroyed and the survivors run away in defeat, the local population had a change of mind about the "superiority" of the Portuguese forces. Commenting on one such attack, a party member reported:

> Oh, it went well. We had three weapons. There were ten of us. We ambushed three of their vehicles and killed seven of them. We took eight weapons, mostly Mauser rifles but two automatics as well, and a lot of ammunition and stores. We lost one man killed. But the comrades took courage from this first action. All of them are still alive, I think, but for the one we lost then, and another since.
>
> Quoted in Davidson, *The Liberation of Guiné*

By the end of 1962 the revolution included preparations for full-scale war. It was from this time that the peasants

> discovered for themselves the need to revolt, when they made the revolt their own, they entered the ranks of the guerrillas in large numbers. . . . In our struggle, we established our principles after having become thoroughly familiar with our country's conditions. For instance, we decided that we should never struggle from

outside our own country, for which reasons we never
had armed forces outside our own country. And, for
the same reason, in 1963 we started the armed struggle
in the centre of the country, both in the south and in the
north. This means that contrary to what has been done
by other peoples in Africa or elsewhere who are fighting
for national independence, we adopted a strategy that
we might call centrifugal; we started in the centre and
moved toward the periphery of our country. This came
as the first big surprise to the Portuguese, who had stationed their troops on the Guinea and Senegal borders
on the supposition that we were going to invade our
own country.

Cabral, *Revolution in Guinea*

By the middle of 1963 this relatively unknown guerrilla
movement had liberated 15 per cent of their national territory. Faced with a growing number of peasants joining
the guerrillas in the liberated zone, the Portuguese
launched a major offensive in 1964 designed to reconquer
the south-central area of Guinea-Bissau. The Portuguese,
who had by now bolstered the number of soldiers to 10,000,
attacked the PAIGC's Como Island stronghold.

Yes, the big dream of the Portuguese has been to recover
the already liberated territory. For instance, in 1964 they
carried out a big offensive with almost 3,000 men against
Como Island. The recovery of Como would have two
advantages for the Portuguese: first, a strategic advantage, because it is a firm base for the control of the
southern part of the country; secondly, a political advantage, because it would constitute a big propaganda
victory for the Portuguese and would serve to demoralize
our own populations.

But the Portuguese were defeated on Como, where
they lost more than 900 soldiers and much more mate-

rial. They had to withdraw, and Como continues to be free. It is today one of the most developed zones of our liberated areas.

Cabral, *Revolution in Guinea*

The defeat of the Portuguese in the seventy-five-day seige was more than a military victory for the PAIGC. It marked their first defense of Guinean territory against a major offensive by the Portuguese. It also boosted the morale of the guerrillas when they were joined by thousands of men, women, and children from the villages who helped to defend the island from the Portuguese invaders.

The next step for the PAIGC, whose army of a few thousand were already holding down 10,000 Portuguese troops in Guinea, was to hold a party congress to solidify the party organization. In February of 1964 the PAIGC leaders and cadres gathered in Guinea's southern region to hold their first congress. The congress, which lasted seven days, focused on reorganizing the guerrillas into a regular army for organized warfare against the Portuguese.

We decided during the Congress to mobilize part of the guerrilla forces to create regular forces, so as to extend the armed struggle to new areas. It is not necessary, in our opinion, to mobilize everyone for armed struggle; it is enough to mobilize a reasonable proportion of the population. After that you can move on to creating regular forces and mobilize the rest. . . . With the creation of the regular armed forces we opened up new fronts, Gabu and Boé in the East, and São Domingos in the West.

Cabral, *Revolution in Guinea*

During the congress, 2,000 men volunteered for the regular army, and 900 were actually accepted. The men were given new uniforms, better equipment, and new arms including cannons and antiaircraft automatic rifles.

The arms that the PAIGC had been using up to this time were mostly captured Portuguese arms. But as the struggle progressed, the PAIGC received more aid from African countries, as well as from countries in the socialist bloc. With the increasing number of arms and equipment, the People's Revolutionary Armed Forces (FARP) was an effective, well-equipped fighting unit.

The formation of the regular army saw a new phase in the Guinean peoples' struggle against the Portuguese. The successes of the guerrilla war gave the regular army a strong base upon which to lay out strategies and tactics.

> As for our tactics, we follow the fundamental principle of armed struggle, or, if you prefer, colonial war: the enemy, in order to control a given zone, is forced to disperse his forces; he thus becomes weakened, and we can defeat him. In order to be able to defend himself from us he needs to concentrate his forces and when he concentrates his forces he allows us to occupy the areas that are left empty and work on them politically to prevent the enemy from returning.
>
> Cabral, *Revolution in Guinea*

The years 1965 and 1966 brought new successes to the people. By now, half of the national territory had been liberated. The PAIGC had inflicted great losses on the Portuguese. In 1966 alone, the number of Portuguese killed and wounded was estimated between 1,500 and 2,000. The Portuguese were attacked in sixty fortified camps and towns.

> Having delivered more than one hundred attacks on fortified positions, we have succeeded (by December 1966) in ravaging about fifteen enemy camps, several of which were very important, such as those of Madina,

Ollosato, Enxale, Cutia, Medjo and Biambi, as well as
seriously damaging about twenty others, such as those
of Buba, Empada, Mansôa, Beli, Bula, Buruntuma,
Camquelita, Farim, etc. Hastily reconstructed, some
camps have been attacked, destroyed and damaged
several times.

The enemy's growing use of aircraft and helicopters
reflects their growing difficulties in the supply of their
troops. . . .

Quoted in Davidson, *The Liberation of Guiné*

Again in 1967 the army and guerrillas increased the number of attacks on the Portuguese. In their communiqué, the
PAIGC lists 142 major attacks on the Portuguese, including
22 commando operations on airfields, and 476 ambushes;
the army captured 86 G-3 submachine guns, 397 Mauser
rifles, 26 60-mm mortars, and 16 radio transmitters. The Portuguese lost 1,905 men in that year, their worst year since
the war began.

In the same year, the PAIGC lost 86 of its soldiers, along
with 172 civilians. Commenting on these low figures, Basil
Davidson wrote:

One is equally free to disbelieve these low military cas-
ualty figures, as the PAIGC leadership suspects that one
will; but then one will gravely risk misunderstanding
the nature of well conducted guerrilla warfare. PAIGC
warfare is undoubtedly well conducted: its units could
not otherwise have survived and grown. And, as such,
PAIGC tactics are aimed at keeping severe casualties
to an absolute minimum.

Davidson, *The Liberation of Guiné*

The military struggle which the PAIGC waged was, however, not without great difficulties and sacrifices. The struggle to this point was a long and difficult one, with great loss

of life to both the military and civilian population. This brief review of the situation lists the successes of the PAIGC, but it cannot list the hardships and the day-to-day obstacles that the fighters had to overcome.

By the end of 1967 the entire guerrilla force had been incorporated into regular army forces. The liberated areas were protected by the peoples' armed militia while the regular forces were free to fight on the fronts.

By 1968 the Portuguese had 25,000 men in Guinea. Desperate in the face of great losses at the hand of the guerrillas, the Portuguese were beginning to change their tactics and shifted to a greater emphasis on aerial and chemical-biological warfare, similar to the tactics of the United States in Vietnam. This was an attempt to limit the number of Portuguese soldiers in combat and cut down on the already large number of casualties. Subject to attack at almost any time, the Portuguese army was by now completely on the defensive.

> The situation on the level of the armed struggle is therefore generally favorable. The enemy is on the defensive, and we hold the initiative on all fronts. We must not lose sight of the fact, however, that the enemy, economically much stronger than us, has considerable human resources and efficient material means available with which to continue the war against us. They are still firmly established in certain urban areas, particularly in the main towns, and can still count on money, arms, aircraft and other equipment which their allies are supplying.
>
> Cabral, *Revolution in Guinea*

C. The Military Struggle Today

The only enemy camps that have not been the object of the action of our troops in 1971, Bissau, the capital, and Bafatá, the second city of the country, were at-

tacked with success by units of our regular army, the
9th and 26th of June.

These attacks mark a new stage in the politico-military
evolution of our struggle.

During the night of 9th–10th June, a unit of artillery,
aided by infantry groups of our regular army, succeeded
in penetrating the defensive lines of the enemy, in
order to bombard the Portuguese position in Bissau.
Important destruction of material as well as loss of life
were suffered by the enemy, who, surprisingly, did not
put up any reaction.

On the 26th of June, units of the Armed Forces of the
Eastern Front penetrated into Bafatá, submitting enemy
garrisons, the principal airport, and several administration buildings to intense attack. Four barracks, the
meteorologic station and diverse administration buildings of the enemy were destroyed. The colonialist
troops registered many dead and wounded.

The civilians in urban centres, especially the Portuguese, live now in a permanent state of alert, and can
hardly disguise their fear. Most of the officers are sending their families home to Portugal.

PAIGC communiqué (unpublished), January 1, 1972

With the attacks on Bafatá and Bissau, 1971 proved to
be the most successful year of the eight-year-old war against
the Portuguese army. The freedom fighters, who by now
were holding down 30,000 Portuguese troops, are able to
carry the war to the two main Portuguese strongholds. Between January and December of 1971, there were at least
1,495 Portuguese casualties, including 912 killed. Out of the
eighty camps originally occupied by the Portuguese troops,
the people have successfully expelled the troops from over
forty of these camps, while inflicting heavy losses of life
and property to the remaining camps.

We now control all roads except for some in the western and center-eastern regions; they cannot pass and they do not try. What they do try to do is to asphalt the roads to prevent us from mining them. But it is too late to asphalt them: we have good bazookas to destroy them with, and we have developed, over the years, ways of attacking boats on the rivers.

Cabral, *Facts and Reports*, November 30, 1971

The most recent major Portuguese setback came in an operation they named "Safira Solitária":

In the face of the intensification of the action of our soldiers, who, in December of 1971 attacked over and over again all the entrenched camps of the center-north of the country, notably the cities of Farim and Mansôa, and the important garrisons of Bissora and Olossado, the colonialist command was convinced that we were preparing a more intensive offensive toward the end of the year—particularly, a new attack on the capital. They decided to launch an operation of great breadth against our forces in the region: in particular in the Mores sector, known as an important PAIGC base.

On the morning of December 20th, several contingents of the colonialist army, about 800 men from the fortified camps of the region and special commandos helicoptered from Bissau, penetrated into the Mores sector in several directions after an intensive aerial bombardment. In the course of several encounters and ambushes carried out by our regular army, as well as the local armed forces and the people armed, the colonial forces were routed and had to call to their aid jet planes and helicopters to evacuate the dead and the wounded. Our soldiers killed 102 enemy soldiers, wounding many more. The hospitals of Bissau were overwhelmed by the arrival of the wounded, many of whom could not find a place in them. The Portuguese commander who directed the "Safira Solitária" operation committed suicide.

Cabral, in PAIGC communiqué, January 1972

Confident that they can attack and destroy the capital city of Bissau, the PAIGC forces are making efforts to avoid doing so. Realizing the number of civilians who would be killed if they were to bombard and attack the city, the PAIGC has restated its willingness to negotiate:

> We want peace . . . We want to solve this conflict with Portugal by negotiation, but we cannot accept Portuguese rule of our country . . .
> We have fought for nine years—but we have fought for peace and peace means nothing without freedom. We are very sure of the situation in our country. We have liberated more than two thirds of it and we control that even administratively. We are now able to attack Bissau, the capital, and Bafatá, the second town —and we have the means to destroy these towns. If it became necessary to use force to free the town tomorrow, that we would do. But we do not want to take such an action. We would prefer to solve the problem without further destruction. But that depends on the Portuguese.

PAIGC communiqué, January 1972

II. Life in Liberated Guinea-Bissau

Keep always in mind that the people are not fighting for ideas, for the things in anyone's head. They are fighting to win material benefits, to live better and in peace, to see their lives go forward, to guarantee the future of their children. . . .

From the general directives of the PAIGC leadership, 1965

A. The Political Situation

The political conditions in our country before the beginning of our struggle—nationwide oppression, absence of even the most elementary freedoms, police and military repression—determined our actions, forcing us to start the armed liberation struggle. Now it is the latter—as the expression of our determination to free ourselves from the colonial yoke, and thus of our fundamental political choice—which is determining the enemy's political behaviour.

> Cabral, OSPAAL speech, December 1968,
> in *Revolution in Guinea*

Under the guidance of the PAIGC, the people have organized themselves to run their own lives, from the most basic level on up:

We've held elections for a Party committee in each village of the liberated regions. We call it a "tabanca committee" [*tabanca* is Guinea-Creole for village]. In general, it is composed of three men and three women, and is elected by the village assembly, in other words, by the entire adult population of the village. We explain beforehand the way in which they must get organized, the tasks they have to carry out, and, of course, the basic principles of the Party. Young people are often elected. The old people haven't always been happy to see their places in the village leadership taken over by the young. Almost all of our fighters are young, too, of course. But then again, since everybody, old and young, had had enough of the Portuguese, even the old ones who at first dragged their feet finally came around. So anyhow, committee officers are elected by the villagers. We in the Party are consulted, and we decide to support a candidate on the basis of the work she/he has already accomplished for the Party, and of the esteem in which the other peasants hold her/him. In principle, the peasants' choice is respected. If, in our opinion, they have chosen badly, we leave the candidate in office. We wait for the peasants to realize their mistake by themselves. Naturally, the Party reserves the right to remove those who use their prerogatives in their own interests.

We don't want a new chieftainship system. A new committee is elected at the peasants' request; and elections are also held periodically just to avoid what you might call hardening of the arteries.

The village committee has several tasks. At the present stage, one of the most important is to increase agricultural production, so that there will be plenty of rice for both families and fighters. The fighters also produce rice, millet, etc., but their food is supplied mainly by the village. We've created new collective fields so that the villagers can produce for the fighters. The village committee takes care of supervising and administering the work, and it also takes care of the militia. The militia consists of young people who are not FARP fighters but guerrilla partisans with rifles and no uniforms. They are part [of the] village's self-defense group. In certain zones, they play an offensive role. They live in the village and are transferred from place to place according to the requirements of our struggle. Obviously, they are volunteers. They join us because of the political work in the villages. This work is done in the local language.

Political work means getting the people to know about the Party and explaining why we exist and what we want. We explain what colonialism means. At first, we explain that Guinea isn't Portugal and that we can govern ourselves without the Portuguese taking our livestock, without heavy taxes, and blows, and fear of the Portuguese. We explain that what's happening here isn't an act of God, and that it's already happened in a lot of other countries. We have to show our people that the world doesn't end at their villages. Our problem is to make them understand the present level of the struggle, that fact that the struggle doesn't concern just their village but all of Guinea, and that it's not simply a national but also an international struggle. We have to make them aware that in order to advance, *they* must guarantee the struggle's continuity, *they* must take charge of their own destiny by solving their problems on the village level, developing production, sending their children to school, and holding frequent meetings.

> Chico, political commissar for the northern interregion, quoted in Gérard Chaliand, *Armed Struggle in Africa*, 1969

The village committees appoint their representatives to the central committee of the party, the supreme battle council, which consists, at present, of seventy-five members. It was at a meeting of this body, in August of 1971, that the decision was taken to establish popular assemblies at the local, regional, and national levels.

> We have all the elements of an independent state in the areas we now control. We are now concerned with extending the liberated zones and with building independence there. We have judged that the time has come to expand the role of the people in decision-making . . . We wish to reinforce the sovereignty of the people, in giving them an instrument which is different from the Party, but which remains in close relationship with it. Therefore, we made the decision to institute Popular Assemblies, on the local as well as on the national level . . . These Assemblies will proclaim the existence of this State as the representative of the realities being lived by the people of Guinea and Cape Verde.

> Cabral, *Actualités*, August 1968

In the summer of 1972 a United Nations team visiting liberated Guinea-Bissau reported that free popular elections had been held at all levels and that the country had the structure of a democratic state. On the strength of this demonstrated self-government, the PAIGC was accepted as an observer government in the UN General Assembly. Full, formal independence, the final discrediting of Portuguese rule, is a short step away.

B. The Economic Situation

For some time now, we have abolished the system of colonial exploitation over most of our national territory. In 1966, we dealt a heavy blow to the remainder of the [Portuguese] trading system, especially in the eastern (Gabu-Bafatá) and western (Canchungo-São Domingo) regions. In fact, the state of insecurity created by our units in these regions, and our control of certain roads, have made impossible both the growth of groundnuts [the colonial monoculture] and the distribution of warehoused goods in the interior entrepôts [of the Portuguese.] Besides this, our ambushes mounted on the Bissau-Mansôa road have held up the transport of imported goods and local farming products. The greater part of wholesale and retail trade in secondary urban centres has come to a stop, traders and clerks having fled from these centres to the capital. To get some idea of the catastrophic situation of the colonial economy, it is enough to recall that the Companhia União Fabril (CUF), the main commercial enterprise in Guinea, has been in deficit for almost three years, and has had to draw on its reserves to survive. In addition the colonial authorities, in a country which produces more rice than is needed for local consumption, have had to import large quantities of this cereal (10,000 tons from Brazil alone) to feed the troops and the urban population.

In the liberated areas we are continuing to give every attention to economic development, particularly with regard to increasing the production of crops. New areas of land were planted with rice and other crops during the last rainy season. Other products (leather, rubber from the forests, crocodile and other animal skins, and coconuts) have been shipped and sold abroad, although only in small quantities.

We are also trying to develop artisan work and small local industries. Because of technical difficulties (lack of means of transport and spare parts) we have had to postpone the reopening of the sawmills previously belonging to settlers in the forest of Dio. We are currently examining the possibility of starting up in the North a small rudimentary factory to produce ordinary soap, using palm oil.

Cabral, Revolution in Guinea

The work of planting, growing and harvesting is of course greatly affected by the day to day reality of the war:

> The work in the rice fields must be done at dusk and dawn and the rice must be gathered into small bundles and distributed evenly along the edges of the field, to prevent the airplanes from destroying them. Now areas under cultivation may often be found in the jungle, several kilometers from the village, and even water must be fetched from afar.

Mikko Pyhala, "Report of a Visit to the
Liberated Areas of Guinea-Bissau," National
Union of Finnish Students, Helsinki, 1971

In spite of intensified aerial bombardment and warfare, we have succeeded in considerably enlarging the production of food crops, in diversifying cultivation, and in applying new techniques by means of specialized cadres formed during the struggle. Rice growing, our main food base, has had good results in the southern regions, the centre-north, and the north-west, the biggest productive increase being in Quitafine, the most bombed region. Diversification has taken shape mainly through the growing of more cassava, potato and beans, and in the introduction of certain exotic varieties of beans and other vegetables.

Cabral, "Report on the Situation of the Struggle, 1967," quoted in Davidson, *The Liberation of Guiné*

To supply the basic needs of the population, the PAIGC has, since the end of 1964, set up People's Stores throughout the liberated areas:

The form of commerce utilized is that of simple barter. Some products, such as kola nuts, palm nuts, hides, the skin of crocodiles and other animals, are sold outside the country, in order to purchase things which the people need. This exportation is, however, severely limited by the inherent conditions of the war and its material difficulties. Gifts and purchases are held in a central store, and are distributed, according to need, to regional and zonal stores. Selling brigades take charge of direct barter with village producers.

Actualités, February 1971

By the summer of 1968, there were, in all, fifteen People's Stores in the liberated regions: five in the north, seven in the south, two in the east, and one on the frontier with Guinea-Conakry. The main goods they imported were cottons, mosquito netting, machetes, hoe blades, salt, sugar, tobacco, bicycles, saucepans, sewing machines, fish hooks and lines, flashlights, and flashlight batteries. The main goods they exported were kola nuts, skins, coconuts, rubber, beeswax, and large quantities of rice.

C. Education and Health

It would be naïve to pretend that the progress achieved in our liberated areas has brought about a radical change in the social situation of the inhabitants. Our people, who have to face a colonial war whose genocidal intentions spare nobody, still live under difficult conditions. Entire populations have seen their villages destroyed and have had to take refuge in the bush. But everybody has enough to eat, nobody is subject to exploitation, and the standard of living is progressively rising. Demonstrating a political consciousness which is heightened every day, the people live and work in harmony, united in standing up to the evils of the war imposed on us.

Cabral, OSPAAL speech, 1968

In five hundred years of Portuguese colonial domination, a total of fifty-six schools had been established in the country (eleven of these were government schools; forty-five were missionary schools). Ten years of fighting for freedom has meant the setting up of 245 primary schools, attended (in 1970) by 20,000 pupils.

The decision to set up schools throughout the countryside was made at the 1964 PAIGC Congress. Implementing this decision was hard work:

The schools are generally located in an important village, and the school children come in daily from the neighboring villages. We explain the purpose of the school to the village people, and they agree to build a school themselves, as well as the benches and tables. The Party furnishes the rest—things like books, writing tablets, pencils, a blackboard and so forth . . . Some villages have no great comprehension of the meaning or practical use of education. The Party has to explain it again and again. We try to explain it in simple terms, with pictures and concrete examples, that we are going to need a great many educated people after we expel the Portuguese. . . .

Anselmo, age twenty-three, in charge
of educational problems in the north,
quoted in Chaliand, Armed Struggle in Africa

The importance of education for Guinea and the PAIGC, is immeasurable.

> It is apparent that in the social revolution, the most profound transformations concern the new generation: it is sufficient to see the difference between children in the liberated zones and those who arrive from the zones under colonial domination. This is why the PAIGC pays such attention to school age youth. It is in the primary schools in the villages, in the boarding school in the North, in the infant day care centers and in the political school in Conakry, that a new Guinea, master of modern language, molded in new social relations, is being formed.
>
> O. Monteiro, in *AfricAsia*, July 1971

The Portuguese realize this as well: schools have consistently been one of the major targets of their bombing raids. Therefore, schools are located in the shelter of the jungle. Schools must work on two shifts for security reasons; the number of pupils going to school at the same time must be small—below forty. Further, the school must change sites three or four times each year. Despite these precautions, three schools were destroyed by the Portuguese in 1970; in two of them, thirty children were killed.

Against these high costs, the people of Guinea-Bissau recognize the value and the benefit, both to themselves and to their country, of the education drive. A visitor to a village within the liberated zone records the following incident:

> The old man, a member of the tabanca committee, proudly showed us a photo of his son, who had learned to read in a PAIGC school and was now continuing his education in a foreign country. He was clearly aware of the profound transformation his son was a part of.
>
> Monteiro, in *AfricAsia*, July 1971

The Portuguese, in five hundred years of domination, had established a total of three hospitals in the country. These hospitals serviced the colonialist population almost exclusively. Now, in the course of the fight for liberation,

> four hospitals are functioning in the interior of the country (two in the South, one in the North and one in Boé,) with a total of about two hundred beds, and the permanent attendance of doctors helped by sufficient nurses, and having the equipment necessary for surgical operations. Also, dozens of dispensaries established in the various sectors give daily assistance to the combatants and to the people. The hospital at Boé has now been improved and has departments of general medicine, surgery, orthopedics, radiology, anaesthesia and analysis. In the past year, 80 nurses have been trained (30 inside the country and 50 in Europe), and 30 more are being trained at the moment. We are soon going to set up a new rural hospital exclusively for orthopedics.
>
> Cabral, OSPAAL speech, 1968

These hospitals are extremely important for the continuation and the success of the war for liberation:

> Before every important attack, a meeting takes place between the military leaders and the doctors of that region's hospital, to organize a plan of evacuation and rapid treatment of the wounded. Often, mobile units capable of carrying out a variety of surgical operations are found in proximity to the combat zone.
>
> "Hygiene in the Liberated Zones," unpublished, n.s.d.

The hospitals of the PAIGC, like the schools, are located in the shelter of the jungle. A visitor to Guinea-Bissau describes what he saw of health facilities in December of 1970:

> The hospitals are modest straw cottages where the wounded and the sick may rest in shade. In one of these

hospitals, with no electricity nor any running water, surgeons performed fourteen operations during the last two months—all of them successful. The population of the liberated areas has approximately ten doctors at their disposal. All of them are military physicians at the same time, and supervise the nursing school, which works closely with the hospital. In general, the nursing staffs are equally divided as to men and women. The doctor must also visit sanitary stations that are very far from the hospitals. The work seems unending, and there is a considerable shortage of medicine. Malaria is a constant disease, and the same is true for skin diseases, which are increasing because of the lack of vitamin B. This vitamin is found in meat, but the Portuguese killed the cattle, and the bombers have scared away wild animals. There are, however, a number of army surgeons who have studied abroad, and who are now working among the people. Each year, the hospital schools produce more sanitary personnel, too. Each village has a sanitary brigade, which works under the supervision of the Commissioner of Social Matters in the region.

Pyhala, "Report of a Visit to the Liberated Areas"

In 1972 the peasants of Guinea-Bissau grow rice to eat instead of peanuts to sell to the Portuguese. They trade their rice for merchandise they need at People's Stores, which make them independent of the Portuguese economy. Men and women together participate in village discussions to direct their communal agricultural work. Men and women together "talk politics" to clarify in their own minds the reasons for their struggle. In the midst of Portuguese bombing raids, they are building schools and hospitals, they are learning to read and learning the skills needed by their people. And they are preparing to set up the formal structure of statehood, through elections on the local, regional, and national levels. These are the specific conditions of life in Guinea-Bissau today.

III. The Development of Revolutionary
Strategy in Guinea-Bissau

"Every person must have a clear understanding of the struggle."

From the "specific conditions" described above—the concrete realities of their daily lives—the Guinean people have developed a general understanding of their historical position. They understand that Portuguese colonialism has caused the underdevelopment of their country and has meant the exploitation of their people. They understand that their war for national liberation is aimed at ending this exploitation. And because they are fighting to put the development of their country back into their own hands, they understand that they must take the responsibility for making village self-government work, as well as for developing a People's Army; that the struggle means trading at their own People's Stores to develop their own economy, as well as refusing to trade with the Portuguese or to pay taxes to them. They know that the never-ending battle to liberate themselves touches almost every aspect of their everyday lives.

The people also know that their efforts in Guinea-Bissau are not aimed solely at the achievement of political independence. The national liberation struggle, which is itself an affirmation of the vitality of their indigenous culture, is a fight to regain control over their unique historical development and simultaneously to end all forms of social exploitation in the country. This knowledge of why they are fighting, together with the idea, which comes out of daily experience, of *how* to do so most effectively, is the basis for the theory that guides their revolution.

Theory is crucial in providing continuity and direction.

It makes individual actions understandable by putting them in the framework of a total vision of the purpose and method of the struggle and provides a guide for future actions—for revolutionary strategy.

Revolutionary theory can never be separated from revolutionary practice. All successful revolutionaries of modern times have insisted on this point. Theories separated from action are merely idle or irrelevant, but action separated from theory is blind. This is why Cabral emphasizes that:

> Every practice produces a theory, and if it is true that a revolution can fail even though it be based on perfectly conceived theories, nobody has yet made a successful revolution without a revolutionary theory.

Cabral, Revolution in Guinea

Praxis is a dynamic relationship between knowledge and action. It is the close combination of acting in the world and reflecting upon that action to understand it in a framework or perspective which influences further action. It is a conception of knowing and doing which stresses the unity, rather than the separateness, of the two.

This concept of thinking and acting as an interrelated process is essential in understanding contemporary revolutionary struggles. Under colonialism in Guinea-Bissau, for example, people's everyday experience gave them a concrete knowledge of exploitation. Reflecting on this knowledge, Guineans came to see that Portuguese colonialism and social inequality were historical problems—in other words, that these problems were products of the development of historical forces at a particular time and were not inevitable or unchangeable. This understanding led people to act to change their situation.

It is the specifics of each situation—the knowledge that comes from experience, not any universal theory—that determines what needs to be changed and how best to do it. Cabral says that

> however great the similarity between various cases and however identical are the enemies, national liberation and social revolution are not exportable commodities; they are, and increasingly so every day, the outcome of local and national elaboration, more or less influenced by external factors but essentially determined and formed by the historical reality of each people.
>
> Cabral, *Revolution in Guinea*

The *praxis* of making a revolution, which is unique in each different situation, is a constantly developing process. Theory is proven right or wrong only by acting on it. A revolutionary theory is valid only if it is successful in directing the transformation of reality towards the desired end— for example, changing colonial domination into national liberation. If the analysis of the people's present situation and the strategy of how to transform that situation does not lead to improved material conditions, it is incorrect theory and has to be modified. Revolutionary militants, whether in China, Cuba, Mozambique, or Guinea-Bissau, refine their theories by referring back to the concrete realities of their specific situations and reflecting more deeply upon them in the light of their successes and failures.

The rest of this chapter on building freedom in Guinea-Bissau highlights the relation of theory to practice and the importance of theory in the revolutionary struggles of the people of Guinea-Bissau.

A. Colonialism and the Birth of the PAIGC

In a speech given in Conakry to the United Nations Special Committee on Territories Under Portuguese Administration, the PAIGC outlined the meaning of Portuguese presence in Guinea-Bissau this way:

The basic strength of Portuguese colonialism, whether or not assisted by favorable historical circumstances, lies, and has always lain, in its *moral and physical propensity for repressive practices*, based on an absolute refusal to regard the African as a human being.

The cannon and other firearms of the era of discovery and conquest, the palmatoria, the whip, the pistol, the modern rifle, the machine gun, the mortar, bombs of all kinds, including napalm bombs and torture, are the instruments of that strength. The navigators and mariners of former days, the mercenaries, the Captains General, the soldiers of the "pacification," the *chefes do pôsto*, the Administrators, the Governors, the modern colonial troops (army, navy and airforce) and the political police are its agents.

From the time of the slavehunts until the massacres of today, the people of Guinea have been the constant victims of these crimes of Portuguese colonialism:

More than a million Africans were carried off by the slave traders from the Guinea region.

Tens of thousands of Africans in Guinea were killed in the colonial wars of conquest and occupation.

Few adult Africans—the so-called natives—have escaped the palmatoria or the whip.

On August 3rd, 1959, fifty African workers who had gone on strike were massacred on the docks at Pijiguiti (Bissau) . . .

Hardly a day passes, in town or countryside, without the rattle of machine guns, the thud of mortars or the roar of aircraft engaged in the unceasing hunt for nationalists . . .

Quoted in Cabral, *Revolution in Guinea*

The early Portuguese in Guinea were concerned mainly with slaves, a concern that continued for 400 years. Duarte

Pacheco Pereira reported back to Portugal in 1506: "Here you can buy slaves at the rate of six or seven for a horse, even a bad horse; you can also buy gold, though not much . . ." Portuguese built small trading stations along the coast but knew almost nothing about the country, except that its population was hostile to them, until the end of the nineteenth century. When they attempted to settle the territory at that time, they met with determined African resistance.

The Portuguese fought eleven major wars against the peoples of Guinea-Bissau in the period from 1880 to 1915 in order to occupy the colony effectively. Other Portuguese "campaigns of pacification" continued almost yearly until 1936, and even then the Portuguese had only a feeble hold over significant sections of the country. But once Portuguese domination was finally achieved, it meant rapidly worsening living conditions for the people of Guinea-Bissau. Economically, the colony served the direct interests of Portugal which got cheap imports from Guinea-Bissau on extremely favorable terms. Because there were few Portuguese settlers in Guinea-Bissau there was little of the plantation-style forced labor. But, as in Angola and Mozambique, a large segment of the rural population was forced to grow crops for export at fixed prices. The high level of malnutrition in the country under Portuguese rule was largely due to this fact—most families forced to cultivate peanuts for sale could not grow enough crops for their own consumption.

Almost none of the Portuguese profits were reinvested in the country, and the Portuguese provided almost nothing for the African populations' needs. The resulting situation meant that in the 1950s, for example, 600 out of every 1,000 babies born died within one year. Two fifths of the population was afflicted with sleeping sickness and almost everyone suffered from malaria and various forms of dysentery.

There were never more than eleven doctors for the entire rural population, or one doctor for every 100,000 Africans. There was only one hospital outside of the capital city of Bissau, and even that one was primarily for the use of the colonialists.

The educational situation, as we have seen, was similar to that of health: during all the years of Portuguese rule 99 per cent of the population remained illiterate. Throughout the history of Portuguese rule, African living conditions were never improved. Although international pressure forced the Portuguese to liberalize several of their laws (such as those on forced labor), the actual condition of the laborers did not change at all.

Portuguese colonial policy forbade Africans to express any political opinions. No political parties, gatherings, debates, or demonstrations of any kind were allowed. Africans were also forbidden to form trade unions. There was no way open to them to work for reform of these oppressive conditions. Africans were faced with only two alternatives: to accept the foreign domination quiescently or to revolt.

In a speech to the United Nations Special Committee referred to above, the Central Committee of the PAIGC outlined the history of African response to colonial domination in the 1950s:

> Starting in 1953, Africans of Guinea attempted to organize themselves in order to take up, in an orderly manner and by collective action, the defense of their rights and interests (economic, political, moral and cultural) against the injustice, discrimination and despotism of the Portuguese administration. Although they were concerned with the situation of the so-called indigenous masses with which they had close links (principally in the urban areas) they were forced to confine these attempts at organization, at least in appearance, to those Africans who at the time were called *assimilados* or

civilizados. These attempts coincided with the return to Guinea of some Africans who, abroad and for the most part in Europe, had closely followed the evolution of colonial policy and the international situation after the Second World War. In Portugal, they had taken their first steps along the path of "re-Africanization" and development of national consciousness together with African students from other Portuguese colonies.

All these attempts failed in the face of opposition from the administrative authorities, who went so far as to forbid the establishment of a sports and recreational association for Africans. Sensing that something new was occurring that affected the "tranquillity" of the population, especially in Bissão [Bissau], the authorities decided to keep close watch on suspect Africans. However, the vanguard of this nationalist movement (composed primarily of Guinean and Cape Verdian civil servants and business employees) began secretly to mobilize the workers of Bissão into an organization called the Movement for the National Independence of Guinea (MING).

In 1956, all attempts at lawful action having failed and because of the weakness of the MING, this same group of Africans, together with several craftsmen and manual workers, decided to create a clandestine organization of the political party type to carry on the struggle for national liberation. Thus was born, in September of that year, the Partido Africano da Independência da Guiné e Cabo Verde (PAIGC)—African Party for the Independence of Guinea and the Cape Verde Islands— the central organization of the peoples of those colonies in the struggle for national liberation.

Having proclaimed in its manifesto, its intention to create the means necessary to "build peace, happiness and progress" in Guinea and the Cape Verde Islands, the PAIGC defined a minor program of "unity and struggle" and drew up a major program along the following general lines: immediate and total independence;

national unification of Guinea and the Cape Verde Islands; African unification; a democratic and anti-colonialist regime; economic independence, building up the economy and developing production; justice and progress for all; strong national defense with the participation of the people; an independent international policy, in the interests of the nation, Africa, peace and progress of mankind.

Starting in 1958, after overcoming not only the difficulties of building up a clandestine military organization while exposed to the dangers of Portuguese repression, by then reinforced by the active presence of the political police, but also the resistance to be expected in a society in which political organizations had always been forbidden, the PAIGC undertook to broaden the struggle for liberation both in Guinea and in the Cape Verde Islands, limiting itself primarily, however, to the working masses and employees in the urban areas.

The strikes of July–August 1959, suppressed by the massacre of the Pijiguiti dock, showed that the course followed [by the PAIGC] until then had been a mistaken one. The urban centers proved to be the stronghold of colonialism, and mass demonstrations and representations were found to be not only ineffectual but also an easy target for the repressive and destructive operations of the colonialist forces.

Quoted in Cabral, *Revolution in Guinea*

The Portuguese massacre of striking African dock workers at Pijiguiti in 1959 marked an important turning point in Guinean resistance to colonial domination. After the massacre the PAIGC re-evaluated its position and strategy and decided to wage war against the Portuguese:

Having reviewed these three past years of clandestine political work [since the foundation of the PAIGC in 1956] and analysed the political situation, the enlarged

meeting of September 19 concluded, in the light of the
Pijiguiti experience and the nature of Portuguese colonialism, that the only way to liberate the country is
through struggle by all possible means including war.

Quoted in Davidson, The Liberation of Guiné

This decision moved the opposition struggle to a qualita-
tively new level and necessitated a new strategy. The
strategy of the PAIGC in the period 1956–59 had been to
create a strong resistance organization (composed mainly
of urban workers) intent on the national liberation of
Guinea-Bissau. The party reasoned that mass demonstrations and other protest would force the Portuguese to de-
colonize the country. Although they were in fact building a
clandestine military organization during this period, the
PAIGC's tactics were not yet aimed at using physical force
to liberate the country.

The basis of the PAIGC's decision to liberate the country
"by all possible means" provides an important example of
how revolutionary groups revise their theories—and their
strategies based on them—in the light of experience. In the
period 1956–59, the PAIGC's efforts had centered on the
organization of laborers in the cities. The inadequacy of
this strategy, culminating in the Pijiguiti massacre, made
the Party reassess its analysis of Portuguese colonialism.
First, the PAIGC realized that colonialism (and the people's
acceptance of it) was much stronger in the cities than they
had believed: people in the cities were under the influence
of Portuguese customs and were often under direct Portuguese control. Second, they saw that they had under-
estimated the amount of force necessary to convince
Portugal to change its colonial policy. Third, the strategy of
organizing mainly in the cities and towns was seen to be
incorrect on the additional grounds that it played into the
hands of Portuguese repression: mass demonstrations

proved to be very easy for the Portuguese to control and suppress. And finally, the PAIGC strategy in this period had left the nine tenths of the population who lived outside the cities and who were not as deeply separated from their cultural roots without an active role in the movement for national liberation.

The PAIGC's two important decisions of 1959—that armed struggle would be necessary and that the struggle could not be organized from the cities—came directly out of the evaluation of their three years' experience in urban organizing and from their subsequent reanalysis of the character of Portuguese colonialism. But how was the war to be fought, and what role would the different parts of the population play in it? The answer to these questions of strategy rested on an all-inclusive analysis of the characteristics of Guinean society.

B. Critical Analysis: Organizing the Struggle

Movements for national and social liberation, revolutionaries believe, develop out of their unique historical settings. The theoretical component of each struggle must therefore be grounded in the specific characteristics of the individual society. Analysis of the make-up of the society is a crucial part of revolutionary theory, for strategy stands or falls on how people are disposed toward the struggle for self-government and liberation.

"Critical analysis" is the term we will use for the process of examining the disposition of different social groupings toward directed social change in their societies. The socioeconomic position of a group of people in society is the most important category of such an analysis, for it determines the greatest part of the group's material living conditions and the degree of control it exercises over the direction of its own life. Most societies are stratified into *classes* of differing economic position. In industrial societies, the class of people who own the factories, banks, and the other means of producing the wealth of the society is called the bourgeoisie or capitalist class. Wage laborers—people who work in factories, for example, and who have no share in the ownership of industry—comprise the class called the proletariat. A third class is the petty bourgeoisie, which is made up mainly of civil servants, salespeople, and shopkeepers.

In most of the underdeveloped countries of the world, however, only a small percentage of the population can be classified as bourgeoisie or proletariat. In Guinea-Bissau, for example, almost nine tenths of the population are peasants. But peasant farmers definitely do have socioeconomic interests individually and as a group, and this is what is important for the leaders of a movement for social change to determine. People's individual or collective material interests are usually strong influences on the way they act.

The economic dynamics explained by a *class* analysis are fundamental, but a comprehensive analysis of a society's structure must take other factors into account. In an important theoretical statement, PAIGC Secretary General Cabral explained the matter this way:

> In the thorough analysis of social structure which every liberation movement should be capable of making in relation to the imperatives of the struggle, the cultural characteristics of each group in society have a place of prime importance. For, while the culture has a mass character, it is not uniform, it is not equally developed in all sectors of society. The attitude of each social group toward the liberation struggle is dictated by its economic interests, but it is also influenced profoundly by its culture. It may even be admitted that these differences in cultural levels explain differences in behavior toward the liberation movement on the part of individuals who belong to the same socio-economic group.

"National Liberation and Culture," speech
at Syracuse University, February 1970

Experience has shown the PAIGC that loyalties or antagonism among ethnic groups, religious beliefs, and cultural practices often have a significant bearing on people's disposition to accept or reject social change. In some feudal societies, for example, social organization and custom compels people to follow their chiefs in rejecting changes that would materially benefit them in the long run (but would not benefit their chiefs).

To be able successfully to mobilize Guineans to join the struggle, the PAIGC found it necessary to know in detail the traditions, interests, and discontents of all the different groups of the population. They accordingly made an assessment of the interests of the different groups as determined by their relative wealth or poverty, their relative political power or impotence vis-à-vis both Portuguese rule and their traditional social organization. PAIGC Secretary General Cabral emphasized the importance of this analysis of the social structure in the actual direction of the struggle:

> You [the reader] will understand that this [very brief analysis of the general situation in Guinea] has no value unless it is related to the actual struggle. In outline, the methodological approach we have used has been as follows: first, the position of each group must be defined—to what extent and in what way does each group depend on the colonial regime? Next we have to see what position they adopt towards the national liberation struggle. Then we have to study their nationalist capacity and lastly, envisaging the post-independence period, their revolutionary capacity.
>
> Cabral, *Revolution in Guinea*

The leaders of the PAIGC relied heavily on this critical analysis in their attempt to involve Guinea's large rural population in the struggle for national liberation.

1. ARE THE PEASANTS REVOLUTIONARY?

The Guinean's struggle for national liberation did not pass to the stage of armed revolt until January 1963. But the more than three years between the party's decision to wage war and organize the rural population in 1959 and the start of the actual fighting were absolutely crucial to the PAIGC's later military and political success. They were years of mobilizing peasant discontent with Portuguese rule into a functioning revolutionary organization.

It was evident that any successful revolutionary effort in Guinea-Bissau would have to involve the country's rural population, which was over 90 per cent of the total. The question was how. The attitudes of the population were so complex that the actual task of developing a strategy out of an analysis of the society had to proceed with caution. Should the peasants be organized first because they were the most exploited group and the majority of the population?

> Obviously, the group with the greatest interest in the struggle is the peasantry, given the nature of the various different societies in Guinea (feudal, semi-feudal, etc.) and the various degrees of exploitation to which they are subjected; but the question is not simply one of objective interest.
>
> Given the general context of our traditions, or rather the superstructure created by the economic conditions in Guinea, the Fula peasants have a strong tendency to follow their chiefs. Thorough and intensive effort was therefore needed to mobilise them. The groups without any defined form of state organization [i.e., no definite social hierarchy] put up much more resistance against the Portuguese than the others and they have maintained intact their tradition of resistance to colonial penetration. This is the group we found most ready to accept the idea of national liberation.
>
> Cabral, *Revolution in Guinea*

The point here is that even overt exploitation or oppression may not be enough to mobilize certain groups to revolutionary action—especially when political or cultural traditions encourage acceptance of present conditions. A further complexity is that even among the parts of the population in favor of national liberation, the levels of commitment to the struggle may vary widely. It is clearly crucial to involve the most committed people in the most active and demanding parts of the campaign—and, similarly, not to challenge the more reluctant people before they are ready. The PAIGC's analysis of the revolutionary potential of the peasantry shows this concern:

> Here I [Cabral] should like to broach one key problem, which is of enormous importance for us, as we are a country of peasants, and that is the problem of whether or not the peasantry represents the main revolutionary force. I shall confine myself to my own country, Guinea, where it must be said at once that the peasantry is not a revolutionary force—which may seem strange, particularly as we have based the whole of our armed liberation struggle on the peasantry. A distinction must be drawn between physical force and a revolutionary force; physically, the peasantry is a great force in Guinea: it is almost the whole of the population, it controls the nation's wealth, it is the peasantry which produces; but we know from experience what trouble we had convincing the peasantry to fight . . . All the same, in certain parts of the country and among certain groups we found a very warm welcome, even right at the start. In other groups and in other areas all this had to be won.

> Cabral, *Revolution in Guinea*

This all-important judgment that the peasantry could not be the leaders of the movement for national liberation was the result not just of knowledge of the peasants' socioeconomic situation, but of the experience of trying to mobilize them. And it was the same with the work of moving people to take revolutionary action: the PAIGC's strategy here began with detailed knowledge of the characteristics of the population but was refined only in the course of talking with the people.

Winning a commitment to national liberation struggle from the Guinean peasantry depended partly on knowing how to approach them—knowing not just how to speak to their needs, but how to do it in a way acceptable to their individual traditions. The party leaders, and especially Cabral, knew how to speak to the different groups of peasants in the country because of having lived among them and observed them intensively. Cabral, who spent the years 1952–54 taking an agricultural census for the Portuguese, used that opportunity to get to know the traditions, the interests, and discontents of most of the different rural groups of the country. When it came time to train people to go among the peasants to do the political work of convincing them to fight against the Portuguese, Cabral had an analysis, developed from precise information, to direct his instruction of the cadres. Antônio Bana, one of hundreds of PAIGC political workers (cadres), describes learning the strategy of winning peasant support:

> We were sent into the countryside (in 1960, in this case) to mobilize the peasants. We used to make contact with the elders, the *homems grandes*. They were the men with influence, and afterwards they talked to the others. Portuguese oppression was bad enough for them to take us seriously, we young men, when we talked to them of independence; and they listened to us. We explained what the Party was. The Balante were the worst oppressed: they were the ones who had to build the roads. They understood us more quickly than the others.
>
> For the mobilization, Cabral used to make us play a

scene. In his presence, each of us had to pretend he was
going into a village and talking to an elder. While each
of us was doing this, the others listened. If we got it
wrong, if it didn't work, Cabral made us begin again
until we'd found the right arguments to use. Sometimes
we had to do this several times over.

Before going into a village to meet the elder, we asked
for information about him. You had to be very careful.
You found out about his everyday life, his standing in
the village, his relations with the Portuguese. At the
beginning we didn't go into villages where the elders
were hostile . . .

So you go into a village after finding out about the
elder, the *homme grande,* the man who has moral authority in the village; and you're dressed as a peasant.
First of all, I ask for the elder. Then I greet him and
ask for hospitality. The Balante are very hospitable. The
elder answers my greetings and shouts for food to be
prepared.

When the food arrives, I look at what they've brought.
It's rare they bring rice or chicken. If there's only rice
with palmoil sauce, I say to the elder:

"Father, why do you give me only rice? The Balante
are a hospitable people."

"I'm a poor man. No chickens."

"But how's that, father? You've been working all your
life and you haven't even a single cock in your yard?"

"My son, why ask such things. I used to have cows,
lambs too, but the whites have taken them for tax."

"And does it suit you, father, what the whites are
doing?"

"It doesn't suit me. But what can I do? They're too
strong."

So far I've been getting an idea about what the old
man is like. He's already told me that he doesn't like
the colonialists. But I have asked no big questions, I've
said nothing important yet. Now I go a bit further.

"Father, if by chance there's something that could give

you a better life tomorrow, would you be in favour of it?"

"I would be in favour."

"Well then, think about it. For now we have a Party that fights the Portuguese so we can be free and so you can keep what you get by your work. If you have a son or daughter, the Party will send him or her to school. But keep the secret of this, for if the Portuguese find out they'll kill you. That doesn't mean you can't talk to other people about it. But only talk to people you can trust. Me, for instance, I've trust in you, father, and that's why I came to talk to you . . ."

Then I leave after telling him that I want to meet the trustworthy people of the village in a quiet place, and talk with them . . .

The second time I meet them, the elder has called the trustworthy people . . . and I ask them to question me on what I've told the elder. Often they'll say:

"We're blacks, we don't even know how to make a safety-match. The whites have guns, aeroplanes. However can we get rid of them? . . ."

Quoted in Davidson, *The Liberation of Guiné*

Thousands of such discussions were necessary before armed struggle could begin. Sala N'tonton, a PAIGC soldier, tells how he was convinced to join:

I was a farmer [Balante, from Quinara in the central area of Guiné], and our village was a poor one. We'd pigs and chickens. The Portuguese bought these, but they gave us bad prices. We had to pay a lot of taxes without ever seeing the benefit of them . . . Where was the school, the clinic? There weren't any, no matter what taxes we paid. So I joined the Party (in 1963). I wanted to have a hand in putting things right . . .

Yes, before that I'd been in the army, the Portuguese I mean. That was in 1957, maybe I was 20, in Balamo. Two years and six months I served them. They didn't

treat us well. The whites had all the promotion. We
had the dirty jobs. Then I went back to my village and
I stayed there. That was the time that a comrade from
the Party came to our village. He began talking about
how things were and what we had to do to put things
right. I listened to him. I knew he wasn't telling lies.
I know that things were like he said. I'd seen it for myself. I joined the Party after that . . .

Quoted in Davidson, *The Liberation of Guiné*

To assist in the training of cadres to do the political work
of initiating discussions of national liberation among the
Guinean population, the PAIGC started a political school
in Conakry, capital of the neighboring Republic of Guinea.
PAIGC leaders selected people to study both the details of
the social situation under Portuguese rule in Guinea, and
the international setting of their fight against colonialism.
It was at school in Conakry that Antônio Bana learned the
specific situations of most of the ethnic groups of his country and how to mobilize the peasants to break out of those
situations:

I came back more solid, more confident. But now we
began to be hunted by the Portuguese. Repression
started. Some of the people in the villages grew afraid,
others grew rougher: "The Portuguese have killed my
father—or my brother—or my son. The Portuguese are
our enemies, we must fight them." We used the repression to explain what the Portuguese really were. Then
the more violent their repression, the more obvious was
their true face—and they themselves confirmed what we
had said about them.

But of course there were difficulties. Some peasants
said that all this trouble was our fault: that if we'd stayed
quiet they could have lived in peace by paying their
taxes. Cabral told us clearly that we shouldn't think that
the peasants would rise with enthusiasm if we talked

about independence. There was distrust. To meet the
Mandinka you had to dress as a Mandinka: to meet the
Balante as a Balante. You had to watch out for Portuguese agents who would at once betray you. You talked
in a village and then you went out of that village and
slept in the bush.

You had to get yourself known and the Party known.
Little by little the Party sympathizers in the village
would come into the bush with food for you. Later you
could hold village meetings in the bush: talk to them,
explain the struggle, ask for their help. After a while
there were those who were with the Party and others who
sympathized—then the neutrals and the suspects. Little
by little, you had to find a way, thanks to the determined
ones, of getting amongst the neutrals and the suspects
and seeing that they did us no harm.

The mobilization was far more difficult than the war
itself . . .

Quoted in Davidson, *The Liberation of Guiné*

2. CLASS INTERESTS AND REVOLUTIONARY POTENTIAL

One part of the PAIGC's strategy of how to organize the
war came out of an analysis of the peasants' social and economic position in Guinea-Bissau and was further developed
by the actual work of mobilizing the rural population. It
proved possible to move some peasants to fight the Portuguese and to move others to at least support the fighters.
But if the theory that the peasantry was not the main revolutionary force in Guinea-Bissau was correct, who would
lead the struggle?

The work of mobilizing the rest of the population also
began with a careful study of its socioeconomic character
and revolutionary potential. The PAIGC considers this
analytical work as the foundation of the action of the struggle. It is vital because the success or failure of the revolution

—life and death—depend on the workability of the strategy that comes from it.

Then there are the positions vis-à-vis the struggle of the various groups in the towns to be considered. The Europeans are, in general, hostile to the idea of national liberation; they are the human instruments of the colonial state in our country and they therefore reject a priori any idea of national liberation there. It has to be said that the Europeans most bitterly opposed to the idea of national liberation are the workers, while we have sometimes found considerable sympathy for our struggle among certain members of the European petty bourgeoisie.

As for the Africans, the petty bourgeoisie can be divided into three sub-groups as regards the national liberation struggle. First, there is the petty bourgeoisie which is heavily committed and compromised with colonialism: this includes most of the higher officials and some members of the liberal professions. Second, there is the group which we perhaps incorrectly call the revolutionary petty bourgeoisie: this is the part of the petty bourgeoisie which is nationalist and which was the source of the idea of the national liberation struggle in Guinea. In between lies the part of the petty bourgeoisie which has never been able to make up its mind between the national liberation struggle and the Portuguese. Next comes the wage-earners, which you can compare roughly with the proletariat in European societies, although they are not exactly the same thing: here too, there is a majority committed to the struggle, but, again, many members of this group were not easy to mobilize—wage earners who had an extremely petty-bourgeois mentality and whose only aim was to defend the little they had already acquired.

Next comes the déclassés. The really déclassé people, the permanent layabouts, the prostitutes and so on, have been a great help to the Portuguese police in giving

them information: this group has been outrightly against
our struggle, perhaps unconsciously so, but nonetheless
against our struggle. On the other hand, the particular
group I mentioned earlier, for which we have not yet
found any precise classification (the group of mainly
young people recently arrived from the rural areas with
contacts in both the urban and the rural areas), gradually comes to make a comparison between the standard
of living of their own families and that of the Portuguese; they begin to understand the sacrifices being
borne by the Africans. They have proved extremely
dynamic in the struggle right from the beginning and it
is among the group that we found many of the cadres
whom we have since trained.

Cabral, *Revolution in Guinea*

The people who took the leadership of the liberation
struggle were able to get a perspective on the exploitation
of their people by comparing the position of Africans and
Europeans in the towns. It is important to notice that most
of the "revolutionary petty bourgeoisie" Cabral speaks of
here were relatively new to urban colonial experience. This
meant that on the one hand their ties to their rural African
culture were stronger, while on the other hand their ties to
the more Europeanized urban African culture were weaker
than the long-time town dwellers who had been forced to
assimilate some degree of Portuguese custom and colonial
mentality. As a result, this group was more readily able to
see not just the Portuguese exploitation of labor, but also
the repression of African culture in favor of a European one.

The PAIGC found that it was not just exploitation that
produced revolutionary consciousness, but rather a specific
social situation that allowed people to compare their living
conditions with those of more privileged classes, especially
the Europeans in the towns.

The importance of this urban experience lies in the fact
that it allows comparison: this is the key stimulant required for the awakening of consciousness. As far as
Guinea is concerned, the idea of the national liberation
struggle was born in our own country, in a milieu where
people were subjected to close and incessant exploitation. Many people say it is the peasants who carry the
burden of exploitation: this may be true, but so far as
the struggle is concerned it must be realized that it is
not the degree of suffering and hardship involved as
such that matters: even extreme suffering in itself does
not necessarily produce the *prise de conscience* required
for the national liberation struggle. In Guinea the peasants are subjected to a kind of exploitation equivalent
to slavery; but even if you try and explain to them that
they are being exploited and robbed, it is difficult to
convince them by means of an unexperienced explanation of a technico-economic kind that they are the most
exploited people; whereas it is easier to convince the
workers and the people employed in the towns who
earn, say, 10 escudos a day for a job in which a European
earns between 30 and 50 escudos that they are being
subjected to massive exploitation and injustice, because
they can see. To take my own case, as a member of the
petty-bourgeois group which launched the struggle in
Guinea, I was an agronomist working under a European
who everybody knew was one of the biggest idiots in
Guinea; I could have taught him his job with my eyes
shut but he was the boss: this is something which counts,
this is the confrontation which really matters. This is of
major importance when considering where the initial
idea of the struggle came from.

                              Cabral, *Revolution in Guinea*

   In the work of determining how to structure the liberation struggle,

another major task was to examine the material interests
and the aspirations of each group after the liberation, as
well as their revolutionary capacities. As I have already
said, we do not consider that the peasantry in Guinea
has a revolutionary capacity. First of all, we had to make
an analysis of all these groups and of the contradictions
between them and within them so as to be able to locate
them all vis-à-vis the struggle and the revolution.

The first point is to decide what is the major contradiction at the moment when the struggle begins. For us
the main contradiction was that between, on the one
hand, the Portuguese and international bourgeoisie
which was exploiting our people and, on the other hand,
the interests of our people.

Cabral, *Revolution in Guinea*

Cabral uses the term "contradiction" here to help explain the dynamics of the social situation in Guinea-Bissau.
By "contradiction," he means an opposition or point of tension between social groupings. Because the interests of the
Portuguese colonialists are opposed to the interests of the
African people of Guinea-Bissau, for example, there is a
contradiction between them. If a contradiction tends toward the disunity of the social whole, it is called an
"antagonistic contradiction." Antagonistic contradictions
develop around structural weaknesses in society and lead,
through worsening conditions, to some restructuring of
relations between different social interests. If the clash of
opposing interests and forces can be identified, the necessary resolution or restructuring can perhaps be directed toward social progress.

Identifying contradictions is an important part of
strategy. Existing points of conflict in a society can often
be built on to achieve a desired end. For example, in a semifeudal society the difference between the interests of the
people and those of their chiefs can be used to mobilize the

people to build a more egalitarian society. If, on the other hand, existing points of tension are not identified and accommodated in some way, they can lead, through worsening conditions, to uncontrollable situations fatal to the emerging revolutionary society. In the case of Guinea-Bissau, the PAIGC clearly realized that the Portuguese were not the only source of exploitation:

There are also major contradictions within the country itself, i.e., in the internal life of our country. It is our opinion that if we get rid of colonialism in Guinea, the main contradiction remaining, the one which will then become the principal contradiction, is that between the ruling classes, the semifeudal groups, and the members of the groups without any defined form of organization. There are other contradictions, such as that between the various feudal groups and that between the upper and lower. All this is extremely important for the future, and even while the struggle is still going on we must begin to exploit the contradictions (for example) between the Fula people and their chiefs who are very close to the Portuguese.

There are other contradictions which we consider secondary: you may be surprised to know that we consider the contradictions between the tribes a secondary one; we could discuss this at length, but we consider that there are many more contradictions between what you might call the economic tribes in the capitalist countries than there are between the ethnic tribes in Guinea. Our struggle for national liberation and the work done by the Party have shown this contradiction is really not so important; the Portuguese counted on it a lot but as soon as we organized the liberation struggle properly the contradiction between the tribes proved to be a feeble, secondary contradiction.

That, in brief, is the analysis we have made of the situation; this has led us to the following conclusion: we

must try to unite everybody in the national liberation
struggle against the Portuguese colonialists; this is where
our main contraction lies, but it is also imperative to
organize things so that we always have an instrument
available which can solve all the other contradictions.
This is what convinces us of the absolute necessity of
creating a party during the national liberation struggle.

Quoted in Cabral, *Revolution in Guinea*

C. Critical Analysis: The Goals of Liberation

1. INDEPENDENCE DOES NOT MEAN LIBERATION

The PAIGC defines its movement as a struggle for national
liberation rather than just for political independence from
colonial rule. This definition is based on an analysis of the
dynamics of the Guinean social situation.

Who will govern the country after the achievement of
political independence? If the goal of the national struggle
is just to end the exploitation of the people by the Portuguese, this all-important question may be ignored during
the anti-colonial campaign. It cannot be simply presumed
that the end of colonial exploitation will also be the end of
social inequality in the country.

The experiences of many African countries which became
independent in the 1950s and 1960s show this clearly. Most
of these countries are now governed by small classes of
elites who enjoy considerable privileges at the expense of
the bulk of the population. Many of these same countries
are economically dependent on the former colonial powers
and thus do not yet have full control of their own resources
or the direction of their own development.

National liberation, on the other hand, is specifically
aimed at putting the entire population of a country in control of its own resources, thus ending the exploitation of
some people in the society by others. Cabral explained

this clearly in a talk he gave, sometime in 1966, to a group of peasants inside Guinea-Bissau:

> There is no point to our struggle if our only goal is to drive out the Portuguese. We want to drive them out, but we are also struggling to end the exploitation of our people, both by whites and by blacks . . . As far as we're concerned, no one has the right to exploit labor . . . You were working for the chiefs and the Portuguese. We're going to recover our whole country and work hard in it, but the beneficiaries of this work will be the workers themselves.
>
> Quoted in Chaliand, *Armed Struggle in Africa*

Thus the PAIGC is involved in an essentially political struggle to transform the country rather than a solely military fight to destroy colonialism.

This political struggle involves the awareness that most of the populations of the African countries that became independent without undergoing any social transformation are rarely better off materially now than they were under colonial rule. This problem centers around the elites that now govern these countries. Most of these elites came from the class called the petty bourgeoisie; they had been small shop owners, merchants, civil servants, and petty administrative officials. They were usually the best off of all the indigenous African classes. As in most underdeveloped countries, the real owners of the factories, mines, and plantations (and other means of producing the country's internationally exchangeable wealth) were the colonizers. When the colonial administrators and big wealth-holders withdrew, the class left to assume administration of the country was the petty bourgeoisie.

In fact, many of these new social elites have become representatives of the mother country's business interests in the now "independent" countries. These people, compro-

mised with status and relative affluence, usually find it in
their interest to oppose any transformation of society
toward more social equality or more democratic government.

This system that allows the former colonial powers and
other developed countries to maintain significant interests
in the economies of independent underdeveloped countries
through the co-operation of an indigenous class has been
described as neo-colonialism. The PAIGC specifically identified the possible evolution of a neo-colonial situation in
Guinea-Bissau as a problem to be programmatically
avoided. The PAIGC's emphasis on village self-government
and on the creation of an economy based on People's Shops
is partly in response to the danger of this problem.

It was not just the experience of other underdeveloped
countries that led the PAIGC to formulate its anti-
neo-colonial strategy. The strategy also came out of the
party's analysis of the position and function of the petty-
bourgeois class in Guinean society. Because of their relative
affluence and their proximity (in many cases) to the Portuguese colonialists, the PAIGC reasoned, the people of this
class could not as a whole be counted on to continue to work
for the transformation of the country after the achievement
of political independence. And of course it was the actual
practice of trying to mobilize this class to join the national
liberation struggle that further developed the party's theory
here: although there were significant exceptions, the petty
bourgeoisie as a class was not strongly committed to carrying out the revolution.

2. THE ECONOMIC BASIS OF LIBERATION

The PAIGC asserts that true political and cultural freedom
will be achieved only when *all* the people of the country,
not just a class or social elite, have a say in the development
of the resources of the country. More specifically, they are

insisting that the entire population must democratically control the country's *forces of production*—the means by which the wealth of the country is produced.

In Guinea-Bissau most of the people are farmers, and almost all of the country's wealth comes from agriculture. The wealth of many other underdeveloped countries (such as Libya, for example) comes from extracted minerals or oil. In industrialized countries like the United States or the Soviet Union, factories are the main forces of production, and most of those countries' wealth comes from industrial operations. The historical evolution of a nation or people, their culture and living conditions, are directly shaped by the level of development of the nation's productive forces.

Foreign domination, whether directed from the mother country or mediated through an indigenous elite of administrators, exerts control on the country's economic activity and therefore stops or diverts that people's free historical development. In a speech titled "The Weapon of Theory" delivered in Havana in 1966, PAIGC Secretary General Cabral summed up this point:

> . . . The violent usurpation of the freedom of the process of development of the productive forces of the dominated socio-economic whole constitutes the principal and permanent characteristic of imperialist domination, whatever its form. We have also seen that this freedom alone can guarantee the normal development of the historical process of a people. We can therefore conclude that national liberation exists only when the national productive forces have been completely freed from every kind of foreign domination.
>
> Cabral, *Revolution in Guinea*

But even in an independent national state, questions of freedom and exploitation are still crucial. Assessment of these conditions will always involve determination of people's relationship to the control of the country's productive forces.

In Guinea-Bissau the wealth produced by agriculture (essentially what was left after the subsistence needs of the people were met) was long controlled by the Portuguese and/or the chiefs or ruling elites of the different ethnic groups. The Portuguese took away almost all autonomy and forced the cultivation of certain crops. But even in their traditional societies most Guineans were prevented from using the wealth created by their labor for common social progress; providing for the extra consumption by elites, for example, cornered resources that might have been used for education or for raising the living standard of the entire population. Now the PAIGC has organized the struggle in Guinea-Bissau so that the war for national liberation from Portuguese rule is also a struggle to enable the workers themselves to be the beneficiaries of their own work.

3. CULTURE AND NATIONAL LIBERATION

These two points about the mechanisms of exploitation and the economic basis of liberation are foundation stones in the PAIGC's analysis of the scope of its struggle. This understanding further buttresses the theory that the goal of independence can not be separated from the goal of transforming the society. The goal had to be to put the entire population in democratic control of their resources and development. In his 1970 speech "National Liberation and Culture," Cabral explained:

> The chief goal of the liberation movement goes beyond the achievement of political independence to the superior level of complete liberation of the productive forces and the construction of economic, social and cultural progress of the people.

In Guinea-Bissau this has necessarily been a democratic struggle, both in form and in content. The mobilization of the population to revolutionary action, for example, has proceeded democratically through discussion. The people couldn't be forced to fight a guerrilla war; they made the necessary sacrifices only when they understood the reasons and benefits for doing so. The effect of the mobilization has been to break down social hierarchies and conflicts between ethnic groups in the face of a common enemy. And in place of the traditional social structure that was incapable of being mobilized to fight a national liberation struggle, the PAIGC has instituted (again by discussion and common consent) truly democratic village self-government, the full equality of women, and equal economic and educational rights for all.

In the speech referred to above, Cabral explains why the actual process of fighting the armed liberation struggle must lead to social transformation:

> As we know, the armed liberation struggle requires the mobilisation and organization of a significant majority of the population, the political and moral unity of the various social classes, the efficient use of modern arms and of other means of war, the progressive liquidation of the remnants of tribal mentality and the rejection of social and religious rules and taboos which inhibit development of the struggle (gerontocracies, nepotism, social inferiority of women, rites and practices which are incompatible with the rational and national character of the struggle, etc.). The struggle brings about profound modifications in the life of the populations. The armed liberation struggle implies therefore a veritable forced march along the road to cultural progress.
>
> Consider these features inherent in an armed struggle: the practice of democracy, of criticism and self-criticism, the increasing responsibility of populations for

the direction of their lives, literacy work, creation of schools and health services, training of cadres from peasant and worker backgrounds—and many other achievements. When we consider these features, we see that the armed liberation struggle is not only a product of culture but also a *determinant of culture*. This is without doubt for the people the prime recompense for the efforts and sacrifices which the war demands.

The new life in the liberated zones of Guinea-Bissau and the unique Guinean culture and social liberation being created there have been brought about by careful planning and organization. The detailed theory behind this organization encompasses the international historical context of the struggle as well as the dynamics of the indigenous social structure. But it is artificial to conceive of the theoretical thinking and careful analysis that guide the struggle as separate from the day-to-day prosecution of the war. The theory that guides the war for national liberation comes from action and experience, is tested in action, and is constantly rethought. A social revolution is in the most profound sense a product of praxis.

CONCLUSION

THE WORLD LOOKS AT SOUTHERN AFRICA

The struggle between the forces of White supremacy and the forces of African liberation does not end at the borders of Southern Africa. Every African nation has been drawn into the conflict. In addition, because of the vast resources, market potential, and land area concerned, the major capitalist powers find the conflict in Southern Africa an increasingly important part of their foreign policy.

As the successes of the liberation movements grow, the Western capitalist powers have moved more toward support of South Africa and Portugal. The movements in the Portuguese colonies, through the concrete example of the political, social, and economic institutions that have been set up in the liberated areas, have shown that what they mean by independence is firm control over their own resources and lives. They reject the option of development in which a few at the top make the basic political and economic decisions. Therefore, what is developing in Southern Africa is more than a struggle over employment, wages, or housing conditions. It is instead a question of who will make decisions, in what way, and how these decisions will be implemented.

The overtures by a few United States businesses or "progressive" White South Africans to modify apartheid, or the reforms toward nominal "autonomy" in the Portuguese colonies, are largely responses to the concrete successes of the liberation movements and the growing community around the world which supports them. These are efforts of liberal interests in Portugal, South Africa, and the Western supporting nations to reform the system in order to preserve the existing power relationships. These reformist proposals are a clear rejection of the legitimacy of the efforts of the African people to determine their own destiny.

Western government and corporate powers argue that change is of course necessary and that their continued presence in South Africa will help to "soften" apartheid. But change is not the major question at stake; rather it is *what kind of change*. What the corporations are in fact doing is (1) supporting the governments in power, both financially and politically; (2) attempting, by these piecemeal reforms, to reduce the anger and frustrations of Africans under White rule in Southern Africa; (3) trying to take some of the outside pressures off by showing "world opinion" that change is taking place; and (4) depoliticizing the conflict (both inside and outside South Africa) by diverting it into a discussion of isolated issues—wages, employment opportunities, trade, education, or housing—while avoiding discussion of basic power relationships.

Corporations like IBM, General Motors, Mobil, Gillette, and General Electric are paving their way to prolonged economic investment in South Africa by contributing money to "liberal reforms" in the name of improving conditions. An article in *Fortune* magazine, July 1972, outlined this new corporate strategy for American businesses in South Africa:

> Top managements that want to protect the future of their companies in a changing South Africa will face a

difficult, perhaps painful, task. One important step would be to quit judging local managers solely by the size of their current profit margins. Instead, they should be encouraged to act in the longer-term interest of the company, with power to increase wages and improve the benefits of African workers. In most cases, the profits from the South African operations are so substantial that the increased labor costs would not be overly burdensome—especially since productivity would be likely to improve.

The Nixon administration has taken firm steps to bring American foreign policy closer to support of the White minority regimes of Southern Africa. The White House has warmly endorsed Prime Minister Vorster's "outward policy," even though the South African government has made clear its belief that this policy will strengthen apartheid. There have been a series of relaxations recently in American adherence to the arms embargo. The United States remained silent in 1970 when Britain reversed its own policy on exporting arms to South Africa. The Nixon administration is said to be re-evaluating the strategic importance of South Africa to the American presence in the Indian Ocean, along with the political consequences of acknowledging South Africa more openly as an American ally. There has been some discussion in NATO of admitting South Africa or of setting up a complementary South Atlantic Treaty Organization to include South Africa, Argentina, Brazil, and "Portuguese" Africa.

In his 1970 State of the World message, President Nixon condemned the use of violence on the part of the African people in Southern Africa. Yet in the period following this statement, the Nixon administration made these policy moves affecting that region:

1. Embargoes were ended on the sale of strategic and military equipment to Portugal and South Africa by the

United States. This led to the sale of Boeing 707s and 747s and Bell helicopters to the Portuguese for use in military operations.

2. The United States greatly escalated its sales of herbicides to the Portuguese government. In 1970 alone, Portugal purchased more than $225,000 worth of herbicides.

3. The Azores Pact of December 1971 between the United States and Portugal provides Portugal with $436 million in economic aid from the United States in return for continued use of its air and naval base in the Azores. The base, of questionable military significance, has been occupied for years by the United States without payment.

4. In 1971 the United States Congress effectively ended the ban on the importation of Rhodesian chrome ore which had been part of a United Nations embargo. Within months the first shipments of Rhodesian chrome ore arrived in an American port.

5. The United States agreed in 1970 to allow South Africa to sell its gold to the International Monetary Fund, after a suspension of almost two years. This was an economic victory for South Africa, which was having serious foreign exchange shortages.

6. At the United Nations, the United States has consistently voted against resolutions condemning White supremicist racial policies in Southern Africa. The United States used its veto in the Security Council for the first time in 1970 —to defeat a proposal strengthening the condemnation of Rhodesia.

The United States government is not alone in condemning violence in Southern Africa while at the same time reinforcing the violent rule of White governments there. Other capitalist nations including Great Britain, Japan, Israel, France, and West Germany are bolstering these regimes by providing arms and increased trade and investments.

But as the capitalist powers develop new strategies to reinforce their presence in Southern Africa and continue to endorse the policies of the White-ruled countries, worldwide opposition to these policies is growing. Individuals, groups, and governments have understood that the internationalization of support for White domination in Southern Africa extends responsibility to them. They have taken action to support the African people fighting for liberation and to undermine the forces buttressing minority rule. Much of the military and financial aid to liberation movements comes from socialist countries, primarily the Soviet Union and the People's Republic of China. Increasingly, aid is also coming from organizations and groups in the United States, Canada, and Western Europe. This support takes many forms: The Liberation Support Movement, with offices in the United States and Canada, has sent three shipments equaling about six tons of clothing, technical books, uniforms, and over $10,000 in medical supplies to the MPLA of Angola. They have also sent shipments to Mozambique. In 1971 the World Council of Churches allocated more than $120,000 in aid to the liberation movements. In Holland, the Angola Comité has launched nationwide campaigns to collect food and clothing for the liberation movements. Support groups in England, such as the Committee for Freedom in Mozambique, Angola, and Guiné, have provided material support to the Southern African struggles. These are only a few of the support campaigns which have been initiated over the past years.

At the same time, protests against White domination are increasing, the principal targets being the governments and corporations involved in supporting minority rule in Southern Africa. These protest actions make it more difficult for capitalist interests to aid White rule and they alert public attention to the situation in Southern Africa. A few of these specific actions are listed below.

—The Angola Comité in the Netherlands initiated a successful boycott of Angolan coffee.

—In the United States, boycotts of Gulf Oil and Polaroid products have been organized to protest corporate collaboration with Southern African countries.

—In Louisiana, Black dockworkers refused to unload chrome ore arriving from Rhodesia in 1972 and 1973.

—Throughout the world (and particularly in Great Britain and Australia), there have been countless demonstrations against South African sports teams, which are of course segregated. South Africa has been barred from many international competitions, including the 1972 Olympic Games, because of its racial policies. Rhodesia was ousted from the 1972 Olympics as a result of pressure by African and Black American athletes.

—The World Council of Churches voted in August 1972 to divest itself of all stocks of corporations involved in the Portuguese colonies.

—In spring 1972 the Pan African Liberation Committee, a Black activist group, took over Harvard University's administration building to protest Harvard's investments in Gulf Oil because of Gulf's presence in Angola.

—Also in 1972, 20,000 Black people marched through the streets of Washington, D.C., to express their solidarity with the liberation movements of Africa and to condemn White minority rule. The Pan African Liberation Day Committee raised $22,000 through activities surrounding the march and presented this money to Amilcar Cabral of the PAIGC in the fall of 1972.

Each of these actions has widened the network of people actively concerned with the Western role in the dynamics of domination and liberation in Southern Africa. Of course, the real forces for change in that region are and will continue to be the African people themselves. Whatever happens there affects their lives first. It is they who will determine how best to shape their struggle. At the same time, however, world-wide attention to the future of the region is crucial.

It is of course impossible to foresee the details of the evolution of the situation in Southern Africa. We have only outlined the forces at work in the region, where the growing entrenchment of minority domination rigidly confronts the successes of popular resistance. As in Indochina, the conflict here opposes the needs of capitalist expansion and struggles for self-determination. In this sense, the struggle in Southern Africa is a continuation of the wars in Asia. The sharpening of conflict makes it more and more likely that international political pressures will assume critical importance in determining the future of Southern Africa. It is already certain that whatever happens there will have world-wide repercussions, and, as with the Vietnam war, there will be no way to remain unaffected.

REFERENCES AND SUGGESTIONS FOR
FURTHER READING

Chapter One. South Africa: Life Under
Apartheid

A. *Race Classification and Geographical Segregation*

For documentation of the rights and privileges denied people on the basis of race, see *Apartheid and Racial Discrimination in Southern Africa*, UN OPI/335, United Nations, New York, 1968.

For a detailed breakdown of population and other statistical representations of life in South Africa, see *Facts and Figures on South Africa*, UN No. 7/71, United Nations, New York, 1971. Also see Barbara Rogers, *The Standard of Living of Africans in South Africa*, UN No. 45/71, United Nations, New York, 1971.

For background on the development of geographical segregation, see *Land Ownership in South Africa*, UN No. 40/71, United Nations, New York, 1971; and *'Native Reserves' in South Africa*, UN No. 6/70, United Nations, New York, 1970.

A general study of the "native reserves" is Christopher R. Hill, *Bantustans: The Fragmentation of South Africa*, Oxford University Press, London, 1964. A detailed study of one Bantustan, the Transkei, is Gwendolen M. Carter, Thomas Karis, and Newell M. Stultz, *South Africa's Transkei: The Politics of Domestic Colonialism*, Northwestern University Press, Evanston, 1967.

For a critique of geographical segregation, see Leslie Rubin, *Bantustan Policy: A Fantasy and a Fraud*, UN No. 12/71, United Nations, New York, 1971.

The information on the resettlement camp at Morsgat and other personal accounts of the effects of the resettlement necessitated by apartheid can be found in Cosmos Desmond, *The Discarded People*, Penguin African Library, Harmondsworth, 1971.

A statistical survey of the effects of the pass laws can be found in Muriel Horrell, ed., *A Survey of Race Relations in South Africa, 1968*, South African Institute of Race Relations, Johannesburg, 1969, pp. 159–78.

B. *History of South Africa*

1. *Early History*

For a general and well-documented, readable history, see Monica Wilson and Leonard Thompson, eds., *The Oxford History of South Africa*, Vol. I, Oxford, London, 1969.

2. *The Nineteenth Century*

For a history of White settlement, African resistance, and English-Afrikaner hostility, see the following: Monica Wilson and Leonard Thompson, eds., *The Oxford History of South Africa*, Vol. II, Oxford, London, 1971; H. J. Simons and R. E. Simons, *Class and Colour in South Africa 1850–1950*, Penguin African Library, Harmondsworth, 1969; G. H. L. LeMay, *British Supremacy in South Africa, 1899–1907*, Oxford, London, 1965.

3. *The Twentieth Century*

A good account of the formalization of apartheid and the rise of the Nationalist government is found in Brian Bunting, *The Rise of the South African Reich*, Penguin African Library, Harmondsworth, 1969.

An account of African resistance to White domination in the twentieth century and especially of the formation of the African National Congress (ANC) is Mary Benson, *South Africa: The Struggle for a Birthright*, Penguin African Library, Harmondsworth, 1966.

The ANC's own history of its development in the twentieth century is in *A Short History of South Africa*, African National Congress, London, 1970.

For the biographies of two important South African government figures that reveal much about the development of apartheid, see Alan Paton, *Hofmeyr*, Oxford, Cape Town, 1964; and Alexander Hepple, *Verwoerd*, Penguin, Harmondsworth, 1967.

C. Religion and Apartheid

A survey, with a good section on the support that the Dutch Reformed Church gives to the maintenance of apartheid, is found in Rev. Kenneth N. Carstens, *Church and Race in South Africa*, UN No. 23/71, United Nations, New York, 1971.

D. Signs of Strain in the Policy of Apartheid

A discussion of the effect of apartheid on the South African economy may be found in Sean Gervasi, *Poverty, Apartheid and Economic Growth*, UN No. 30/71, United Nations, New York, 1971.

An outline of the tension between apartheid legislation and economic needs is in Marvine Howe, "Apartheid Attacked on Economic Grounds," New York *Times*, August 4, 1970.

The weekly South African business journal, *The Financial Mail*, consistently complains that apartheid legislation hinders economic development. The lead article in each issue is usually a critique of the government's economic policy, with special attention to the various aspects of apartheid's encumberment of the economy. As representatives of the multinational wing of South Africa's corporate elite, the editors favor some liberalization of certain apartheid laws while still supporting White superiority and White rule. *The Financial Mail*, an excellent source of economic information on South Africa, is indexed and available in libraries in the United States.

E. Industrialization, Labor, and Wages

The relationship of apartheid to South Africa's recent industrialization is discussed, with the help of detailed tables on the structure of the economy, in Sean Gervasi, *Industrialization, Foreign Capital, and Forced Labor in South Africa,* UN ST/PSCA/SER. A/10, United Nations, New York, 1970.

Statistics on wages and employment are available in Ruth First, *Work, Wages and Apartheid,* UN No. 22/70, United Nations, New York, 1970; and Alexander Hepple, *Workers Under Apartheid,* International Defence and Aid Fund, London, 1971. A useful outline of the development of labor legislation in South Africa is found in *Africa Today: A Special Report on American Involvement in the South African Economy,* American Committee on Africa, New York, 1966; available from ACOA.*

F. *Education*

Detailed statistical information on education in South Africa is available annually in Muriel Horrell, ed., *A Survey of Race Relations in South Africa,* Institute of Race Relations, Johannesburg. See also *Apartheid and Education,* UN No. 13/70, United Nations, New York, 1970.

For a study of the development of Bantu education, see Muriel Horrell, ed., *Bantu Education to 1968,* South African Institute of Race Relations, Johannesburg, 1968. For a political analysis of that system, see I. B. Tabata, *Education for Barbarism in South Africa,* Pall Mall Press, London, 1960.

A more general study of education in South Africa can be found in Brian Rose, ed., *Education in Southern Africa,* Collier-Macmillan, London, 1970.

For a detailed study of one aspect of White indoctrination, see F. E. Auerbach, *The Power of Prejudice in South African Education,* Balkema, Cape Town, 1966.

G. *Resistance, Repression, and the Police State*

1. *African Resistance*

The history of African resistance to White invasion and settlement is recounted in Edward Roux, *Time Longer Than Rope: A History of the Black Man's Struggle for Freedom in South*

---

* For the addresses of this and other organizations cited in this bibliography, see list beginning on p. 318.

Africa, University of Wisconsin Press, Madison, 1964. Also see *A Short History of South Africa*, African National Congress, London, 1970.

African resistance to White domination in the twentieth century is documented in Mary Benson, *South Africa: The Struggle for a Birthright*, Penguin African Library, Harmondsworth, 1966. Also in A. J. Luthuli, *Let My People Go*, MacGraw-Hill, New York, 1962. Nelson Mandela, *No Easy Walk to Freedom*, Heinemann, London, 1965, contains speeches, articles, and trial addresses of the African National Congress leader who is now serving a life term of imprisonment on Robben Island in South Africa.

M. P. Naicker, *The Defiance Campaign Recalled*, UN No. 11/72, United Nations, New York, 1972, relates the main events and political significance of one specific resistance campaign.

The Freedom Charter, UN No. Special, 1970, is an important document in the history of African people's struggle in South Africa.

Govan A. N. Mbeki, *South Africa: The Peasant's Revolt*, Penguin, Baltimore, 1964, is an account of rural resistance to White rule. Accounts of more recent African resistance can be found in "Southern Africa: A Smuggled Account from a Guerrilla Fighter," *Ramparts*, October 1969; and in *South African Studies I: Guerrilla Warfare*, African National Congress, London, 1970.

2. Repressive Legislation

The Suppression of Communism Act is outlined in considerable detail in *Repressive Legislation in South Africa*, UN ST/PSCA/SER. A/7, United Nations, New York, 1968.

The "Terrorism Act" is outlined in *South Africa's "Terrorism Act,"* UN No. 18/70, United Nations, New York, 1970.

3. Government Control

Statistical information on detentions and trials under the security laws and other information on the government's control of persons is found annually in Muriel Horrell, ed., *A Survey of Race Relations in South Africa*, South African Institute of Race Relations, Johannesburg. See also Patrick Duncan, *South Africa's Rule of Violence*, Methuen, London, 1964.

Information on the capability and preparedness of South Africa's military and police forces is available in *Military and Police Forces in the Republic of South Africa*, UN ST/PSCA/ SER. A/3 and A/AC 115/L. 203–204, United Nations, New York, 1967, as well as in Abdul S. Minty, *South Africa's Defense Strategy*, Anti-Apartheid Movement, London, 1969.

H. *General Sources*

Ernest Cole, *House of Bondage*, Random House, New York, 1967, is a powerful photo essay on the everyday realities of apartheid.

William Frye, *In Whitest Africa: The Dynamics of Apartheid*, Prentice-Hall, Englewood Cliffs, N.J., 1968, is a noted journalist's account of his visit to South Africa.

Two African autobiographical accounts are Bloke Modisane, *Blame Me on History*, Dutton, New York, 1963, and Ezekiel Mphahlele, *Down Second Avenue*, Faber & Faber, London, 1959.

South African Writing Today, Penguin African Library, Harmondsworth, 1967, is a collection of short stories, poems, and essays written by White and Black South Africans.

Chapter Two. Life Under Portuguese Colonialism

A. *Historical Background*

For general histories of the Portuguese presence in Africa, see Ronald H. Chilcote, *Portuguese Africa*, Prentice-Hall, Englewood Cliffs, N.J., 1967, and James Duffy, *Portugal in Africa*, Penguin African Library, Baltimore, 1963.

For background information on history, culture, and geography with maps, see David M. Abshire, and Michael A. Samuels, eds., *Portuguese Africa: A Handbook*, Part I, Praeger, New York, 1969.

For a historical account of colonial Mozambique, see Eduardo Mondlane, *The Struggle for Mozambique*, Penguin African Library, Harmondsworth, 1969.

For a historical account of Portuguese colonialism in Angola, see David Birmingham, *The Portuguese Conquest of Angola*, Oxford, London, 1965.

For a historical account of Portuguese policy under Salazar, see A. de Oliveira, "Salazar's Portugal," in *Angola: A Symposium*, Institute of Race Relations, London, 1962.

Perry Anderson, "Portugal and the end of Ultracolonialism," *New Left Review*, 15, 16, and 17, 1962.

B. *Economic and Political Relations*

For background information on the government and economy of the Portuguese colonies, see Abshire and Samuels, eds., op. cit., Parts II and III.

Facts and Reports, a biweekly summary of news clippings, is published by the Angola Comité, in Amsterdam, providing valuable information on political and economic developments in Portugal and the colonies.

For an examination of Portuguese economic and political policies in Mozambique, see Mondlane, op. cit.

For a collection of papers examining the case for and against Portuguese policy with particular emphasis on Angola, see *Angola: A Symposium*.

C. *Social Relations*

For a general survey of social relations, see Michael A. Samuels, and Norman A. Bailey, "Education, Health, and Social Welfare," in Abshire and Samuels, eds., op. cit. See also Mondlane, op. cit.; and James Duffy, *Portuguese Africa*, Harvard University Press, Cambridge, 1961, esp. chs. 12 and 13.

D. *Resistance*

For a more detailed bibliography, see listings for Chapters Seven, Eight, and Nine.

The following are short introductions to the situation at present: Ruth First, *Portugal's Wars in Africa*, International Defense and Aid Fund, London, 1971; and *War on Three Fronts*, Committee for Freedom in Mozambique, Angola and Guiné, London, 1972.

E. *General*

For general facts and information about Portuguese colonialism in brief form, see "Portugal in Africa: Information Sheet," available from the American Committee on Africa.

Chapter Three. *Portugal and the West*

A. *Portugal's Dilemma*

1. *General Sources*

Information on the internal Portuguese economy and its relations to the colonial wars can be found in the following:

For an excellent overview of Western involvement in Portuguese colonies, see William Minter, *Portuguese Africa and the West*, Penguin African Library, Harmondsworth, 1972.

Portuguese and Colonial Bulletin is a monthly bulletin of facts and analysis of domestic and international dimensions of Portuguese policy; available from K. Shingler, 10 Fentiman Road, London S.W.8.

Quarterly Economic Review: Supplement (*Portugal and the Overseas Provinces*), Economist Intelligence Unit, 1969, contains statistics and analyses of the economies of Portugal and the colonies examined by sector. (The Economist Intelligence Unit issues these reviews periodically.)

Portugal, 1970: Capitalist Strategy, Workers Offensive and Colonial Wars is a monograph on the colonial wars considered in the perspective of Portugal's domestic economy and class struggle; available from Philadelphia Solidarity, c/o S.C.C., PO Box 13011, Philadelphia, Pa. 19150.

See also Research Group for the Liberation of Portuguese Africa, *Dependency and Underdevelopment Consequences of Portugal in Africa*, University of California, Riverside, Calif., 1971.

A news analysis of Portugal's dilemma in late 1971 can be found in Hugh O'Shaughnessy, "War and Emigration a Drain on Resources," *Financial Times* (London), November 19, 1971.

See also Eduardo de Sousa Ferreira, "The Government of Marcelo Caetano and the Role of the Colonies in the Portuguese Economy," in *Portuguese Colonialism from South Africa to Europe* (1972), available from the Committee for Freedom in Mozambique, Angola and Guiné, London.

2. The Portuguese Position and Colonial Policy

A recent policy statement is contained in a speech delivered by Portuguese Premier Marcelo Caetano, "Portugal Belongs to Us All: We All Go to Make Up Portugal," September 27, 1970, available from the Portuguese Ministry of Information, Lisbon.

See also *The Growing Economy of Portugal,* Overseas Companies of Portugal, available from Overseas Companies of Portugal, Rua Victor Cordon 36–1, Lisbon, Portugal; and *Opportunity in Portugal,* Overseas Companies of Portugal, of the same address.

B. Western Involvement in the Colonies

1. Trade and Investments

The following are general sources of statistics and economic analysis: *International Financial News Survey* (weekly) is available from the International Monetary Fund, 19th and H Streets, Washington, D.C. 20431. *Quarterly Economic Review: Supplement (Portugal and the Overseas Provinces),* Economist Intelligence Unit, 1969; available from The Economist, 27 St. James's Place, London S.W.1. *Standard Bank Review* (monthly) is available from the Standard Bank Ltd., 52 Wall Street, New York, N.Y. 10005. *Overseas Business Reports* are available on individual countries from U. S. Department of Commerce.

See also Eduardo de Sousa Ferreira, "The Development of the Portuguese Economy and International Capital in Portugal and the Colonies," in *Portuguese Colonialism from South Africa to Europe.*

2. Western Involvement, By Country

(a) United States involvement

A comprehensive analysis of U. S. investments, trade, and military aid in Portuguese Africa, with a list of American corporations in Angola and Mozambique, can be found in "Allies in Empire: The U.S. and Portugal in Africa," in *Africa Today,* Vol.

17, No. 4 (July–August), 1970; available from the American Committee on Africa.

A news analysis of recent developments in U. S.–Portuguese relations is "Pact with Portugal Aids Colonial Wars," *American Report*, December 24, 1971.

A listing of U. S. corporate involvement can be found in "U.S. Corporate Subsidiaries and Affiliates," Report of the Special Study Mission on Southern Africa, Hon. Charles C. Diggs, Jr., August 10–30, 1969; available from the U. S. Government Printing Office.

(b) *German involvement*

Eduardo de Sousa Ferreira, "Development of the West German Economy and Its Interests in Portugal and the Colonies," in *Portuguese Colonialism from South Africa to Europe*.

(c) *British involvement*

The most recent, comprehensive study is *British Economic Involvement in Portugal, Angola, Mozambique and Guiné* (1972) available from the Committee for Freedom in Mozambique, Angola and Guiné, London.

(d) *French involvement*

"La France et l'Afrique Australe," *Revue Française d'études politiques Africaines*, December 1970.

(e) *South African involvement*

See listings for Chapter Four.

3. *Case Studies of Western Involvement*

Two analyses of NATO involvement are S. J. Bosgra, and Chr. van Krimpen, *Portugal and NATO*, Angola Comité, Amsterdam, 1967; and "NATO and Africa," *The Nationalist* (Tanzania), May 6, 1971.

The involvement of Gulf Oil Company has been documented in Committee of Returned Volunteers, *Gulf Oil: A Study in Exploitation* (1970), available from the Dayton Gulf Boycott Coalition, Box 123, Dayton View Station, Dayton, Ohio 45406. See also "Cabinda Successes Encourage Further Oil Exploration," *Financial Times* (London), July 19, 1971.

The two major hydroelectric projects, the Cunene River project and the Cabora Bassa dam have been researched and documented in the following: *Cunene Dam Scheme* (1971), available from the World Council of Churches, 150 Route de Ferney, 1211 Geneva 20, Switzerland; Eduardo de Sousa Ferreira, "Namibia and the Cunene Project in Angola," in *Portuguese Colonialism from South Africa to Europe;* "Où vont les diamants d'Angola?", *AfricAsia,* December 21, 1970–January 3, 1971; *Cabora Bassa and the Struggle for Southern Africa* (1971), available from the World Council of Churches; Eduardo de Sousa Ferreira, "Cabora Bassa as a Test Case," in *Portuguese Colonialism from South Africa to Europe.*

C. *General Sources of Information on Portugal and the West*

See listings for Chapter Two, especially *Facts and Reports,* Angola Comité.

Chapter Four. *Apartheid Takes the Offensive: The Regionalization of Southern Africa*

A. *Military Regionalization*

Some examples of South Africa's military interventions to ensure the security of a White-controlled Southern African bloc are related in Douglas Brown, *Against the World,* Doubleday, Garden City, N.Y., 1968, Chap. 10.

More recent details can be obtained from South African newspapers and sometimes from U. S. newspapers, e.g., "South African Police Chase Guerrillas into Zambia," Boston *Globe,* October 8, 1971.

B. *Economic Regionalization*

Details on trade between South Africa and the rest of Africa, including tabular information on the emergence of a Southern African economic bloc, can be found in Sean Gervasi, *Industrialization, Foreign Capital and Forced Labor in South Africa,* UN ST/PSCA/SEP. A/10, United Nations, New York, 1970.

For a historical study of the three former British high-commission territories of Botswana, Swaziland, and Lesotho that discusses the control that South Africa has over these territories, see Jack Halpern, *South Africa's Hostages,* Penguin African Library, Harmondsworth, 1965.

Information on South Africa's economic ties to the rest of Africa is contained in "The Breakthrough," *The Financial Mail* (Johannesburg), November 13, 1970.

South Africa's economic control over Lesotho and Swaziland is outlined in "Shabby Treatment," *The Financial Mail,* April 7, 1972.

South Africa's economic control of Rhodesia is discussed in *The Financial Mail,* October 23, 1970. See also "Rhodesia Losing Economic Freedom," *Times of Zambia,* January 23, 1967.

A description of Lesotho's economy *and* its reliance on South Africa is in "Lesotho," *The Financial Mail,* January 1971, p. 308.

The effect of South Africa's economic power on small African states is illustrated in Anthony Martin and Alan Rake, "Question Mark over Lesotho," *African Development,* March 1970.

A general article that argues that South African economic expansion has scarce begun is "South Africa's Economic Network," *African Development,* October 1970.

C. *Analysis of Outward Policy*

The best and most succinct statement on the outward policy is R. Molteno, *Africa and South Africa,* African Bureau, London, 1971.

Further sources of information are Jack Spence, "South Africa and the Modern World," in Monica Wilson and Leonard Thompson, eds., *The Oxford History of South Africa,* Vol. II, Oxford, London, 1971; Giovanni Arrighi and John Saul, "Nationalism and Revolution in Tropical Africa," *Socialist Register,* Merlin Press, London, 1969; Larry W. Bowman, "South Africa's Southern Strategy and Its Implications for the U.S.," *International Affairs,* Vol. 47, No. 1, January 1971, and "The Subordinate State Systems of Southern Africa," *International Studies Quarterly XII,* September 3, 1968; Richard Hall, *The High Price of Principles: Kaunda and the White South,* Columbia University Press, New York, 1969.

Chapter Five. South Africa and the West

A. Corporate Interests and South Africa

The significance of foreign capital in the South African economy and the extent of South Africa's trade with the rest of the world is analyzed, with the help of extensive tables, in Sean Gervasi, *Industrialization, Foreign Capital, and Forced Labor in South Africa,* UN ST/PSCA/SER. A/10, United Nations, New York, 1970.

For information on investment in South Africa, see *Foreign Investment in the Republic of South Africa,* UN ST/PSCA/SER. A/11, United Nations, New York, 1970.

A complete list of the more than 500 British firms and subsidiaries operating in South Africa is available from the Anti-Apartheid Movement in London.

A similar list of the almost 400 American firms and subsidiaries operating in South Africa is available from the American Committee on Africa.

A candid appraisal of the importance of both British and American investment to the South African economy is found in "Sell Out or Shell Out?" *The Financial Mail* (Johannesburg), June 18, 1971.

American support of the South African economy is discussed and the domestic American campaigns pressuring U. S. firms to withdraw their investments from South Africa is evaluated from a South African businessman's point of view in "Dear Mr. Diggs: an Open Letter to Congressman Charles Diggs," *The Financial Mail,* August 13, 1971.

U. S. contributions to the industrialization of South Africa are documented in Richard Thomas, "U. S. Economic Involvement in South Africa," unpublished mimeo, available from the American Committee on Africa.

A good study of American corporate involvement in South Africa, including interviews with both U. S. and South African business leaders is Timothy H. Smith, *The American Corporation in South Africa: An Analysis and A Foundation for Action,* available from the Southern Africa Committee, New York.

An excellent study of U. S. economic interests in South Africa is *Apartheid and Imperialism: A Study of U.S. Corporate Involvement in South Africa,* a special issue of *Africa Today,* Vol. 17, No. 5, September–October 1970.

American business support for apartheid is documented in "U. S. Business in South Africa," *Newsweek,* March 29, 1971.

The "Polaroid experiment" and the campaign to pressure Polaroid to terminate its operations in South Africa are documented and discussed in "Special Committee on Apartheid Holds Hearings on 'Polaroid Experiment'," UN No. 6/71, United Nations, New York, 1971, and also in Ray Vicker, "Experiment in South Africa: Some U. S. Firms Ignore Urgings to Leave, Instead Seek to Upgrade Status of Blacks," *The Wall Street Journal,* September 22, 1971, p. 38.

Further references on the Polaroid issue are Robert Maynard, "Polaroid's Challenge: Racism or Morality?" Washington *Post,* January 17, 1971; Jo Ann Levine, "Polaroid Dispute Echoes," *The Christian Science Monitor,* December 1, 1970, which considers the implications of Polaroid's action for other U. S. businesses involved in South Africa; for a South African evaluation of the experiment, "Progress or Propaganda?" *The Financial Mail,* January 22, 1971. See also George Houser, "U. S. Business Should Leave South Africa: Investment Dollars Bolster Apartheid," letter to the Financial Editor, New York *Times,* April 18, 1971, which places the Polaroid issue in the context of the continuing campaign to persuade U. S. business to disengage from South Africa.

American financial support for South Africa after the Sharpeville massacre is detailed in *Partners in Apartheid: United States Policy on South Africa,* a special issue of *Africa Today,* Vol. 11, No. 3, March 1964.

For a justification of continued foreign economic involvement in South Africa by a British analyst, see Norman MacCrae, "The Green Bay Tree," *The Economist,* 29, June 1968; and by the same author, "What Will Destroy Apartheid?" *Harper's,* March 1970.

B. *National Interests and South Africa*

1. *Military Ties*

For a discussion of South Africa's ties with NATO, see *NATO and Southern Africa: The Growth of a Military Bloc* (1971) American Committee on Africa.

Abdul S. Minty, *South Africa's Defence Strategy*, Anti-Apartheid Movement, London, 1969. This study discusses the build-up of South Africa's military might, the international arms embargo against South Africa, Western help for South Africa's militarization, and South Africa's military calculations.

France has been one of South Africa's major military suppliers in spite of the UN arms embargo. Details of French arms sales to South Africa can be found in *Economic Relations Between France and South Africa, 1966–1969*, a government study made by the Republic of Zambia in 1970 and available from the Zambian Consulate General, 13 Piazza S. Silvestro, 00100 Rome.

2. *Strategic Considerations*

South Africa's value in U. S. defense calculations is discussed by an American military historian, S. L. A. Marshall, in *South Africa: The Strategic View*, a publication prepared in 1967 for the American-African Affairs Association, 550 Fifth Ave., New York, N.Y. 10036.

The importance of oil to South Africa, the strategic aspects of the Cape route for oil shipment from the Middle East to Europe, and American interests in oil exploration in South Africa are all surveyed in "Oil: Supplement to *Financial Mail*" (Johannesburg), March 5, 1971.

Prime Minister Vorster is quoted as revealing South Africa's intention to develop nuclear weaponry in Minty, op. cit.

Peter Calvocoressi, *South Africa and World Opinion*, Oxford, London, 1961, examines the world's reactions to South Africa's racial policies.

Colin and Margaret Legum, *South Africa: Crisis for the West*, Praeger, New York, 1964, Part II, discusses international power and South Africa with special attention to possible world action against South Africa.

Waldemar A. Nielsen, *African Battleline: American Policy Choices in Southern Africa,* Harper & Row, New York, 1965, was prepared for the Council on Foreign Relations, an influential advisory group to the U. S. government on foreign policy matters.

George F. Kennan, "Hazardous Courses in Southern Africa," *Foreign Affairs,* Vol. 49, No. 2, January 1971, is an assessment of the current situation in Southern Africa and its implications for U. S. policy.

William A. Hance, ed., *Southern Africa and the United States,* Columbia University Press, New York, 1968, is a collection of essays dealing with U. S. relations in Southern Africa.

3. *Economic National Interests*

The importance of both British and American economic involvement with South Africa relative to their respective economies is assessed by South African businessmen in "Sell Out or Shell Out," *The Financial Mail* (Johannesburg), June 18, 1971. The article also compares the importance and profitability of U. S. investment in South Africa with U. S. investment in other countries around the world.

Ronald Segal, ed., *Sanctions Against South Africa,* Penguin, Harmondsworth, 1964, a collection of papers that was prepared for the International Conference on Economic Sanctions against South Africa in April 1964, examines the implications of sanctions from legal, political, and ethical points of view and gives a thorough consideration of the needs of smaller nations who presently trade with that country.

Chapter Six. Mozambique

Mozambique Revolution is the official English-language journal published by FRELIMO in Dar es Salaam, Tanzania. It is available in North America from Liberation Support Movement/ Canada.

Mozambique Information is the official French-language journal published by FRELIMO in Algiers.

Eduardo Mondlane, *The Struggle for Mozambique,* Penguin

African Library, Harmondsworth, 1970, was written by the first president of FRELIMO shortly before his assassination in 1969. It is the single best description and analysis of Portuguese colonialism and the struggle for freedom in Mozambique.

Also useful are an interview by Boubaker Adjali of Marcelino dos Santos published by the Liberation Support Movement in 1971, and FRELIMO, "Education in Mozambique," *Tricontinental*, No. 73, April 1971.

Chapter Seven. Angola

1. Portugal and Angola

See listings for Chapters Two and Four.

2. History of the Liberation Movement

A general overview of the MPLA's struggle, extensively documented inside Angola, can be found in Basil Davidson, *In the Eye of the Storm*, Doubleday, Garden City, N.Y., 1972.

Ronald Chilcote, *Portuguese Africa*, Prentice-Hall, Englewood Cliffs, N.J., 1967, provides general background.

A shorter general introduction can be found in Kapiassa Husseini, "M.P.L.A. . . . 15 years toward Independence," *Motive*, February 1971.

Angola in Arms, the official English-language journal of the MPLA, published in Tanzania, frequently carries historical articles; it is available from Liberation Support Movement (op. cit.).

The massacres of Angolans are documented in John Marcum, *The Angolan Revolution*, M.I.T. Press, Cambridge, 1969.

Differences between MPLA and other Angolan movements can be found in the following: Marcum, op. cit., and Al J. Venter, *The Terror Fighters*, Purnell, Cape Town, 1969.

An introduction to the movement by MPLA's president is Agostinho Neto, "Angola: People in Revolution," *Tricontinental*, No. 12, 1969.

See also Rev. S. Gilchrist, "Angola Awake," *Transition Magazine*, 1968.

3. *Racism*

Sources for this topic are documented in James Boggs, *Racism and the Class Struggle*, Monthly Review Press, New York, 1970, and Basil Davidson, *The African Slave Trade*, Little, Brown, Boston, 1961.

4. *Growth of the MPLA*

For a military chronology and history, see Donald L. Barnett and Roy Harvey, *The Revolution in Angola*, Bobbs-Merrill, New York, 1972.

See also an interview with Iko Carreira in the *Standard* (*Tanzania*), April 23, 1971, and Basil Davidson, "Angola in the Ninth Year," *African Affairs* (London), January 1971, and an interview with Humberto Traca by *Liberation News Service*, March 6, 1971.

An exposition of guerrilla fighting in Angola by a hostile White South African is Venter, op. cit.

Documentation on the use of defoliants and herbicides can be found in *Medical Assistance Services*, prepared and printed by Liberation Support Movement Information Center, Seattle, Wash. This pamphlet and other relevant information is available from SAM, P.O. Box 1595, Lusaka, Zambia.

Portuguese strategies are discussed by Neto, op. cit.

5. *Life in the Liberated Areas*

Village life and organization is described in Barnett and Harvey, op. cit., "Economy of the Country," and Mikko Lohikoski and Börje J. Mattsson, *A Report of a Trip to Angola*, Helsinki, Finland, February 4, 1971.

Production in the villages is documented in Barnett and Harvey, op. cit., "Interview with Commander Setta Likambuila," and Lohikoski and Mattsson, op. cit.

The role of women is discussed in Barnett and Harvey, op. cit., "Interview with Commander Setta Likambuila" and "Marsha—A Fourteen-Year-Old Guerrilla."

Descriptions of health care can be found in Boubaker Adjali, "Inside Liberated Angola: A Survey of Medical Services," *Southern Africa*, published by the Southern Africa Committee/ New York, August–September 1971; *Medical Assistance in the*

Liberated Regions, available from SAM, P.O. Box 1595, Lusaka, Zambia; and *Memorandum of Activities of Medical Assistance Services of the MPLA in the Liberated Regions of the Eastern Front,* prepared and printed by Liberation Support Movement Information Center, Seattle, Wash. June 1970, available from SAM.

The new educational system in the liberated zones is described in "Education: A Strategy Factor of Liberation," in *Angola in Arms,* Vol. 1, No. 1, February 1971. For material on literacy, see *Victory Is Certain,* MPLA literacy manual, 1968.

6. *Additional Sources*
The most recent source on Gulf Oil is *"Gulf Oil in Angola,"* a pamphlet published by the American Committee on Africa, New York, 1973.

A further recent study of Portuguese strategies in Angola is Douglas Wheeler and René Pélissier, *Angola,* Praeger, New York, 1971.

Chapter Eight. Guinea-Bissau

1. *Armed Struggle in Guinea-Bissau*
For background material on the history of the armed struggle for the liberation of Guinea-Bissau, see Amilcar Cabral, *Revolution in Guinea,* Monthly Review Press, New York, 1971, particularly "The Development of the Struggle," "Practical Problems and Tactics," and "Towards Final Victory." See also Gérard Chaliand, *Armed Struggle in Africa,* Monthly Review Press, New York, 1969, and Basil Davidson, *The Liberation of Guiné,* Penguin African Library, Harmondsworth, 1969.

For information on the current military situation, see *Actualités,* an information bulletin published monthly by the PAIGC. *Actualités* is available in French directly from the PAIGC, P.O. Box 298, Conakry, Republic of Guinea, or in English translation from Liberation Support Movement, Box 15210, Seattle, Wash. 98115.

In addition, the PAIGC publishes "Monthly Communiques" and yearly "Reports on the Situation of the Struggle," available from the PAIGC in Conakry. Further information, compiled from the international press, is published monthly in *Facts and Reports*, Angola Comité in Amsterdam.

2. *Life in Liberated Areas*

For background information on the political, economic, and social aspects of life in Guinea-Bissau, see Cabral, op. cit., particularly "The Development of the Struggle," a speech made by Cabral at the December 1968 meeting of the Organization for the Solidarity of Peoples of Asia, Africa and Latin America (Ospaal), in Havana. See also Davidson, *The Liberation of Guiné,* particularly ch. 3, 4, 6, 7, and Chaliand, op. cit.

For information on the current situation and plans for the future, see *Actualités* and *Facts and Reports.* Also see "Talk with a Guinean Revolutionary," in *Ufahamu,* Vol. I, No. 1, spring 1970.

3. *The Development of Revolutionary Strategy*

A. *Theory and Practice*

Amilcar Cabral, op. cit., "The Weapon of Theory." Cabral emphasizes the importance of revolutionary theory in this speech to the first tricontinental meeting of the OSPAAL held in Havana in January 1966.

An excellent consideration of the concept of praxis, and especially its development in the thought of Hegel and Marx, is found in Richard Bernstein, *Praxis and Action,* University of Pennsylvania Press, Philadelphia, 1972.

An essay on the relation between knowledge and practice, between knowing and doing is in Mao Tse-tung, "On Practice," in *Selected Works,* Vol. I, Foreign Languages Press, Peking, 1967, pp. 295–311.

B. *Colonialism and the Birth of the PAIGC*

Cabral's outline of the meaning of Portuguese presence in Guinea-Bissau was taken from his speech made in Conakry, Republic of Guinea, in 1962 to the United Nations Special Committee on Territories under Portuguese Administration, which is reprinted in toto in Cabral, op. cit.

A synopsis of Portuguese colonialism in Guinea-Bissau, including mention of the major colonial wars and the education and health situations under colonial rule, is in Davidson, op. cit.

Background to the PAIGC's decision to wage war against the Portuguese and to their shift in organizing strategy may be found in Cabral, op. cit., pp. 29–32, and in Davidson, op. cit., pp. 29–42.

C. *The Theory and Practice of Organizing the Struggle*

How the analysis of a society is linked to the revolutionary campaign is explained in Cabral, op. cit., "Brief Analysis of the Social Structure in Guinea."

Personal accounts of the cadres who took responsibility for mobilizing the peasantry are found in Davidson, op. cit.

The disposition of other groups in Guinean society towards revolution is analyzed in Cabral, op. cit., pp. 50–61. Here, he also talks about the relationship between exploitation and the revolutionary *prise de conscience* and analyzes the contradictions in Guinean society that the PAIGC mobilizes around.

The PAIGC's goal of national liberation is defined in Chaliand, op. cit.

Cabral's major theoretical statement, "National Liberation and Culture," was delivered on February 20, 1970, as part of the Eduardo Mondlane Memorial Lecture Series at Syracuse University. Copies may be obtained from the Program of Eastern African Studies, Syracuse University, Syracuse, N.Y. 13210.

A recent collection of speeches made by Cabral in London in 1971, is *Our People Are Our Mountains,* Committee for Freedom in Mozambique, Angola and Guiné.

For a collection of Cabral's last speeches, see *Return to the Source,* edited, with an introduction, by the Africa Information Service, New York, September 1971.

Partial List of Organizations Working on Issues Related to Southern and Colonized Africa

Africa Information Service, 112 West 120th Street, New York, N.Y. 10027

African Activist Association, African Studies Center, University of California, Los Angeles, Calif. 90024

African Information Bureau, P.O. Box 1554, East Lansing, Mich. 48823

African Information Center, 1016 East 75th Street, Chicago, Ill. 60621

African Liberation Support Committee/Boston, 25 Holyoke Street, Boston, Mass. 02116

African Liberation Support Committee/New York, 261 West 125th Street, New York, N.Y. 10027

African Liberation Support Committee/Washington, 1648 Roxanna Road, N.W., Washington, D.C. 20012

—African Youth Movement for Liberation and Unity (House of Kuumba), 108 West 112th Street, New York, N.Y. 10027

Afro Asian Peoples Solidarity Organization, 89 Abdel Aziz al Saud, Cairo, U.A.R.

All African News Service, P.O. Box 21366, Greensboro, N.C. 27420

American Committee on Africa, 164 Madison Avenue, New York, N.Y. 10016

Angola Comité, Da Costastraat 88, Amsterdam, Netherlands

Anti-Apartheid Movement, 89 Charlotte Street, London, W.1, England

Black Concern, Box 513, Bronx, N.Y. 10472

Black Unity and Freedom Party, 15a Lausanne Rd., Peckham, London S.E.15, England

Chicago Area Committee for the Liberation of Angola, Mozambique, and Guiné, 2546 North Halsted Street, Chicago, Ill. 60614

Committee for a Free Mozambique, 616 West 116th Street, Apt 1-A, New York, N.Y. 10027

Committee for Freedom in Angola, Mozambique, and Guiné, 12 Little Newport Street, WC2AH 7JJ, London, England

Interreligious Foundation for Community Organization, Room 560, 475 Riverside Drive, New York, N.Y. 10027

Liberation Support Movement/California, Box 814, Oakland, Calif. 94604

Liberation Support Movement/Canada, Information Center, Box 338, Richmond, B.C., Canada

Madison Area Committee on Southern Africa, 731 State Street, Madison, Wisc. 53703

Pan African Information Bureau, c/o Nairobi Bookstore, 1621 Bay Road, East Palo Alto, Calif. 94303

Pan African Liberation Committee, P.O. Box 514, Brookline Village, Mass. 02147

Pan African Skills Project, Room 560, 475 Riverside Drive, New York, N.Y. 10027

Southern Africa Committee/New York, 224 West 27th Street, New York, N.Y. 10001

Southern Africa Committee/South, 213 Gregson Street, Durham, N.C. 27701

Southern African Liberation Committee, 310 Triphammer Road, Ithaca, N.Y. 14850

Youth Organization for Black Unity, Box 20826, Greensboro, N.C. 27420

Race to Power: The Struggle for Southern Africa
Written and edited by:
David Olsen
Nancy Barnes
Elsa Roberts
John Auerbach
Carol Bengelsdorf
Jenny Clift
Craig Howard
Marjorie Jacobs
Alan Kellock
Margaret   Marshall
Wendy Sisson

INDEX

Actualités (information bulletin), 235, 250, 253, 315

Adjali, Boubaker, 157, 170, 208, 225

African Development (British trade journal), 90

"African homelands" (Bantustans). See Reserves (reservations), native

African League, 53–54

African National Congress (ANC), 31, 34, 35, 37–39, 98, 117–18

African Party for the Liberation of Guinea and the Cape Verde Islands. See PAIGC

African Research Group, ii

Africans (Blacks), 3 ff., 135–37, 139–81, 183–234, 235–88, 289–95 (*see also* specific aspects, countries, people, places); coming of Whites to Africa and, 14–16 (*see also* Europeans; Whites; specific countries, people, places); and development of revolutionary strategy (*see* Strategy, revolutionary); educational system and, 27–29, 51–52, 192–99 (*see also* Education); history of colonial racism and slavery and, 14 15, 29–30, 101–3, 192–99, 260–67 (*see also* specific aspects, developments, people, places); and national liberation movements (resistance to White minority rule), 29–40, 101–3, 135–38, 139–81, 183–234, 235–88, 289–95

(*see also* specific countries, organizations, people, places); Portuguese colonialism and, 41–60, 61–82, 85–87 (*see also* Portugal; specific people, places); role of the West in domination and liberation movements in Africa and, 99–100, 101–31, 289–95 (*see also* West, the); South African apartheid system and, 3–40 (*see also* Apartheid system); South African regionalization of Southern Africa and, 85–100 (*see also* specific aspects, places)

African Slave Trade, The (Davidson), 193, 194

African Studies Center, 186

Afrikaners (Boers), 3, 14–16, 17–40, 86, 123; Anglo-Boer War (1899–1912), 102; "Great Trek" and, 14–15

Agriculture (crops, farming), 22 (*see also* Peasants; specific aspects, crops, groups, people, places); Angola, 185, 195; goals of liberation and, 285–88; Portuguese colonialism and, 43–48, 60, 66, 68, 69, 156–57, 159, 260; resistance movement in Mozambique and, 156–57, 159, 160, 161, 179–80; South African apartheid and, 22

Aid programs (*see also* military aid): liberation movements and, 233–34, 242, 293–95; Portuguese colonialism and,

65–66, 71–72, 73–75, 104, 232–33, 291–93

Air Force, Portuguese, 174–75, 180, 189, 205, 210, 237, 243, 253, 254, 292 (*see also* Bombings, air); in Angola, 189, 205; and chemical warfare, 205–9; in Mozambique, 174–75, 180

Aldeamentos, 171–72. *See also* Strategic hamlets

Algeria, 148

Allis-Chalmers, 125

Ambrosio, Miguel, 154

American Committee on Africa, 112

American Metal Climax, 111

American Motors, 125

American-South African Investment Corporation, 117

ANC. *See* African National Congress (ANC)

Anglo-American Corporation of South Africa, 76, 77–79, 113

Angola, xv, 41 ff., 45–48, 51, 53–54, 136, 183–234; background to resistance to Portuguese oppression in, 185–86; and beginning of armed struggle, 190–92; development of slavery and racism in, 192–99; education in, 222–32; GRAE, 137; health care in, 218–22; history and resources of, 183–86; liberation and changes in, 209–34; literacy in, 227–32; MPLA and, 137, 184–85, 186 ff. (*see also* MPLA); political organizations, 186–89, 191–92; Portuguese colonial rule and, xv, 41 ff., 45–48, 51, 53–54, 55–56, 58, 59–60, 61, 64, 68, 69–

71, 73–74, 76–77, 80, 81, 183–234; resistance to Portuguese colonial rule in, 136, 172, 176, 183–234, 293, 294; role of women in, 214–18; South Africa's regionalization policy and, 84, 86–87, 91; UNITA, 137; village life and production in, 210–14; war in, 199–209

Angola in Arms (journal), 191, 192, 201, 205, 313

Angola Comité, 293, 294, 318

Antagonistic contradictions, development of revolutionary strategy and, 280–82

Apartheid system, South Africa and, 5–13, 82, 85, 87, 93, 96, 97, 101–31; Bantustan policy, 6–9, 19–22; defined, explained, 5–13; economic aspects of, 20–22, 23–27, 89–93, 127–31 (*see also* specific aspects, developments); educational system and, 27–29; foreign corporations (capital investment) and, 101–31, 290–95; foreign policy and national interests and, 122–31; geographical segregation and, 6–9; history of colonialism and, 14–16; labor and, 4, 10–13, 23–27, 31, 106–7, 111 ff.; life in South Africa and, 3–40; migratory labor and pass laws, 10–13; military ties and, 123–26; national interests and foreign policy and, 122, 127–31; race classification and, 5–6; and regionalization of Southern Africa, 85–100; resistance, repression, and the police state, 29–40; signs of strain in, 20–22; strategic considerations and, 126–27; White view of, 17–18; world opinion and, 122–23

Arantes e Oliveira (Mozambique governor-general), 173–74, 177

Argentina, 291

Armed Struggle in Africa (Chaliand), 250, 254, 283

Arms embargoes, 123–25, 127, 291–92; UN and, 123–25, 127, 291–92

Army, people's (*see also* Militia, people's): Angola, 170–72, 190–92, 199–209, 210–14; development of revolutionary strategy and, 258–88; Guinea-Bissau, 236, 238–47, 258–88; Mozambique, 139, 142–81

Army, Portuguese, 61, 62, 63, 68, 71–73, 75, 79–82, 170–81 *passim;* and Angola, 184, 189, 190–99, 203–9; and Guinea-Bissau, 237–47; and Mozambique, 144, 150–81 *passim;* tactics in Angola, 203–9; United States and training of, 75

Army, South African, 35–36, 86–90

Arrests, 35, 37, 187, 189, 238

Asians (Indians), 149; apartheid and, 5, 6, 7–9, 10–13, 17, 24, 32, 34, 36

Assimilation (*assimilados*), Portuguese colonialism and, 48–50, 51–52, 54, 197, 263–64

Atlantic Ocean, 73, 126

Australia, 294

Automobile industry, 107–8, 118–19. See also specific corporations

Azores, 64–65, 292; Pact (1971), 292

Bafatá, Guinea-Bissau, 244–45, 247, 251

Baixa de Cassange, Angola, 191

Bakongo tribe (Angola), 191, 193, 204

Balante people (Guinea-Bissau), 272–74, 276

Bana, Antônio, 272–74, 275–76

Banda, Dr. Hastings Kamuzu, 95, 96

Banning orders, South Africa and, 32–34

Bantustans. See Reserves (reservations), native

"Bantu" universities, 27–28

Basuto people, 31

Beech Aircraft Corporation, 125

Belgium, 124

Bell Helicopter, 78, 292

Bié, Angola, 202

Bissau, Guinea-Bissau, 237–38, 244–45, 247, 251, 263, 264

Bissora, Guinea-Bissau, 246

Blacks. See Africans (Blacks)

Boers. See Afrikaners (Boers)

Boggs, James, 192–93, 195, 196

Bombings, air, Portuguese and, 174–75, 180; Angola, 189, 205, 210; Guinea-Bissau, 255

Botswana, 84, 87, 88, 91, 97, 308

Bourgeoisie, 268, 277. See also Petty bourgeoisie

Boycotts, economic, 118–19, 294

Brazil, xvi, 291

Bride price, abolition in liberated Angola of, 217
British. *See* Great Britain
British Commonwealth, 96
Business. *See* Corporations; Industry; specific places

Cabinda, Angola, 67–70, 200–1, 202
Cabo Delgado, Mozambique, 146, 148, 150, 154, 162, 169, 170, 174, 179
Cabora Bassa project, 77–79, 81, 87, 150, 151, 306–7
Cabral, Amilcar, 235, 236–37, 240–41, 242, 244, 245, 247, 248, 250, 252, 253, 254, 256; "National Liberation and Culture" speech, 268, 286, 287–88, 317; "open letter" to the Portuguese government, 236–37; on revolutionary theory and strategy, 259, 260, 261, 265, 269, 270–71, 272–73, 277–78, 279–83, 285–88; speech to UN Special Committee on Territories and Portuguese Administration, 260–61, 263–64, 316–17; "Weapon of Theory" speech, 285, 316
Cadres, political, 272–76, 278; Angola MPLA, 224–32; Guinea-Bissau, 241–42, 249, 272–76, 278; Mozambique, 158–61, 178; revolutionary strategy and, 272–76, 278
Caetano, Marcelo, 71–72, 76, 80, 81, 305
Caltex, 108
Canada, 77, 118–19, 130, 293
Cape Colony, 15–16

Cape Masters and Servants Law of 1865 (South Africa), 24–25
Cape of Good Hope, 101
Cape Town, South Africa, 14
Cape Verde Island, 41, 42, 137, 189, 235, 236, 237, 264–65; PAIGC and liberation of (*see* PAIGC)
Capital investment, foreign (*see also* Corporations, foreign): and Portuguese colonial rule, 63 ff., 69–79, 184, 188, 232–33; role in domination and liberation in Southern Africa, 91 ff., 102–31, 289–95; and South Africa and apartheid, 101–31, 290–95; and South Africa and regionalization of Southern Africa, 91–93, 95, 96
"Capitalist powers," use of term, xvi
Capitalist societies, development of revolutionary strategy and changes in, 268
Carreira, Iko, 201, 202, 203, 206
Cassava production, 206–9, 213–14, 252
Cassinga iron ore center, 71
Catholic Church, 79
Centers of Revolutionary Instruction (CIR), Angola, 209, 216, 218, 223–32
Chaliand, Gérard, 250, 254, 283
Change(s), economic and social, liberation movements and, 289–95; critical analysis of revolutionary strategy and, 267–88; culture and, 286–88; development of revolutionary strategy and, 258–88 (*see also* Strategy, revolutionary); eco-

nomic base, 284–86; goals of liberation and, 282–88; liberated Angola and, 209–34; liberated Guinea-Bissau and, 247–57; role of Western powers and domination and, 289–95

Chase Manhattan Bank of New York, 111, 117

Chattel slavery, 194. *See also* Slavery (slave trade)

Chemical Construction Company, 109

Chemical warfare, Portuguese use of, 205–8, 244, 292

Chiefs: Guinea-Bissau, 12, 70, 280–81, 283, 286; Mozambique, 158; revolutionary strategy and, 280–81, 286

China, Nationalist, xvi

China, People's Republic of, 293

Chipande, Alberto-Joaquim, 56–57, 144–49

Chipenda, Daniel, 200

Chrome ores (Chromium), 122, 120, 292, 294

Chrysler South Africa, 112

Chuabos people (Mozambique), 154

Church, the. *See* Catholic Church; Dutch Reformed Church; World Council of Churches

Cities and towns (rural population), revolutionary strategy and (Guinea-Bissau), 266–67, 276–82

Civilizados, 264. *See also* Assimilation (*assimilados*)

Class structure, development of revolutionary strategy and

changes in, 267–69 ff.; class interest and revolutionary potential, 276–82; goals of liberation and, 282–88

Coates, Austin, 82

Coffee production, 69

Collective education (Angola), 226

Collective farming (Angola), 212–13

Colonialism, 29 ff. (*see also* specific aspects, developments, movements, people, places); economy and (*see* Economy); history of (*see* specific aspects, people, places); Portuguese (*see* Portugal); resistance to, 29 ff. (*see also* specific aspects, movements, people, places); role of the West in (*see* West, the); and slavery (*see* Slavery); South Africa and, 14–16 (*see also* South Africa, Republic of); South Africa and Portuguese colonies and, 75–77, 81–82, 85–87

Coloreds, apartheid in South Africa and, 5, 6, 8–9, 10–13, 14, 16, 17, 24, 25, 32, 33, 34

Committee for Freedom in Mozambique, Angola, and Guinea, 273

Communism, 32, 100, 126, 301. *See also* Socialist countries

Comocmin, 176

Como Island, 240–41

Compania União Fabril (CUF), 251

Conakry, Republic of Guinea, 253, 255, 260–61, 275

CONCP (Conference of the Nationalist Organizations of the Portuguese Colonies), 137–38

Congo, People's Republic of (formerly Congo-Brazzaville), 97, 99, 199, 219

Congo-Kinshasa. *See* Zaire (formerly Congo-Kinshasa)

Congo River, 185

Contract labor, 46, 187

Contradictions, use of term in critical analysis and development of revolutionary strategy, 280–82

Contrato, 189. *See also* Forced labor

Copper mining, 22

COREMO (Revolutionary Committee of Mozambique), 137

Corporations, foreign (*see also* Industry): and Portuguese colonialism, 232–33, 289–95; role in domination and liberation in South Africa, 91 ff., 103–31, 232–33, 289–92, 294; and Southern Africa and United States foreign policy, 120–22 ff., 289–92, 294

Correctional labor, 46

Cotton production, 43–48, 56, 62, 146, 161, 195

Craveirinha, José, 54–55

Critical analysis, revolutionary strategy and, 267–88: goals of liberation and, 282–88; organization of the struggle and, 267–82

Cuando-Cubango, Angola, 201, 202

Cuba, xvi, 128

Culture, goals of national liberation and, 286–88

Cunene River project, 233, 306–7

Dams. *See* Hydroelectric power projects (dams); specific projects

Dar es Salaam, Tanzania, 141, 146, 147, 148, 149

Davidson, Basil, 193, 194, 204, 237, 238, 243, 253, 266, 275–76

Déclassés, revolutionary strategy and use of, 277–78

Decolonization movements, 53–60, 61–82, 96–97. *See also* Colonialism; Liberation movements; specific organizations, people, places

"Defiance campaign" (South Africa, 1952), 33–34

Defoliants, use by Portuguese of, 205–8

Delgado. *See* Cabo Delgado, Angola

Deolinda, Natacha, 46–47

Development aid programs (development funds), 63, 71–72

DIAMANG, 71

Diamonds (diamond mining), 16, 22, 102, 128

Dingaan's Day, 15

Dingane, King, 15

Diseases, 262–63. *See also* Health (medical) care

Dos Santos, Marcelino, 157, 169–70

Douglas-Home, Sir Alec, 126

Dow Chemical, 207–8

Durban, South Africa, 39–40; workers' strike (1972–73), 39–40

Dutch, the, and South Africa, 3, 14–40, 101. *See also* Afrikaners (Boers); Netherlands (Holland, the Dutch)

Dutch Reformed Church, 17–18, 299

East Africa, 101

Economy (economic aspects, economic structures), White minority rule and colonial exploitation and, 3, 4, 7, 20–22, 23–27, 43–48, 61–82 *passim*, 127–31 (*see also* specific aspects, developments, groups, people, places): aid programs and (*see* Aid programs); change and (*see* Change[s]); foreign capital investment and (*see* Capital investment; Corporations); goals of liberation and, 284–86; Portuguese Africa and, 43–48, 61–82 *passim*, 183–84, 192–99, 202, 289–95 (*see also* specific people, places); role of the West in, 102–31, 289–95; South African apartheid system and, 3, 4, 7, 20–22, 23 ff.

Education (schools): development of revolutionary strategy and, 272 ff.; liberated Angola and, 197, 209, 220–21, 222–32; liberated Guinea-Bissau and, 253–56, 257; liberated Mozambique and, 152–53, 161, 163, 164, 178, 179, 180; literacy (*see* Literacy); medical, 220–21; Portuguese colonial rule and, 50, 51–52, 60, 222–23, 263; resistance movements and, 152–53, 161, 163, 164, 178, 179, 180, 222–23, 253–56, 257 (*see also* specific organizations, people, places); South African apartheid system and, 27–29; women and, 162–65, 216

Ehnmark, Anders, 198

Eisenhower, Dwight D., 110

Elders, village (*hommes grandes*), 272–74

Elites, 236, 282–84, 286

Embargoes, 291–94. *See also* Arms embargoes; Boycotts, economic

Employment (jobs), 111–12 (*see also* Labor [workers]); South African apartheid system and, 4, 10–13, 20–22, 25–27, 31, 106–7, 111 ff.; United States in South Africa and, 111–12

Engelhard, Charles, 117

England. *See* Great Britain

Esso, 108

Ethnic groups, 187, 191–92, 270, 281. *See also* Tribes

Europeans (*see also* Whites, the; specific developments, people, places): African resistance to domination and, 135 ff., 184 ff., 238 ff. (*see also* specific aspects, people, places); and colonialism (*see* Colonialism; specific people, places); control and apartheid system in South Africa and, 3–40, 101–31 (*see also* Apartheid system); development of revolutionary strategy and, 277 ff. (*see also* Strategy, revolutionary); and Portuguese Africa, 41 ff. (*see also* Portugal); role of the West in domination and liberation of Southern Africa, 289–95 (*see also* specific people, places); and slave trade (*see* Slavery [slave trade])

Eviction orders, geographical segregation in South Africa and, 7–9, 10

Exploitation, goals of liberation and ending of, 282–88

Export labor, 46

Facts and Reports, 303

Family life: apartheid system and, 11, 23–24; Portuguese colonial rule and, 47–48

Fanon, Frantz, 196

Farim, Guinea-Bissau, 246

Farmers. *See* Agriculture; Peasants (peasantry); specific kinds, places

Farming, subsistence, 45–48

FARP (People's Revolutionary Armed Forces), Guinea-Bissau, 242, 249

Fernandes, Gil, 236

Financial Mail, The, 299, 308, 309, 312

Fingo-Xhosa feuds, 31

First National City Bank of New York, 117

Foote Mineral, 121

Forced cultivation, 46

Forced labor, 45–48, 53, 184, 189, 197–98, 263

Forces of production, economic base of liberation movements and, 285–86

Ford Motor Company, 107, 118–19, 125

Foreign policy, national interests and South African apartheid system and, 120–31 *passim*

Fortified camps, Portuguese, 203–5, 242–43, 244–47

Fortune magazine, 290–91

France (the French), 14, 95, 100, 104, 123, 124, 233, 292–93, 311; and Portuguese colonialism, 62, 73–74, 77, 233, 292–93; and South Africa, 95, 100, 104, 123, 124, 292–93, 311

Freedom Charter for South Africa (1955), 34

"Freedom demands" (South Africa, 1955), 34

Freedom movements, 135 ff. *See also* Independence movements; Liberation movements; specific people, places

Free trade, South Africa and regionalization of Southern Africa and, 89–93

"Free World", use of term, xvi

FRELIMO (Front for the Liberation of Mozambique), v, 58–60, 78, 86, 137, 138, 139, 141–81; and armed struggle and nation building, 157–58; and call to arms (mobilization), 143–44; character and organization of the army and, 152–57; Council of the Presidency of, 169–70; First Congress and statement of aims, 141–44; leadership of, 165–70; military operations and, 150–51 ff., 170 ff.; Mondlane and, 165–70; and political structure, 158 ff.

Fula people (Guinea-Bissau), 270, 281

Gambia, 96
GEC-English Electric, 77–78
General Electric, 78, 290
General Motors, 107–8, 110, 111, 115, 116, 119, 120, 125, 290
Germany. See West Germany
Ghana, 96, 201
Gilchrist, Reverend S., 199
Gillette, 290
Ginga Mbandi, Queen, 216
Goan League, 189
Gold (gold mining), 16, 22, 102, 128, 262, 292
Gordian Knot Operation, 173–75
Gowon, Yakubu, 95
GRAE (Revolutionary Government of Angola in Exile), 137
Great Britain (the British), xv, 62, 66, 69, 96, 292, 293, 294; capital investment in dollars in South Africa, 105; and Portuguese colonialism, 62, 66, 69, 81, 171, 186, 233; and South Africa and apartheid, 14, 15–16, 17, 22, 23, 29, 30–31, 87, 88, 94, 100, 101–2, 104–5, 107, 111, 123, 124, 126, 130–31
Greece, xvi
Guebuza, Armando, 145
Guerrilla movements (guerrilla warfare), 203 (see also specific developments, organizations, people, places); Angola, 190–92, 109–209 ff.; development of revolutionary strategy and, 258–88; Guinea-Bissau, 238 ff.; Mozambique, 151–81; role of

the West in colonial domination and liberation and, 289–95; and South Africa, 38–40, 86–87, 89, 97–99; women and, 214–18
Guinea, Republic of, 41, 47, 73, 253. See also Conakry, Republic of Guinea
Guinea-Bissau, xiii–xiv, xv, 41, 42, 47, 56, 58, 59, 60, 61, 73, 136–37, 189, 235–88; armed struggle for independence in, 236–47; development of revolutionary strategy in, 258–88; early history of Portuguese colonialism and slavery in, 260–67; education and health in, 253–57; goals of liberation and, 282–88; life in liberated areas of, 247–57; map, 42; military struggle today, 244–47; PAIGC, 137, 189, 235, 236 ff. (see also PAIGC); resistance to Portuguese rule in, 136–37, 172, 176, 235–88
Guinea-Conakry. See Conakry, Republic of Guinea
Gulf Oil Company, 69–70, 111, 232–33, 294, 306; "Gulf Oil in Angola" (pamphlet), 315

Harvard University, 294
Health (medical) care, 262–63; liberated Angola and, 218–22; liberated Guinea-Bissau and, 256–57; Portuguese colonial rule and, 262–63
Helicopters, use of, 78, 292
Herbicides, Portuguese use of, 205–8, 292
Higgins, Milton P., 114

Holden, Roberto, 191
Hospitals (hospital care). *See* Health (medical) care
Houphouet-Boigny, Felix, 94–96, 100
Houser, Reverend George, 113
Housing, South African apartheid and, 26–27
Hurd, John G., 123
Husseini, Kapiassa N., 189, 201
Hydroelectric power projects (dams), 69, 77–79, 81, 91, 183, 233, 306–7

IBM, 108, 110–11, 290
Icolo-E-Ibengo (Angola), "massacre of," 189
Illiteracy. *See* Literacy (illiteracy)
Independence movements, 18, 19–20, 54–60, 61–82, 135 ff. (*see also* Guerrilla movements; Liberation movements; specific organizations, people, places); Angola, 136, 137, 183–234; culture and, 286–88; economic base of, 284–86; development of revolutionary strategy and, 258–88; goals of liberation and, 282–88; Guinea-Bissau, 136–37, 235–88; Mozambique, 136, 137, 139–81; role of the West in domination and liberation and, 289–95 (*see also* West, the); support from Socialist countries for, 293–95
Independent African countries, exploitation and goals of liberation and, 282–88
India, 101

Indian Ocean sphere, 73, 102, 126–27, 291
Indians (Asians). *See* Asians (Indians)
Indigenous Africans, 263–64, 284–88; class structure and goals of liberation and, 284–85; South African indigenas, 49–50
Indochina, xiii, 122, 295. *See also* Vietnam war
Industrial and Commercial Workers' Union (ICU, South Africa), 31
Industrial society, class structure and changes in, 268–69, 285
Industry (industrialization), 268–69, 285 (*see also* Corporations); apartheid system in South Africa and, 18, 21–27, 28–29, 89–93, 102–31; Portuguese colonialism and, 43–48, 61–79; and role of the West in colonial Africa, 102–31 (*see also* West, the; specific countries); South African apartheid and regionalization and, 89–93
Ingersoll-Rand, in South Africa, 78
International Harvester, in South Africa, 115
International Monetary Fund, 292
Investment (capital investment). *See* Capital investment, foreign
Iron ore, 66, 68, 71
Irrigation. *See* Hydroelectric power projects (dams)
Israel, 292
Italy, 111, 124
Ivory Coast, 94–96, 97

Japan, xv, xvi, 81, 292
Job Reservation Act, 25
Jobs. *See* Employment (jobs); Labor (workers)

Kaffir, use of term, 17
Kaulza de Arriaga, General, 174
Kaunda, Dr. Kenneth, 95, 98, 99
Kavandame, Lazaro, 169
Kenya, 96, 97
Khoi people (South Africa), 14
Kipling, Rudyard, 17
Krupp mines, 71

Labor (workers), 10–13, 20–22, 23–27, 31 (*see also* Agriculture; Economy; Employment; Peasants); Angola, 184, 189, 197–98, 222–32; apartheid in South Africa and, 4, 10–13, 20–22, 23–27, 31, 106–7, 111 ff.; development of revolutionary strategy and, 258–88; education (literacy) and, 27–29, 222–32; goals of liberation and, 283–88; Guinea-Bissau, 203, 266; migrant, 10–13, 92–93; Mozambique, 140–81 *passim;* Portuguese colonialism and liberation movements and, 43–48, 55, 56–57, 140–81 *passim,* 203, 222–32, 266; resistance to apartheid and, 29–40; and revolutionary consciousness, 277–82; role of the West in domination and liberation of, 290–91, 293–94
Land (land use, land policy), 30, 31 (*see also* Agriculture; Economy; Mines and mining); Portuguese colonialism and,

43–48, 79; resistance to White domination and, 135–81 *passim,* 183–234 *passim;* South African apartheid and, 3, 6–10, 12–13, 15, 19–22
Laws (legislation), 23–25, 31, 117; migratory labor and, 10–13; Portuguese colonialism and, 45–48 ff.; South African apartheid and, 3, 4, 5–6, 10–13, 17, 20, 23–25, 31–35, 37, 112, 113, 117
Lesotho, 30, 87, 88, 89, 92, 94, 97, 308
Let Us Discover Angola Movement, 186
Liberation movements, 53–60, 61–82, 97–99, 135–288 *passim,* 289–95 (*see also* Guerrilla movements; Independence movements; specific aspects, organizations, people, places); Angola, 136, 137, 183–234; culture and, 286–88; development of revolutionary strategy and, 258–88; economic base, 284–86; goals of, 282–88; Guinea-Bissau, 136–37, 235–88; Mozambique, 136, 137, 139–81; role of the West in, 289–95 (*see also* specific people, places); South African apartheid and the West and, 101–31; South African regionalization of Southern Africa and, 86–100; support from the West for, 293–95
Liberation News Service, 185
Liberation of Guiné, The (Davidson), 237, 238, 243, 253, 266, 275–76

Liberation Support Movement, 293, 312, 313
Likambuila, Setta, 213, 214, 217
Lisbon, 137, 165, 186, 193, 223
Literacy (illiteracy), 142, 152, 197, 227–32, 255. *See also* Education (schools)
Loans, 71–72
Lohikoski, Mikko, 212, 220–21
Lomes (Mozambique people), 154
Lourenço Marques, 75
Luanda, Angola, 56, 186, 187, 190, 202–3; massacre in (1961), 56
Luthuli, Chief Albert J., 118

Machel, Samora, 155–56, 157, 159–61, 169
Maguni, D. S., 140
Malagasy, 97
Malange, Angola, 202
Malawi, 84, 92, 95–96, 97
Malnourishment (malnutrition), 26, 218, 262
Mandela, Nelson, 38–39
Mandinka people (Guinea-Bissau), 276
Mani-Congo, Kingdom of, 185
Mansôa, Guinea-Bissau, 246, 251
MANU (Mozambique African National Union), 141, 146
Manufacture (manufacturing). *See* Industry (industrialization)
Maquival, Joachim, 47–48
"Marching to Pretoria" (song), 16
Marcum, John, 74
Marriage, liberation movements and changes in, 164–65, 217

"Massacre of Icolo-E-Ibengo" (Angola), 189
Massacres, 140–41, 189, 192, 197–99, 261, 265–66
Mattsson, Börje, 212, 220–21
"Mayibuye i' Africa" ("Africa must come back to us"), 40
Medical care. *See* Health (medical) care
Middle East, 122, 126
Migrant labor, South Africa's apartheid policy and, 10–13, 21, 75, 92–93; pass laws and, 10–13
Military aid, foreign, colonial rule and, 36, 75, 123–26, 184, 207, 232–33, 291–92
Military Assistance Advisory Group, U. S., 75
Militias, people's (*see also* Army, people's): Angola, 190–92, 199–209; Guinea-Bissau, 238–47; Mozambique, 154–55, 158, 179
MINA (Movement for the National Independence of Angola), 187
Mineral mining (mineral resources), 22, 66, 68, 69, 71, 128, 183. *See also* Mines and mining; specific kinds
Mines and mining, 4, 6, 10, 13, 16, 22, 23–26 (*see also* Mineral mining; specific kinds, places); Portuguese colonialism and, 66, 68, 69, 71, 75, 184, 185, 233; South Africa and, 4, 6, 10, 13, 16, 22, 23–26, 46, 92–93, 102, 105–7, 122
Mines and Work Act of 1911, 25
MING, 264

Minigiedi, João, 198

Minnesota, 3M Company of, 115

Mobil Oil, 108–9, 290, 294

Mondlane, Eduardo, v, 44, 47, 48, 49, 52, 57–58, 141, 142, 149, 153, 155, 158, 159; assassination of, v, 166–70; and FRELIMO and Mozambique liberation movement, 165–70

Monteiro, O., 255

Mores sector, Guinea-Bissau, 246

Morsgat, South Africa, 8–9

Motsoaledi, Elias, 38

Movement for the National Independence of Angola (MINA), 187

Movement for the National Independence of Guinea (MING), 264

Moxico, Angola, 201, 202

Mozambique, xv, 41 ff., 46–48, 51–61 passim, 68, 69, 73–74, 75–76, 78–79, 81, 136, 139–81, 182, 293; armed struggle and nation-building in, 157–58; COREMO, 137; FRELIMO, 137, 138, 139, 141–81, 182 (see also FRELIMO); life in liberated zones of, 179–81; military operations, 150–51 ff., 170 ff.; resistance to Portuguese rule in, 136, 139–81

Mozambique Revolution (journal), 143, 144, 163, 168, 175, 170, 101, 312

MPLA (Popular Movement for the Liberation of Angola), 56, 80, 86, 137, 184–85, 186–234; aid from the West to, 293; and beginning of armed struggle, 190–92; birth of, 186–89; Dec-

laration to the Portuguese Government (1960) by, 189; and education, 222–32; and health care, 218–22; and literacy, 227–32; manifesto of, 187–88; and military strategy and organization, 200; role of women in, 214–18; and war, 199–209

Mshoeshoe, King, 30

Mueda, Mozambique, 56–57; massacre in (1960), 140–41, 146, 147

Mulder, Dr. C. P., 89, 99, 100

Muller, Dr. Hilgard, 99

Muthemba, Josina, 52

Nader, Ralph, 110

Namibia (South West Africa), 77, 84, 86, 87–88, 135–36, 233; resistance in, 135–36

Nantombo, Gabriel Mauticio, 43

Napalm, use of, 74, 261

Natal, 15–16, 30

National independence and liberation movements, 135 ff. See also Independence movements; Liberation movements; specific people, places

National interest, foreign policy and South Africa's apartheid system and, 122–31

Nationalist Party (South Africa), 4, 12, 17, 18, 27, 31, 114

"National Liberation and Culture" speech, Cabral's (Syracuse University, 1970), 268, 286, 287–88

Native reserves (native reservations). See Reserves (reservations), native

Natives Land Act, 31

NATO, 72–74, 124–25, 207, 233, 291

Navy, Portuguese, 73–74

Neo-colonialism, 284

NESAM (Nucleus of African Secondary Students of Mozambique), 55, 165

Netherlands (Holland, the Dutch), 14, 293, 294; in South Africa, 14–40 (see also Afrikaners (Boers)

Neto, Dr. Agostinho, 56, 185–86, 187, 189, 190, 191, 192, 199, 210, 211, 233–34; on strategies and prospects of the MPLA, 233–34

Neto, Eugenia, 214–15

Nganje, Maria, 163–65

Niassa, Mozambique, 150–51, 154, 162, 170, 174, 179

Nigeria, 95, 99

Nixon (Richard M.) administration, and foreign policy and Southern Africa, 291–92

Nogueira, Alberto Franco, 65–66

North Atlantic Treaty Organization. See NATO

Nuclear power development, 125–26

Numumbi, Kapingo, 179

Nyanjas (Mozambique people), 154

N'Zinga, Queen, 186

OAU (Organization of African Unity), 93–94, 96, 137, 199, 201, 223

Obligatory labor, 46. See also Forced labor

Oil (oil industry), 68, 69–70, 108–9, 126, 183, 184, 200, 232–33. See also specific countries, places

Olossado, Guinea-Bissau, 246

Orange Free State, 15, 16

Ore mining, 105–7, 122. See also Mines and mining; specific kinds, places

Organization of African Unity. See OAU (Organization of African Unity)

OMA (Organization of Angolan Women), 215–17

Organizations, and work on issues related to Southern and colonized Africa (listed), 318–19

Outward policy, South Africa's, 93–100

"Overseas provinces," Portuguese, 41–42

PAC (Pan Africanist Congress), 35, 37–39, 117–18

Pacheco Pereira, Duarte, 261–62

PAIGC (African Party for the Independence of Guinea and the Cape Verde Islands), v, 137, 189, 235, 236–88; colonialism and birth of, 260–67; and development of revolutionary strategy, 258–88; and education and health, 253–57; First Congress (1964) of, 241–42, 254; and goals of liberation, 282–88; and life in liberated Guinea-Bissau, 247–51; and military development and armed struggle, 236–47; and military struggle today, 244–47; program of, 264–65; publications of, 315–16

País, Economia do, 219

Paiva, João, 198
Pan Africanist Congress (PAC), 35, 37–39, 117–18
Pan African Liberation Committee, 294; march in support of liberation movements (Washington, D.C., 1972), 294
Parliament, South Africa, 4, 33, 39
Partido Africano da Independência da Guiné e Cabo Verde. See PAIGC
Party for the United Struggle of the Angolan Africans (PLUA), 187
Pass laws, South Africa's, 11–13, 23–24, 35
Peanut crop, 262
Peasants (peasantry), oppressive colonialism and liberation and: Angola, 171–72, 210–14; development of revolutionary strategy and, 258–88; Guinea-Bissau, 236, 238 ff., 247 ff., 270–88; mobilization of, 271–76, 279–82 ff.; Mozambique, 140–81 passim; revolutionary potential of, 270 ff.
People's militias. See Militias, people's
People's Revolutionary Armed Forces (FARP), Guinea-Bissau, 242, 249
People's Shops (People's Stores), 240, 244, 253, 257, 264
Petty Bourgeoisie, 268, 277, 278, 279, 283, 284; revolutionary, 277, 278, 279, 283, 284
PIDE (Portuguese secret police), 141, 147, 172, 184, 187, 189, 238

Pijiguiti, Bissau, massacre in, 261, 265–66
Poisons, chemical, Portuguese use of, 205–9
Polaroid Corporation, 110–111, 113–14, 116, 294, 310
Police state, South Africa as, 36–37
Political movements (political organizations): development of revolutionary strategy and, 258–88; Portuguese colonialism and, 54–60, 61 ff., 156–61 ff., 178, 186–89, 191 (see also specific aspects, organizations, people, places)
Political relations, Portuguese colonialism and, 43–50
Political repression, South Africa and, 35–40
Politics, foreign corporate investments in South Africa and, 112–31
Polygamy, 217
Popular Movement for the Liberation of Angola. See MPLA
Poqo (Pure), PAC and formation of, 38
Portugal (Portuguese colonialism), xiii, xiv, xv, xvi, 41–60, 61–82, 85–87, 135–288 (see also specific aspects, people, places); development of revolutionary strategy and, 258–88; early history of, 53, 192–99, 260–67; economic and political relations, 43–50; and education, 50–51; map, 42; military expenditures, 183, 232–33; resistance to, 53–60, 61–82, 135–288 (see also specific organiza-

tions, people, places); and role of the West in, 61–75, 232–33, 289–95; social relations, 48–50; South Africa and, 75–77, 81–82, 85–87, 184, 233; United States and (see under United States); wars in the colonies and, 79–82

"Portugal Belongs to Us All . . ." (speech by Marcelo Caetano, 1970), 305

Potato crop, 213–14

Praxis, 259–60, 288

Pretoria, South Africa, 7–8, 16

Production, agricultural (see also Agriculture, specific crops): economic base of liberation and, 285–86; liberated Angola and, 210–14

Proletariat, 268, 277

Public Security Police (PSP), Portuguese, 172

Pyhala, Mikko, 252, 257

Quitafine, Guinea-Bissau, 252

Race classification, South Africa's and apartheid system: education and, 27–29; geographical segregation, 6–9; and migratory labor and pass laws, 10–13, 23–24, 35; racial groupings, 5–6; resistance to repression and the police state, 29–40

Race Classification Board, 5

Racism (racial discrimination): Angola, 186, 192–99; Portuguese colonialism and, 48–50, 186, 192–99 (see also specific people, places); South Africa

and (see Apartheid system; Race classification); Western and world opinion and, 292–95

Racism and the Class Struggle (Boggs), 192–93, 195, 196

Raimundo, Lourenço, 148

Rand Daily Mail, 96–97

Reading. See Literacy (illiteracy)

Reform movements, capitalist powers and, 290–91; colonial oppression and, 141, 204

Regionalization of Southern Africa, South Africa and, 85–100: economic, 89–93; military, 85–89; outward policy, 93–100; settlers and satellites, 87–89

"Report of a Visit to the Liberated Areas of Guinea-Bissau" (Pyhala), 252, 257

Reserves (reservations), native (Bantustans), 6–9, 10, 12–13, 18–22, 26, 31, 297; map of, 19

Resettlement villages, 8–9, 10, 204

Resistance movements, 29 ff., 135 ff. (see also Guerrilla movements; Independence movements; Liberation movements); Angola, 136, 137, 183–234; development of revolutionary strategy and, 258–88; Guinea-Bissau, 136–37, 235–88; Mozambique, 136, 139–81; role of the West and, 289–95 (see also West, the); to Portuguese colonial rule, 53–60, 61–82, 135–38, 139–81, 183–234, 235–88; to South

Africa and apartheid, 29–40, 135–36

Revolutionary movements (*see also* Guerrilla movements; Liberation movements): critical analysis (goals of liberation), 282–88; critical analysis (organizing the struggle), 267–82; development of revolutionary strategy and, 258–88 (*see also* Strategy, revolutionary)

Revolution in Angola (Barnett and Harvey), 200, 210, 211, 213, 214, 217, 219, 222

Revolution in Guinea (Cabral), 240–41, 242, 244, 248, 252, 259, 260, 261, 265, 269, 270–71, 277–78, 279–82, 285

Rhodes, Cecil, 101

Rhodesia, 75, 76, 84, 121, 292, 294. *See also* Zambia; Zimbabwe

Rice production, 213–14, 251, 252

Road building, 67–68, 176–77

Rural population, development of revolutionary strategy and, 270–71, 276 ff.

Russia. *See* Soviet Union

Sabotage, 39, 136, 238

Sabotage Act, 39

"Safira Solitária" Operation, 246

Salazar, António Oliveira, 45, 48, 54, 63, 66, 76, 237

SAM (Medical Assistance Services), Angola, 219–22

São Tomé, 194

Schools. *See* Education (schools)

Security Branch, South Africa, 36–37

Sekhukuni, King, 30

Self-government, 18, 136 (*see also* Independence movements); Angola, 183–234; Guinea-Bissau, 235–88; Mozambique, 136, 139–81; villages, 248–51, 255, 284, 287–88

"Sell Out or Shell Out" (article), 312

Seme, Dr. P. I., 31

"Separate development" policy, South Africa's apartheid and, 18

Settlers. *See* Afrikaners (Boers); Europeans; Whites; specific people, places

Sharpeville, South Africa, 35, 36; massacre in, 35, 36, 116

Siemens, 78

Sierra Leone, 96

Simango, Uria, 169

Simonstown Naval Base (South Africa), 126

Sita, Nana, trial of, 7–8

Slavery (slave trade), 29 30, 45, Portuguese in Angola and, 45, 185–86, 192–99; Portuguese in Guinea-Bissau and, 45, 261–62; South Africa and, 3, 16, 29–30

Social change. *See* Change(s)

Socialist countries (*see also* individual countries): and aid to liberation movements, 242, 293

Social structure, revolutionary strategy and changes in, 258–88

South Africa, Republic of, xiii, xiv, 3–40, 75 ff., 85–100, 101–

31, 135–36, 289–95; apartheid system, 3–40, 101–31 (*see also* Apartheid system); corporate interests and, 103–31 *passim;* and creation of buffer zones, 85–100; early history, 14–15, 29–30, 101–3; military (police) expenditures and preparation, 36, 124–26; outward policy, 93–100, 291; and Portugal, 75–77, 81–82, 85–87, 184, 233; and regionalization of Southern Africa, 84, 85–100; regional offensive (map) of, 84; resistance to White domination in, 29–40, 135–36; and the West, 99–100, 101–31, 289–95
South Africa, Union of, 16, 30–31, 102
South Africa Foundation, 115
South African Institute of Race Relations, 26
South Atlantic Treaty Organization (proposed), 291
Southern Africa: map, viii; Portuguese and (*see* Portugal; specific people, places); resistance to White domination in, 135 ff. (*see also* specific movements, people, places); role of the West in, 289–95 (*see also* West, the); South Africa and regionalization of (*see* Regionalization of Southern Africa)
South West Africa. *See* Namibia (South West Africa)
Soviet Union, 126, 285, 293
"Special hunters," Portuguese, 174

Strategic hamlets (strategic villages), 171–72, 204, 210
Strategy, revolutionary, development of (Guinea-Bissau), 258–88: critical analysis (goals of liberation), 282–88; critical analysis (organizing the struggle), 267–82; importance of theory, 258–59; PAIGC and, 260–67; *praxis* of, 259–60; revolutionary potential of peasantry and, 270 ff.; social and class structure and, 267–82 ff.
Strikes, 25, 39, 55, 112, 136; massacres and, 261, 265–66
Struggle for Mozambique, The (Mondlane), 44, 47, 48, 49, 52, 57–58, 141, 142, 149, 153, 155, 158, 159, 166
Students, and resistance movements, 136, 140, 142
Subsistence farming, 45–48
Suez Canal, 126
Sugar production, 128
Suppression of Communism Act, South Africa's, 32, 301
Swaziland, 87, 88, 94, 97, 308
Sweden, 77–78, 111
Sweet potato production, 206–7

"Tabanca committees" (Guinea-Bissau), 248–51, 255
Tanganyika. *See* Tanzania
Tanzania (*formerly* Tanganyika), 86, 98, 141, 148, 149
Taxes (taxation), 53, 188–89
Tchiweka (cadre member), 224–25, 226
Teachers (teaching), 225–26

(*see also* Education); in liberated Angola, 225–26

Technical assistance programs, 109–10

Tete, Mozambique, 150, 151, 170, 174, 176

Theory, revolutionary strategy and, 258–59. *See also* Strategy, revolutionary

3M Company of Minnesota, 115

Tongas (South African people), 31

Torture, use by Portuguese of, 172–73, 261

Townships (locations), South Africa's, 11, 12, 29, 35

Traca, Humberto, 185, 203, 205

Trade, 119 (*see also* Economy); economic national interests and apartheid policy, 127–31; free, South Africa's regionalization of Southern Africa and, 89–93, 96; Portuguese colonialism and the West, 69–72; South Africa's apartheid policy and the West, 102–31 *passim*

Trade unions, 25, 31, 186

Traditional medicine, modern medical care and, 221–22

Transmission Lines Construction Company (TLC) of South Africa, 78

Transvaal, 15, 16, 30

Trekkers. *See* Afrikaners (Boers)

Tribes (tribalism), 160, 191–92, 281, 287–88. *See also* Ethnic groups; specific people

Tshaka, King, 15

Tunga, Ariteine, 197–98

Tungsten production, 66

UDENAMO (National Democratic Union of Mozambique), 141

Uganda, 97

Umkhonto We Sizwe (Spear of the Nation), 38–39

UN. *See* United Nations

UNAMI (African Union for an Independent Mozambique), 141

Underdevelopment: liberation movements and change and, 268 ff., 284–88; Portuguese colonial rule and, 194–95, 258

Underground movements, 38–40, 117–18, 135 ff. *See also* Guerrilla movements; Resistance movements

Union Carbide, 105–7, 114, 115, 122

Union of South Africa, 16, 30–31, 102

UNITA (National Union for Total Independence of Angola), 137

United Nations, 41–42, 64–65, 76, 77, 87, 88–89, 93, 95, 96, 103, 123–24, 224, 260–61; and arms embargoes, 123–24, 127, 292; Commission on Human Rights, 172–73; and Guinea-Bissau, 250–51, 260–61; and Mozambique, 142, 166, 172–73; Special Committee on Territories under Portuguese Administration, 260–61, 263, 316–17

United Party (South Africa), 114

United States, role in Southern Africa of, xiv, xv, xvi, 285, 289–92, 294 ff.: American corporate interests and Congress and foreign policy, 120–22 ff., 289–92, 294; Atomic Energy Commission (AEC), 125–26; capital investment in dollars, 105; Export-Import Bank, 78; national interests and foreign policy, 123, 124, 125–31; and Portuguese colonialism, 61, 64–66, 67, 69–70, 72, 74, 75, 81, 100, 174, 183, 184, 200, 207, 232–33, 291–94; and South Africa's apartheid system, 28–29, 100, 105, 120–22 ff., 290 ff.; strategic considerations, 126–27; support for liberation movements from groups in, 293, 294; trade and investment in South Africa, 104–22 ff., 128–31; and Vietnam (see Vietnam war)

UPA (Popular Union of Angola), 56, 191–92

Urban areas and people. See Cities and towns (urban population)

Vauxhall, and South Africa, 119

Venter, Al, 80

Verwoerd, Dr. Hendrik, 88

Victory Is Certain (MPLA literary manual), 227–32

Videira, Dr. Mwambaka, 221–22

Vietnam war, xiii, 120, 122, 203, 205, 207, 244, 295

Villages (villagers), liberation movement in Guinea-Bissau and, 248–51, 255, 258, 272 ff.; and self-government, 248–51, 255, 258, 284, 287–88

Violence, colonialism and, 197–99, 236–37, 291, 292. See also Massacres; Torture

Vorster, John B., 10–11, 36, 82, 93, 95, 97, 98, 124, 291

Wages, 26–27 (see also Economy; Labor); revolutionary consciousness and, 8, 279; South Africa's apartheid policy and, 26–27

"Weapon of Theory" speech, Cabral's (Havana, 1966), 285

"West" ("Western powers"), use of term, xvi

West, the, 61–82 (see also specific countries, people, places); and Portuguese colonialism, 61–85, 184, 207; role in domination and liberation in Southern Africa, 99–100, 101–31, 289–95 (see also specific aspects, countries, places); and South Africa's apartheid system, 101–31; and South Africa's regionalization of Southern Africa, 99–100

West Africa, 41. See also Guinea-Bissau

West Germany, 63, 66, 69, 71, 75, 77, 78, 81, 104, 111, 124, 233, 292

Westmoreland, General William C., 174

"White man's burden," 17

Whites, the, 5, 135–288, 289–95 (see also Europeans; specific groups, people, places); and Portuguese colonialism (see Portugal); and resistance of Africans to, 29–40, 101–3, 135–38, 139–288 passim,

289–95 (*see also* specific movements, people, places); role of the West in Southern Africa and (*see* West, the); and South Africa's apartheid system, 3–40 (*see also* under Apartheid system); and South Africa's regionalization of Southern Africa, 85–100

Williams, G. Mennen, 65

Women, role in liberation movements of: Angola, 211, 214–18; Mozambique, 141, 142, 152, 162–65

Work(ers). *See* Labor (workers)

Work permits, 10

World Council of Churches, 293, 294

World opinion: and apartheid, 122–23; and liberation movements, 290–94

Xhosa-Fingo feuds, 31

Zaire (*formerly* Congo-Kinshasa), 98, 199, 204

Zambesi River, 77–79

Zambezia, Mozambique, 150, 151, 154, 176

Zambia, 86, 95, 98. *See also* Rhodesia

ZAMCO, 77–79

Zeit, Die, 63

Zimbabwe, 84, 86, 87–88, 90, 91, 98. *See also* Rhodesia

Zulus, 15, 30, 31